National Commission on Terrorist Attacks Upon the United States

Monograph on Terrorist Financing

Staff Report to the Commission

John Roth
Douglas Greenburg
Serena Wille

Preface

The Commission staff organized its work around specialized studies, or monographs, prepared by each of the teams. We used some of the evolving draft material for these studies in preparing the seventeen staff statements delivered in conjunction with the Commission's 2004 public hearings. We used more of this material in preparing draft sections of the Commission's final report. Some of the specialized staff work, while not appropriate for inclusion in the report, nonetheless offered substantial information or analysis that was not well represented in the Commission's report. In a few cases this supplemental work could be prepared to a publishable standard, either in an unclassified or classified form, before the Commission expired.

This study is on terrorist financing. It was prepared principally by John Roth, Douglas Greenburg, and Serena Wille, with editing assistance from Alice Falk. As in all staff studies, they often relied on work done by their colleagues.

This is a study by Commission staff. While the Commissioners have been briefed on the work and have had the opportunity to review earlier drafts of some of this work, they have not approved this text and it does not necessarily reflect their views.

Philip Zelikow

Table of Contents

Chapter 1

Introduction and Executive Summary

Introduction

After the September 11 attacks, the highest-level U.S. government officials publicly declared that the fight against al Qaeda financing was as critical as the fight against al Qaeda itself. It has been presented as one of the keys to success in the fight against terrorism: if we choke off the terrorists' money, we limit their ability to conduct mass casualty attacks. In reality, completely choking off the money to al Qaeda and affiliated terrorist groups has been essentially impossible. At the same time, tracking al Qaeda financing has proven a very effective way to locate terrorist operatives and supporters and to disrupt terrorist plots.

As a result, the U.S. terrorist financing strategy has changed from the early post-9/11 days. Choking off the money remains the most visible aspect of our approach, but it is not our only, or even most important, goal. Ultimately, making it harder for terrorists to get money is a necessary, but not sufficient, component of our overall strategy. Following the money to identify terrorist operatives and sympathizers provides a particularly powerful tool in the fight against terrorist groups. Use of this tool almost always remains invisible to the general public, but it is a critical part of the overall campaign against al Qaeda. Moreover, the U.S. government recognizes—appropriately, in the Commission staff's view—that terrorist-financing measures are simply one of many tools in the fight against al Qaeda.

This monograph, together with the relevant parts of the Commission's final report, reflects the staff's investigation into al Qaeda financing and the U.S. government's efforts to combat it. This monograph represents the collective efforts of a number of members of the staff. John Roth, Douglas Greenburg and Serena Wille did the bulk of the work reflected in this report. Thanks also go to Dianna Campagna, Marquittia Coleman, Melissa Coffey and the entire administrative staff for their excellent support. We were fortunate in being able to build upon a great deal of excellent work already done by the U.S. intelligence and law enforcement communities.

The starting point for our inquiry is 1998, when al Qaeda emerged as a primary global threat to U.S. interests. Although we address earlier periods as necessary, we have not attempted to tell the history of al Qaeda financing from its inception. We have sought to understand how al Qaeda raised, moved, and stored money before and after the September 11 attacks, and how the U.S. government confronted the problem of al Qaeda financing before and after 9/11. We have had significant access to highly classified raw and finished intelligence from the intelligence community, have reviewed law enforcement, State Department, and Treasury Department files, and have interviewed at length government officials, from street-level agents to cabinet secretaries, as well as non-government experts, representatives from the financial services industry, and representatives of individuals and entities directly affected by U.S. government action to combat al Qaeda financing.

This monograph does not attempt a comprehensive survey of all known data on al Qaeda financing and every government action to combat it. Rather, we have sought to understand the issues that make a difference, what the 9/11 disaster should have taught us about these issues, and the extent to which the current U.S. strategy reflects these lessons. What we have found is instructive in the larger analysis of what the U.S. government can do to detect, investigate, deter, and disrupt al Qaeda and affiliated terrorist groups bent on mass casualty attacks against the United States.[1]

Executive Summary

September 11 financing

The September 11 hijackers used U.S. and foreign financial institutions to hold, move, and retrieve their money. The hijackers deposited money into U.S. accounts, primarily by wire transfers and deposits of cash or travelers checks brought from overseas. Additionally, several of them kept funds in foreign accounts, which they accessed in the United States through ATM and credit card transactions. The hijackers received funds from facilitators in Germany and the United Arab Emirates or directly from Khalid Sheikh Mohamed (KSM) as they transited Pakistan before coming to the United States. The plot cost al Qaeda somewhere in the range of $400,000–500,000, of which approximately $300,000 passed through the hijackers' bank accounts in the United States. The hijackers returned approximately $26,000 to a facilitator in the UAE in the days prior to the attack. While in the United States, the hijackers spent money primarily for flight training, travel, and living expenses (such as housing, food, cars, and auto insurance). Extensive investigation has revealed no substantial source of domestic financial support.

Neither the hijackers nor their financial facilitators were experts in the use of the international financial system. They created a paper trail linking them to each other and their facilitators. Still, they were easily adept enough to blend into the vast international financial system without doing anything to reveal themselves as criminals, let alone terrorists bent on mass murder. The money-laundering controls in place at the time were largely focused on drug trafficking and large-scale financial fraud and could not have detected the hijackers' transactions. The controls were never intended to, and could not, detect or disrupt the routine transactions in which the hijackers engaged.

---

[1] Our investigation has focused on al Qaeda financing and the country's response to it. Although much of our analysis may apply to the financing of other terrorist groups, we have made no systematic effort to investigate any of those groups, and we recognize that the financing of other terrorist groups may present the government with problems or opportunities not existing in the context of al Qaeda.

There is no evidence that any person with advance knowledge of the impending terrorist attacks used that information to profit by trading securities. Although there has been consistent speculation that massive al Qaeda–related "insider trading" preceded the attacks, exhaustive investigation by federal law enforcement and the securities industry has determined that unusual spikes in the trading of certain securities were based on factors unrelated to terrorism.

One of the pillars of al Qaeda: Fund-raising

Al Qaeda and Usama Bin Ladin obtained money from a variety of sources. Contrary to common belief, Bin Ladin did not have access to any significant amounts of personal wealth (particularly after his move from Sudan to Afghanistan) and did not personally fund al Qaeda, either through an inheritance or businesses he was said to have owned in Sudan. Rather, al Qaeda was funded, to the tune of approximately $30 million per year, by diversions of money from Islamic charities and the use of well-placed financial facilitators who gathered money from both witting and unwitting donors, primarily in the Gulf region. No persuasive evidence exists that al Qaeda relied on the drug trade as an important source of revenue, had any substantial involvement with conflict diamonds, or was financially sponsored by any foreign government. The United States is not, and has not been, a substantial source of al Qaeda funding, although some funds raised in the United States may have made their way to al Qaeda and its affiliated groups.

After Bin Ladin relocated to Afghanistan in 1996, al Qaeda made less use of formal banking channels to transfer money, preferring instead to use an informal system of money movers or bulk cash couriers. Supporters and other operatives did use banks, particularly in the Gulf region, to move money on behalf of al Qaeda. Prior to 9/11 the largest single al Qaeda expense was support for the Taliban, estimated at about $20 million per year. Bin Ladin also used money to train operatives in camps in Afghanistan, create terrorist networks and alliances, and support the jihadists and their families. Finally, a relatively small amount of money was used to finance operations, including the approximately $400,000–500,000 spent on the September 11 attacks themselves.

U.S. government efforts before the September 11 attacks

Terrorist financing was not a priority for either domestic or foreign intelligence collection. As a result, intelligence reporting on the issue was episodic, insufficient, and often inaccurate. Although the National Security Council considered terrorist financing important in its campaign to disrupt al Qaeda, other agencies failed to participate to the NSC's satisfaction, and there was little interagency strategic planning or coordination. Without an effective interagency mechanism, responsibility for the problem was dispersed among a myriad of agencies, each working independently.

The FBI gathered intelligence on a significant number of organizations in the United States suspected of raising funds for al Qaeda or other terrorist groups. Highly motivated street agents in specific FBI field offices overcame setbacks, bureaucratic inefficiencies, and what they believed to be a dysfunctional Foreign Intelligence Surveillance Act (FISA) system[2] to gain a basic understanding of some of the largest and most problematic terrorist-financing conspiracies since identified. The FBI did not develop an endgame, however. The agents continued to gather intelligence with little hope that they would be able to make a criminal case or otherwise disrupt the operations. The FBI could not turn these investigations into criminal cases because of insufficient international cooperation, a perceived inability to mingle criminal and intelligence investigations due to the "wall" between intelligence and law enforcement matters, sensitivities to overt investigations of Islamic charities and organizations, and the sheer difficulty of prosecuting most terrorist-financing cases. As a result, the FBI rarely sought to involve criminal prosecutors in its terrorist-financing investigations. Nonetheless, FBI street agents had gathered significant intelligence on specific groups.

On a national level the FBI did not systematically gather and analyze the information its agents developed. It lacked a headquarters unit focusing on terrorist financing, and its overworked counterterrorism personnel lacked time and resources to focus specifically on financing. The FBI as an organization therefore failed to understand the nature and extent of the jihadist[3] fund-raising problem within the United States or to develop a coherent strategy for confronting the problem. The FBI did not, nor could it, fulfill its role to provide intelligence on domestic terrorist financing to government policymakers and did not contribute to national policy coordination. For its part, the Criminal Division of the Department of Justice had no national program for prosecuting terrorist-financing cases, despite a 1996 statute that gave it much broader legal powers for doing so. The Department of Justice could not develop an effective program for prosecuting these cases because its prosecutors had no systematic way to learn what evidence of prosecutable crimes could be found in the FBI's intelligence files, to which they did not have access.

The U.S. intelligence community largely failed to comprehend al Qaeda's methods of raising, moving, and storing money, because it devoted relatively few resources to collecting the strategic financial intelligence that policymakers were requesting or that would have informed the larger counterterrorism strategy. Al Qaeda financing was in many respects a hard target for intelligence gathering. But the CIA also arrived belatedly

---

[2] This monograph is a survey and analysis of the government's efforts with regard to terrorist financing both before and after 9/11. This necessarily touches on many different aspects of the government's counterterrorism efforts, including the FISA review process and barrier between law enforcement and intelligence information. We did not attempt, however, to conduct an exhaustive review of those issues. Rather, we refer the reader to the 9/11 Commission Report, pp.78-80.

[3] We use the term *jihadist* to include militant Islamist groups other than the Palestinian terrorist groups, such as Hamas and Palestinian Islamic Jihad, and Lebanese Hizbollah. The other jihadist groups who have raised money in the United States appear to loosely share a common ideology, and many of them have been linked directly or indirectly to al Qaeda. These groups raise funds in the United States to support Islamist militants around the world; some of these funds may make their way to al Qaeda or affiliated groups. The Palestinian groups and Hizbollah, which have raised large amounts of money domestically, present different issues that are beyond the scope of our investigation.

at an understanding of some basic operational facts that were readily available—such as the knowledge that al Qaeda relied on fund-raising, not Bin Ladin's personal fortune. The CIA's inability to grasp the true source of Bin Ladin's funds and the methods behind their movement hampered the U.S. government's ability to integrate potential covert action or overt economic disruption into the counterterrorism effort. The lack of specific intelligence about al Qaeda financing frustrated policymakers, and the intelligence deficiencies persisted through 9/11.

Other areas within the U.S. government evinced similar problems. The then-obscure Office of Foreign Assets Control (OFAC), the Treasury organization charged by law with searching out, designating, and freezing Bin Ladin assets, lacked comprehensive access to actionable intelligence and was beset by the indifference of higher-level Treasury policymakers. Even if those barriers had been removed, the primary Bin Ladin financial flows at the time, from the Gulf to Afghanistan, likely were beyond OFAC's legal powers, which apply only domestically.

A number of significant legislative and regulatory initiatives designed to close vulnerabilities in the U.S. financial system failed to gain traction. Some of these, such as a move to control foreign banks with accounts in the United States, died as a result of banking industry pressure. Others, such as a move to regulate money remitters, were mired in bureaucratic inertia and a general antiregulatory environment.

The U.S. government had recognized the value of enlisting the international community in efforts to stop the flow of money to al Qaeda entities. U.S. diplomatic efforts had succeeded in persuading the United Nations to sanction Bin Ladin economically, but such sanctions were largely ineffective. Saudi Arabia and the UAE, necessary partners in any realistic effort to stem the financing of terror, were ambivalent and selectively cooperative in assisting the United States. The U.S. government approached the Saudis on some narrow issues, such as locating Bin Ladin's supposed personal wealth and gaining access to a senior al Qaeda financial figure in Saudi custody, with mixed results. The Saudis generally resisted cooperating more broadly against al Qaeda financing, although the U.S. government did not make this issue a priority in its bilateral relations with the Saudis or provide the Saudis with actionable intelligence about al Qaeda fund-raising in the Kingdom. Other issues, such as Iraq, the Middle East peace process, economic arrangements, the oil supply, and cutting off Saudi support for the Taliban, took primacy on the U.S.-Saudi agenda.

The net result of the government's efforts, according to CIA analysis at the time, was that al Qaeda's cash flow on the eve of the September 11 attacks was steady and secure.

Where are we now?

It is common to say the world has changed since September 11, 2001, and this conclusion is particularly apt in describing U.S. counterterrorist efforts regarding financing. The U.S. government focused, for the first time, on terrorist financing and devoted considerable energy and resources to the problem. As a result the United States now has a far better understanding of the methods by which terrorists raise, move, and use money and has employed this knowledge to our advantage.

With an understanding of the nature of the threat and with a new sense of urgency, the intelligence community (including the FBI) created new entities to focus on, and bring expertise to, the area of terrorist fund-raising and the clandestine movement of money. These entities are led by experienced and committed individuals, who use financial information to understand terrorist networks, search them out and disrupt their operations, and who integrate terrorist-financing issues into the larger counterterrorism efforts at their respective agencies. Equally important, many of the obstacles hampering investigations have been stripped away. The current intelligence community approach appropriately focuses on using financial information, in close coordination with other types of intelligence, to identify and track terrorist groups rather than to starve them of funding.

The CIA has devoted considerable resources to the investigation of al Qaeda financing, and the effort is led by individuals with extensive expertise in the clandestine movement of money. The CIA appears to be developing an institutional and long-term expertise in this area, and other intelligence agencies have made similar improvements. Still, al Qaeda financing remains a hard target for intelligence gathering. Understanding al Qaeda's money and providing actionable intelligence present ongoing challenges because of the speed, diversity, and complexity of the means and methods for raising and moving money; the commingling of terrorist money with legitimate funds; the many layers and transfers between donors and the ultimate recipients of the money; the existence of unwitting participants (including donors who give to generalized jihadist struggles rather than specifically to al Qaeda); and the U.S. government's reliance on foreign government reporting for intelligence.

Since the attacks, the FBI has improved its dissemination of intelligence to policymakers, usually in the form of briefings, regular meetings, and status reports. The creation of a unit focusing on terrorist financing has provided a vehicle through which the FBI can effectively participate in interagency terrorist-financing efforts and ensures that these issues receive focused attention rather than being a footnote to the FBI's overall counterterrorism program. Still, the FBI needs to improve the gathering and analyzing of the information developed in its investigations. The FBI's well-documented efforts to create an analytical career track and enhance its analytical capabilities are sorely needed in this area.

Bringing jihadist fund-raising prosecutions remains difficult in many cases. The inability to get records from other countries, the complexity of directly linking cash flows to terrorist operations or groups, and the difficulty of showing what domestic persons knew about illicit foreign acts or actors all combine to thwart investigations and prosecutions. Still, criminal prosecutors now have regular access to information on relevant investigations, and the Department of Justice has created a unit to coordinate an aggressive national effort to prosecute terrorist financing.

In light of the difficulties in prosecuting some terrorist fund-raising cases, the government has used administrative blocking and freezing orders under the International Emergency Economic Powers Act (IEEPA) against U.S. persons (individuals or entities) suspected of supporting foreign terrorist organizations. It may well be effective, and perhaps necessary, to disrupt fund-raising operations through an administrative blocking order when no other good options exist. The use of IEEPA authorities against domestic organizations run by U.S. citizens, however, raises significant civil liberty concerns because it allows the government to shut down an organization on the basis of classified evidence, subject only to a deferential after-the-fact judicial review. The provision of the IEEPA that allows the blocking of assets "during the pendency of an investigation" also raises particular concern in that it can shut down a U.S. entity indefinitely without the more fully developed administrative record necessary for a permanent IEEPA designation.

The NSC's interagency Policy Coordinating Committee (PCC) on terrorist financing has been generally successful in its efforts to marshal government resources to address terrorist-financing issues in the immediate aftermath of the attacks, although its success likely resulted more from the personalities of its members than from its structure. As the government's response to the problem has evolved over time, the NSC is better situated than an agency or a stand-alone "czar" to take the lead in forming an interagency strategic and operational response to terrorist financing.

The attacks galvanized the international community to set up a near-universal system of laws, tied to United Nations Security Council Resolution 1373, to freeze the assets of terrorists and their supporters. The United States pursued an ambitious course of highly visible asset freezes of terrorists, terrorist supporters, and terrorist-related entities. The State Department embarked on a course of intense diplomatic pressure to ensure that the asset freezes were truly international. Multilateral institutions, such as the Financial Action Task Force, began to develop international antiterrorist finance standards for financial institutions.

Saudi Arabia is a key part of our international efforts to fight terrorist financing. The intelligence community identified it as the primary source of money for al Qaeda both before and after the September 11 attacks. Fund-raisers and facilitators throughout Saudi Arabia and the Gulf raised money for al Qaeda from witting and unwitting donors and divert funds from Islamic charities and mosques. The Commission staff found no evidence that the Saudi government as an institution or as individual senior officials knowingly support or supported al Qaeda; however, a lack of awareness of the problem and a failure to conduct oversight over institutions created an environment in which such activity has flourished.

From the 9/11 attacks through spring 2003, most U.S. officials viewed Saudi cooperation on terrorist financing as ambivalent and selective. U.S. efforts to overcome Saudi recalcitrance suffered from our failure to develop a strategy to counter Saudi terrorist financing, present our requests through a single high-level interlocutor, and obtain and release to the Saudis actionable intelligence. By spring 2003 the U.S. government had corrected these deficiencies. Not just a more effective U.S. message but more especially al Qaeda operations within the Kingdom in May and November 2003 focused the Saudi government's attention on its terrorist-financing problem, and dramatically improved cooperation with the United States. The Saudi government needs to continue to strengthen its capabilities to stem the flow of money from Saudi sources to al Qaeda. A critical part of the U.S. strategy to combat terrorist financing must be to monitor, encourage, and nurture Saudi cooperation while simultaneously recognizing that terrorist financing is only one of a number of crucial issues that the U.S. and Saudi governments must address together. Managing this nuanced and complicated relationship will play a critical part in determining the success of U.S. counterterrorism policy for the foreseeable future.

The domestic financial community and some international financial institutions have generally provided law enforcement and intelligence agencies with extraordinary cooperation, particularly in providing information to support quickly developing investigations, such as the search for terrorist suspects at times of emergency. Much of this cooperation, such as providing expedited returns on subpoenas related to terrorism, is voluntary and based on personal relationships. It remains to be seen whether such cooperation will continue as the memory of 9/11 fades. Efforts within the financial industry to create financial profiles of terrorist cells and terrorist fund-raisers have proved unsuccessful, and the ability of financial institutions to detect terrorist financing remains limited.

Since the September 11 attacks and the defeat of the Taliban, al Qaeda's budget has decreased significantly. Although the trend line is clear, the U.S government still has not determined with any precision how much al Qaeda raises or from whom, or how it spends its money. It appears that the al Qaeda attacks within Saudi Arabia in May and November of 2003 have reduced—some say drastically—al Qaeda's ability to raise funds from Saudi sources, because of both an increase in Saudi enforcement and a more negative perception of al Qaeda by potential donors in the Gulf. However, as al Qaeda's cash flow has decreased, so too have its expenses, generally owing to the defeat of the Taliban and the dispersal of al Qaeda. Despite our efforts, it appears that al Qaeda can still find money to fund terrorist operations. Al Qaeda now relies on the physical movement of money and other informal methods of value transfer, which can pose significant challenges for those attempting to detect and disrupt money flows.

Understanding the difficulties in disrupting terrorist financing, both in the United States and abroad, requires understanding the difference between seeing "links" to terrorists and proving the funding of terrorists. In many cases, we can plainly see that certain nongovernmental organizations (NGOs) or individuals who raise money for Islamic causes espouse an extremist ideology and are "linked" to terrorists through common acquaintances, group affiliations, historic relationships, phone communications, or other such contacts. Although sufficient to whet the appetite for action, these suspicious links do not demonstrate that the NGO or individual actually funds terrorists and thus provide frail support for disruptive action, either in the United States or abroad. In assessing both the domestic efforts of the U.S. government and the overseas efforts of other nations, we must keep in mind this fundamental and inherently frustrating challenge of combating terrorist financing.

Case studies and common themes

The Commission staff examined three significant terrorist-financing investigations in existence prior to September 11 in order to (a) understand U.S. efforts to stem al Qaeda-related terrorist financing before the September 11 attacks, (b) trace the evolution of U.S. policy and operations since the attacks, and (c) illustrate the problems and opportunities in the area of terrorist financing. These case studies—a Somalia-based worldwide money-remitting organization with alleged ties to al Qaeda; two Illinois charities that allegedly raised money for al Qaeda; and an international Saudi-based private charity, with ties to the Saudi government, accused of being a conduit of terrorist money—have given the staff insights into the larger problems and recommendations.

Al-Barakaat: The informal movement of money and its implication for counterterrorist financing

Al-Barakaat (literally, "the blessing"), a money-remitting system centered in Somalia with outlets worldwide, took shape after the collapse of the government and the banking system in Somalia. The intelligence community developed information that Usama Bin Ladin had contributed money to al-Barakaat to start operations, that it was closely associated with or controlled by the terrorist group Al-Itihaad Al-Islamiya (AIAI), and that some of al-Barakaat's proceeds went to fund AIAI, which in turn gave a portion to Usama Bin Ladin.

In the United States the FBI developed an intelligence case on the al-Barakaat network in early 1999, and had opened a criminal case by 2000. Shortly after 9/11 al-Barakaat's assets were frozen and its books and records were seized in raids around the world, including in the United States. Subsequent investigation by the FBI, including financial analysis of the books and records of al-Barakaat provided in unprecedented cooperation by the UAE, failed to establish the allegations of a link between al-Barakaat and AIAI or Bin Ladin. No criminal case was made against al-Barakaat in the United States for these activities. Although OFAC claims that it met the evidentiary standard for designations, the majority of assets frozen in the United States under executive order (and some assets frozen by other countries under UN resolution) were unfrozen and the money returned after the U.S.-based al-Barakaat money remitters filed a lawsuit challenging the action.

The Illinois Charities: Domestic charities used to fund al Qaeda?

Two Illinois-based charities, the Global Relief Foundation, Inc. (GRF), and the Benevolence International Foundation (BIF), have been publicly accused of providing financial support to al Qaeda and international terrorism. GRF, a nonprofit organization with operations in 25 countries, ostensibly devoted to providing humanitarian aid to the needy, raised millions of dollars in the United States in support of its mission. U.S. investigators long believed that GRF devoted a significant percentage of the funds it raised to support Islamic extremist causes and jihadists with substantial links to international terrorist groups, including al Qaeda, and the FBI had a very active investigation under way by the time of 9/11. BIF, a nonprofit organization with offices in at least 10 countries, raised millions of dollars in the United States, much of which it distributed throughout the world for purposes of humanitarian aid. As in the case of GRF, the U.S. government believed BIF had substantial connections to terrorist groups, including al Qaeda, and was sending a sizable percentage of its funds to support the international jihadist movement. BIF was also the subject of an active investigation before 9/11.

After 9/11 OFAC froze both charities' assets, effectively putting them out of business. The FBI opened a criminal investigation of both charities, ultimately resulting in the conviction of the leader of BIF for non-terrorism-related charges. The Immigration and Naturalization Service detained and ultimately deported a major GRF fund-raiser. No criminal charges have been filed against GRF or its personnel.

The cases of BIF and GRF illustrate the U.S. government's approach to terrorist fund-raising in the United States before 9/11 and how that approach dramatically changed after the terrorist attacks: the government moved from a strategy of investigating and monitoring terrorist financing to actively disrupting suspect entities through criminal prosecution and the use of its IEEPA powers to block their assets in the United States. Although effective in shutting down its targets, this aggressive approach raises potential civil liberties concerns, as the charities' supporters insist that they were unfairly targeted, denied due process, and closed without any evidence they actually funded al Qaeda or any terrorist groups.[4] The BIF and GRF investigations highlight fundamental issues that span all aspects of the government efforts to combat al Qaeda financing: the difference between seeing links to terrorists and proving funding of terrorists, and the problem of defining the threshold of information necessary to take disruptive action.

Al Haramain: International charities and Saudi Arabia

Al Haramain Islamic Foundation is a Saudi Arabia–based Islamic foundation. It is a quasi-private, charitable, and educational organization dedicated to propagating a very conservative form of Islam throughout the world. At its peak, al Haramain had a presence in at least 50 countries with estimates of its total annual expenditures ranging from $30 to $80 million. The government of Saudi Arabia has provided financial support to al

---

[4] Legal actions taken by the aggrieved parties have been largely unsuccessful either because, as in the case of al-Barakaat, the government unfroze assets, or because of the highly deferential standard of review afforded to the President in the exercise of his Commander in Chief powers under IEEPA. The issue is not whether the government had the power to conduct the actions that it did. Rather, the issue is whether, based on the nature and quality of the evidence involved, and the threat of likely harm, the government appropriately exercised those powers against U.S. persons.

Haramain in the past, although that has perhaps decreased in recent years. At least two Saudi government officials have supervisory roles (nominal or otherwise) over al Haramain.

Since at least 1996 the U.S. intelligence community has developed information that various al Haramain branches supported jihadists and terrorists, including al Qaeda. Since 9/11 high-level U.S. officials have considered their options regarding al Haramain. As of January 2003 the U.S. government was concerned that personnel in 20 of al Haramain's offices, including personnel within Saudi Arabia, were aiding and abetting al Qaeda and its affiliated terrorist groups.

In March 2002 the U.S. and Saudi governments froze the assets of the Somali and Bosnian offices of al Haramain and, simultaneously, submitted these names to the United Nations for international listing as terrorist supporters. The United States has raised al Haramain's involvement in terrorist financing with the Saudi government repeatedly, in different forms and through different channels, since 1998, but most effectively since 2003. The Saudi government has made some moves to rein in the charity since May 2003, including replacing the executive director of al Haramain, announcing the shutdown of all overseas branches of al Haramain, and changing its relevant laws and regulations. Some of these actions proved to be ineffective and, as a result, the U.S. and Saudi governments froze the assets of four additional branch offices of al Haramain in January 2004 and five additional branch offices in June 2004. The U.S. government took additional action against the U.S. entities in February 2004 and against the former executive director in June 2004. It remains to be seen whether the Saudis have the political will to develop the necessary capabilities to stem the flow of funds to al Qaeda and its related groups and to sustain these efforts over the long haul.

We completed our investigation of al Haramain in early June 2004. Subsequently, the Saudi government announced that it would dissolve the al Haramain Islamic Foundation and that a new Saudi charity commission would "take over all aspects of private overseas aid operations and assume responsibility for the distribution of private charitable donations from Saudi Arabia." We have not assessed the state-of-play or impact of these actions. They are moving targets and it is difficult to come to any final conclusions about the status of al Haramain. Regardless, we believe the discussion in this chapter tells an important story about U.S.-Saudi cooperation on terrorist financing in the post 9/11 period from which important lessons can be drawn.

Findings

The funding of the hijackers

- The 9/11 plot cost al Qaeda approximately $400,000–500,000, of which approximately $300,000 was deposited into U.S. bank accounts of the 19 hijackers. Al Qaeda funded the hijackers in the United States by three primary and unexceptional means: (1) wire transfers from overseas to the United States, (2) the physical transport of cash or traveler's checks into the United States, and (3) the accessing of funds held in foreign financial institutions by debit or credit cards. Once here, all of the hijackers used the U.S. banking system to store their funds and facilitate their transactions.

- The hijackers and their financial facilitators used the anonymity provided by the vast international and domestic financial system to move and store their money through a series of unremarkable transactions. The existing mechanisms to prevent abuse of the financial system did not fail. They were never designed to detect or disrupt transactions of the type that financed 9/11.

- Virtually all of the plot funding was provided by al Qaeda. There is no evidence that any person in the United States, or any foreign government, provided any substantial funding to the hijackers.

- Exhaustive investigation by U.S. government agencies and the securities industry has revealed no evidence that any person with advance knowledge of the 9/11 attacks profited from them through securities transactions.

Raising and moving money for al Qaeda

- Contrary to public opinion, Bin Ladin did not have access to any significant amounts of personal wealth (particularly after his move from Sudan to Afghanistan) and did not personally fund al Qaeda, either through an inheritance or businesses he owned in Sudan. Rather, al Qaeda relied on diversions from Islamic charities and on well-placed financial facilitators who gathered money from both witting and unwitting donors, primarily in the Gulf region.

- The nature and extent of al Qaeda fund-raising and money movement make intelligence collection exceedingly difficult, and gaps appear to remain in the intelligence community's understanding of the issue. Because of the complexity and variety of ways to collect and move small amounts of money in a vast worldwide financial system, gathering intelligence on al Qaeda financial flows will remain a hard target for the foreseeable future.

Intelligence gathering on al Qaeda

- Within the United States, although FBI street agents had gathered significant intelligence on specific suspected fund-raisers before 9/11, the FBI did not systematically gather and analyze the information its agents developed. The FBI as an organization failed to understand the nature and extent of the problem or to develop a coherent strategy for confronting it. As a result the FBI could not fulfill its role to provide intelligence on domestic terrorist financing to government policymakers and did not contribute to national policy coordination.

- Outside the United States, the U.S. intelligence community before 9/11 devoted relatively few resources to collecting financial intelligence on al Qaeda. This limited effort resulted in an incomplete understanding of al Qaeda's methods to raise, move, and store money, and thus hampered the effectiveness of the overall counterterrorism strategy.

- Since 9/11 the intelligence community (including the FBI) has created significant specialized entities, led by committed and experienced individuals and supported by the leadership of their agencies, focused on both limiting the funds available to al Qaeda and using financial information as a powerful investigative tool. The FBI and CIA meet regularly to exchange information, and they have cross-detailed their agents into positions of responsibility.

Economic disruption of al Qaeda

- Before 9/11 the limited U.S. and UN efforts to freeze assets of and block transactions with Bin Ladin were generally ineffective.

- Before 9/11 the Department of Justice had little success developing criminal cases against suspected terrorist fund-raisers, despite a 1996 law that dramatically expanded its power to do so. Because of the "wall" between criminal and intelligence matters, both real and perceived, the prosecutors lacked access to the considerable information about terrorist fund-raising in the United States maintained in the FBI's intelligence files.

- The United States engaged in a highly visible series of freezes of suspected terrorist assets after 9/11. Although few funds have been frozen since the first few months after 9/11, asset freezes are useful diplomatic tools in engaging other countries in the war on terror and have symbolic and deterrence value. The use of administrative freeze orders against U.S. citizens and their organizations may, at times, be necessary but raises substantial civil liberties issues.

- Since 9/11 the FBI has recognized that its investigations of terrorist fund-raising within the United States must have an endgame: to stop the funding or otherwise disrupt the terrorist supporters. The Department of Justice has created a unit to coordinate an aggressive national effort to prosecute terrorist financing and now regularly receives information from the FBI about terrorist fund-raising in the United States, which it lacked before 9/11. Still, prosecuting most terrorist-financing cases remains very challenging.

- The financial provisions enacted after September 11, particularly those contained in the USA PATRIOT Act and subsequent regulations, have succeeded in addressing obvious vulnerabilities in our financial system. Vigilant enforcement is crucial in ensuring that the U.S. financial system is not a vehicle for the funding of terrorists.

- Financial institutions have the information and expertise to detect money laundering, but they lack the information and expertise to detect terrorist financing. As a result, banks and other financial institutions play their most important role by obtaining accurate information about their customers that can be provided to government authorities seeking to find a known suspect in an emergency or investigating terrorist fund-raisers.

- Although the government can often show that certain fund-raising groups or individuals are "linked" to terrorist groups (through common acquaintances, group affiliations, historic relationships, phone communications, or other such contacts), it is far more difficult to show that a suspected NGO or individual actually funds terrorist groups. In assessing both the domestic efforts of the U.S. government and the overseas efforts of other nations, we must keep in mind this fundamental and inherently frustrating challenge of combating terrorist financing.

Interagency cooperation and coordination

- Terrorist financing is, and must continue to be, closely integrated with the broader counterterrorism effort. Terrorist-financing measures both rely on and feed the broader effort. Terrorist financing is neither intrinsically different from nor more complex than other counterterrorism issues. The NSC (as opposed to an agency or a terrorist-financing "czar") is well situated to lead the operational and strategic integration of terrorist financing with counterterrorism generally. The government should resist the temptation to create a terrorist-financing czar or specialized, stand-alone entities focused on terrorist financing, and should support the current NSC-led interagency Policy Coordinating Committee.

Diplomatic efforts and Saudi Arabia

- Before the September 11 attacks, the Saudi government resisted cooperating with the United States on the al Qaeda financing problem, although the U.S. government did not make this issue a priority or provide the Saudis with actionable intelligence about al Qaeda fund-raising in the Kingdom.

- Notwithstanding a slow start, since the al Qaeda bombings in Saudi Arabia in May and November of 2003 and the delivery of a more consistent and pointed U.S. message, it appears that the Saudis have accepted that terrorist financing is a serious issue and are making progress in addressing it. It remains to be seen whether they will (and are able to) do enough, and whether the U.S. government will push them hard enough, to substantially eliminate al Qaeda financing by Saudi citizens and institutions. The highest levels of the U.S. government must continue to send an unequivocal message to Saudi Arabia that the Saudis must do everything within their power to substantially eliminate al Qaeda financing by Saudi sources. The U.S. government must assist by continuing to provide actionable intelligence and much-needed training to the Saudis. At the same time, the Saudis must take the initiative to develop their own intelligence and disrupt terrorist financing without U.S. government prompting.

Overall effectiveness of the U.S. government's efforts on terrorist financing since 9/11

- All relevant elements of the U.S. government—intelligence, law enforcement, diplomatic, and regulatory (often with significant assistance from the U.S. and international banking community)—have made considerable efforts to identify, track, and disrupt the raising and movement of al Qaeda funds.

- While definitive intelligence is lacking, these efforts have had a significant impact on al Qaeda's ability to raise and move funds, on the willingness of donors to give money indiscriminately, and on the international community's understanding of and sensitivity to the issue. Moreover, the U.S. government has used the intelligence revealed through financial information to understand terrorist networks, search them out and disrupt their operations.

- While a perfect end state—the total elimination of money flowing to al Qaeda—is virtually impossible, current government efforts to raise the costs and risks of gathering and moving money are necessary to limit al Qaeda's ability to plan and mount significant mass casualty attacks. We should understand, however, that success in these efforts will not of itself immunize us from future terrorist attacks.

Chapter 2

Al Qaeda's Means and Methods to Raise, Move, and Use Money

There are two things a brother must always have for jihad, the self and money.
An al Qaeda operative[5]

Al Qaeda's methods of raising and moving money have bedeviled the world's intelligence agencies for good reason. Al Qaeda has developed "an elusive network…an unconventional web"[6] to support itself, its operations, and its people. Al Qaeda has demonstrated the ability, both before and after 9/11,[7] to raise money from many different sources, typically using a cadre of financial facilitators, and to move this money through its organization by a variety of conduits, including hawaladars (see the discussion of halawas, below), couriers, and financial institutions. These sources and conduits are resilient, redundant, and difficult to detect.

Contrary to popular myth, Usama Bin Ladin does not support al Qaeda through a personal fortune or a network of businesses. Rather, al Qaeda financial facilitators raise money from witting and unwitting donors, mosques and sympathetic imams, and nongovernment organizations such as charities. The money seems to be distributed as quickly as it is raised, and we have found no evidence that there is a central "bank" or "war chest" from which al Qaeda draws funds. Before 9/11 al Qaeda's money was used to support its operations, its training and military apparatus, the Taliban, and, sporadically, other terrorist organizations. Since 9/11 al Qaeda's money supports operations and operatives and their families.

Since 9/11 the disruption of al Qaeda's sources, facilitators, and conduits, primarily through deaths and arrests, has made funds less available and their movement more difficult. At the same time, al Qaeda's expenditures have decreased since 9/11 because it no longer supports the Taliban, its training camps, or an army. That said, al Qaeda still appears to have the ability to fund terrorist operations.

Intelligence Issues

There is much that the U.S. government did not know (and still does not know) about Bin Ladin's resources and how al Qaeda raises, moves, and spends its money. The combination of Bin Ladin's move to Afghanistan in 1996 and his censure by the

---

[5] Intelligence reporting, Apr. 13, 2004. The discussion of al Qaeda financing in this chapter is derived from an extensive review of documents from State, Treasury and the intelligence community, as well as interviews of intelligence analysts, law enforcement agents, and other government officials.

[6] Intelligence reporting, Apr. 12, 2001.

[7] Our pre-9/11 analysis focuses on al Qaeda after Bin Ladin arrived in Afghanistan in 1996, and especially after he firmly established himself there by 1998.

international community following the 1998 East Africa bombings contributed to the difficulty in tracking this money.[8]

The CIA expressed the extent of the problem in April 2001:

> Usama Bin Ladin's financial assets are difficult to track because he uses a wide variety of mechanisms to move and raise money[;]…he capitalizes on a large, difficult-to-identify network with few long-lasting nodes for penetration. It is difficult to determine with any degree of accuracy what percentage of each node contributes to his overall financial position. Gaps in our understanding contribute to the difficulty we have in pursuing the Bin Ladin financial target. We presently do not have the reporting to determine how much of Bin Ladin's personal wealth he has used or continues to use in financing his organization; we are unable to estimate with confidence the value of his assets and net worth; and we do not know the level of financial support he draws from his family and other donors sympathetic to his cause.[9]

Even after the September 11 attacks, the intelligence community could not estimate the total income or the relative importance of any source of Bin Ladin's revenue stream. High-level policymakers were frustrated and characterized themselves as "seriously challenged…by an inability to obtain on a consistent basis solid and credible background information on targets for blocking of assets[.]"[10] More than a year after 9/11, the head of the government's terrorist-financing coordination effort described this gap in knowledge:

> [S]ometime in the next 3 months a Congressional committee is rightfully going to haul us up to the Hill (or the President is going to call us into the Oval office) and ask us 4 questions:
>
> 1. Who finances al Qaeda?
> 2. How?
> 3. Where is it?
> 4. Why don't you have it (and stop it)?
>
> Paul [O'Neill, secretary of the Treasury] could not [be able to] answer [those questions] today.[11]

---

[8] Mainstream Gulf area donors and the Bin Ladin family generally turned away from Usama Bin Ladin after the East Africa bombings. Additionally, UN Security Council Resolution 1333 in December 2000 called on all member states to freeze funds in accounts associated with al Qaeda, a point discussed more fully later in this monograph.

[9] Intelligence reporting, Apr. 12, 2001.

[10] State Department Memorandum, Dec. 3, 2001.

[11] Treasury Department email, Nov. 14, 2002. The CIA contends it has much better intelligence about al Qaeda financing than is indicated by this Department of Treasury document. In the CIA's view, Treasury was unhappy because the CIA's intelligence was often extremely sensitive, so it could not be released to support public designations.

The volume and quality of the intelligence appear to have improved since the summer of 2002, mostly because a flood of information is being derived from custodial interviews of captured al Qaeda members. Reliance on this information, of course, has its perils. Detainees may provide misinformation and may misrepresent or mischaracterize their roles or the roles of others. As a result, corroborating their information, through other custodial interviews, documentary evidence, or other intelligence collection, is critical in assessing what we know about al Qaeda financing. Even if what detained al Qaeda members tell us is accurate, the information can be stale, as it necessarily describes the state of affairs before their capture, and it is unlikely to be "actionable"—that is, sufficient to create an opportunity for disruption or to enable investigators to follow a money trail forward to operational elements or backward to the donors or facilitators.

Understanding al Qaeda's money flows and providing actionable intelligence present ongoing challenges because of the speed, diversity, and complexity of the means and methods for raising and moving money; the commingling of terrorist money with legitimate funds; the many layers and transfers between donors and the ultimate recipients of the money; the existence of unwitting participants (including donors who give to generalized jihadist struggles rather than specifically to al Qaeda); and the U.S. government's reliance on foreign government reporting for intelligence.

Commission staff evaluated the existing information regarding al Qaeda's financing, before 9/11 and today, in light of these limitations. We describe what we know, acknowledge where the information is simply insufficient, and discuss what we are reasonably certain did *not* occur. The list of purported al Qaeda funding sources is legion: counterfeit trademarked goods, consumer coupon fraud, drug trafficking, insider trading, support from Gulf-area governments, and conflict diamonds are the most common. In many cases, one or two threads of information make such theories tantalizing; but after careful review of all of the evidence available to us, including some of the most sensitive information held by the U.S. government, we have judged that such theories cannot be substantiated.

Al Qaeda's Financing: Sources, Movement, Uses

Where did al Qaeda get its money?

Al Qaeda relied on fund-raising before 9/11 to a greater extent than thought at the time. Bin Ladin did not have large sums of inherited money or extensive business resources. Rather, it appears that al Qaeda lived essentially hand to mouth. A group of financial facilitators generated the funds; they may have received money from a spectrum of donors, charities, and mosques, with only some knowing the ultimate destination of their money. The CIA estimates that it cost al Qaeda about $30 million per year to sustain its activities before 9/11, an amount raised almost entirely through donations.

Dispelling myths

For many years, the United States thought Bin Ladin financed al Qaeda's expenses through a vast personal inheritance or through the proceeds of the sale of his Sudanese businesses. Neither was true. Bin Ladin was alleged to have inherited approximately $300 million when his father died, funds used while in Sudan and Afghanistan. This money was thought to have formed the basis of the financing for al Qaeda.[12] Only after NSC-initiated interagency trips to Saudi Arabia in 1999 and 2000, and after interviews of Bin Ladin family members in the United States, was the myth of Bin Ladin's fortune discredited. From about 1970 until 1993 or 1994, Usama Bin Ladin received about a million dollars per year—adding up to a significant sum, to be sure, but not a $300 million fortune. In 1994 the Saudi government forced the Bin Ladin family to find a buyer for Usama's share of the family company and to place the proceeds into a frozen account. The Saudi freeze had the effect of divesting Bin Ladin of what would otherwise have been a $300 million fortune. Notwithstanding this information, some within the government continued to cite the $300 million figure well after 9/11, and the general public still gives credence to the notion of a "multimillionaire Bin Ladin."

Nor were Bin Ladin's assets in Sudan a source of money for al Qaeda. Bin Ladin was reputed to own 35 companies in Sudan when he lived there from 1992 to 1996, but some may never have actually been owned by him and others were small or not economically viable. Bin Ladin's investments may well have been designed to gain influence with the Sudanese government rather than be a revenue source. When Bin Ladin was pressured to leave Sudan in 1996, the Sudanese government apparently expropriated his assets and seized his accounts, so that he left Sudan with practically nothing. When Bin Ladin moved to Afghanistan in 1996, his financial situation was dire; it took months for him to get back on his feet. While relying on the good graces of the Taliban, Bin Ladin reinvigorated his fund-raising efforts and drew on the ties to wealthy Saudi nationals that he developed during his days fighting the Soviets in Afghanistan.

Financial facilitators and their donors

Al Qaeda depended on fund-raising to support itself. It appears that al Qaeda relied heavily on a core of financial facilitators who raised money from a variety of donors and other fund-raisers. Those donors were primarily in the Gulf countries, especially Saudi Arabia. Some individual donors knew of the ultimate destination of their donations, and others did not; they were approached by facilitators, fund-raisers, and employees of

---

[12] Reporting from November 1998 concluded that although the $300 million figure probably originated from rumors in the Saudi business community, it was a "reasonable estimate" as of a few years earlier, representing what would have been Bin Ladin's share of his family's business conglomerate in Saudi Arabia. The intelligence community thought it had adequately verified this number by valuing Bin Ladin's investments in Sudan as well as what he could have inherited from his fathers construction empire in Saudi Arabia. Finished intelligence supported the notion that Bin Ladin's "fortune" was still intact by concluding that Bin Ladin could only have established al Qaeda so quickly in Afghanistan if he had ready access to significant funds. Intelligence reporting, Nov. 17, 1998.

corrupted charities, particularly during the Islamic holy month of Ramadan. The financial facilitators also appeared to rely heavily on imams at mosques, who diverted zakat donations to the facilitators and encouraged support of radical Islamic causes. Al Qaeda fund-raising was largely cyclical, with the bulk of the money coming in during the Islamic holy month of Ramadan.

Charities

Al Qaeda's charities' strategy before 9/11 had two prongs. In some instances, al Qaeda penetrated specific foreign branch offices of large, internationally recognized charities. In many cases, lax oversight and the charities' own ineffective financial controls, particularly over transactions in remote regions of the world, made it easy for al Qaeda operatives to divert money from charitable uses. These large international Gulf charities donated money to end recipients, usually smaller in-country charities, whose employees may have siphoned off money for al Qaeda. In the second class of cases, entire charities from the top down may have known of and even participated in the funneling of money to al Qaeda. In those cases, al Qaeda operatives had control over the entire organization, including access to bank accounts.

Much has been made of the role of charities, particularly Saudi charities, in terrorist financing. A little context is necessary here. Charitable giving, known as zakat, is one of the five pillars of Islamic faith. It is broader and more pervasive than Western ideas of charity, in that it also functions as a form of income tax, educational assistance, foreign aid, and political influence. The Western notion of the separation of civic and religious duty does not exist in Islamic cultures. The Saudi government has declared that the Koran and the Sunna (tradition) of Muhammad are the country's constitution, and the clergy within Saudi Arabia wield enormous influence over the cultural and social life of the country.

Funding charitable works is ingrained into Saudi Arabia's culture, and Saudi zakat has long provided much-needed humanitarian relief in the Islamic world. In addition, a major goal of Saudi charities is to spread Wahhabi beliefs and culture throughout the world. Thus Saudi efforts have funded mosques and schools in other parts of the world, including Pakistan, Central Asia, Europe, and even the United States. In some poor areas these schools alone provide education; and even in affluent countries, Saudi-funded Wahhabi schools are often the only Islamic schools available.

Since 9/11

Financial facilitators are still at the core of al Qaeda's revenue stream, although there is little question that the arrests and deaths of several important facilitators have decreased the amount of money al Qaeda has raised and have made it more expensive and difficult to raise and move that money. The May 2003 terrorist attacks in Riyadh, moreover, seem to have reduced al Qaeda's available funds even more—some say drastically—for a number of reasons. First, it appears that enhanced scrutiny of donors by the Saudi government after the attacks may be having a deterrent effect. Second, Saudi law enforcement efforts have reduced al Qaeda's cadre of facilitators. Individuals such as Riyadh, an al Qaeda facilitator, and "Swift Sword," known for their ability to raise and deliver money for al Qaeda, have been captured or killed. Lastly, the Saudi population may feel that the fight has come to their homeland, and that they should be more cautious in their giving as a result.

Entirely corrupt charities, such as the Wafa Charitable Foundation, are now out of business, with many of their principals killed or captured. Charities that have been identified as likely avenues for terrorist financing have seen their donations diminish and their activities come under more scrutiny. The challenge is to control overseas branches of Gulf-area charities, prevent charities from reopening under different names, and keep corrupt employees of nongovernmental organizations from corrupting other NGOs as they move from job to job.

Despite the apparent reduction in its overall funding, al Qaeda continues to fund terrorist operations with relative ease. The amounts of money required for most operations are small, and al Qaeda can apparently still draw on hard-core donors who knowingly fund it and sympathizers who divert charitable donations to it.

The exact extent to which the donors know where their money is going remains unknown. Still, substantial evidence indicates that many Gulf donors did know and even wanted evidence that the fund-raisers really were connected to al Qaeda. In addition, some donations, while not completely sinister, are not completely innocent. For example, many donors gave funds to support the families of mujahideen fighters in Afghanistan. Such donors may not have intentionally funded terrorism, but they certainly knew they were supporting the families of combatants. Moreover, there is evidence that donations increased substantially after the United States attacked al Qaeda in Afghanistan, suggesting considerable anti-U.S. sentiment among the donors. At the same time, it seems very likely that facilitators diverted funds from unwitting donors. To stop such revenue from well-intentioned donors, it is necessary to capture or kill the facilitators who raise the funds or to remove the corrupt imans, NGO officials, or others who divert them to al Qaeda.

Allegations of other sources of revenue

Allegations that al Qaeda used a variety of illegitimate means to finance itself, both before and after 9/11, continue to surface. The most common involve the drug trade, conflict diamonds, and state support; none can be confirmed.

After reviewing the relevant intelligence on al Qaeda's involvement in drug trafficking and interviewing the leading authorities on the subject, we have seen no substantial evidence that al Qaeda played a major role in the drug trade or relied on it as an important source of revenue either before or after 9/11. While the drug trade was an important source of income for the Taliban before 9/11, it did not serve the same purpose for al Qaeda. Although there is some fragmentary reporting alleging that Bin Ladin may have been an investor, or even had an operational role, in drug trafficking before 9/11, this intelligence cannot be substantiated and the sourcing is probably suspect. One intelligence analyst described the reporting as "bizarre." Bin Ladin may, however, have encouraged drug traffickers to sell to Westerners as part of his overall plan to weaken the West (though much of that intelligence is also suspect).

It is even less likely that al Qaeda is currently involved in the drug trade. Substantial post-9/11 intelligence collection efforts have failed to corroborate rumors of current narcotic trafficking. In fact, there is compelling evidence the al Qaeda leadership does not like or trust those who today control the drug trade in Southwest Asia, and has encouraged its members not to get involved. Although some individuals with some connection to al Qaeda may be involved in drug trafficking, there is no convincing evidence that al Qaeda plays a major role in it or that it is an important source of revenue.[13] In addition to the lack of affirmative evidence, there are substantial reasons to believe that al Qaeda has no role in drug trafficking: al Qaeda members are geographically hemmed in and are unable to travel as the narcotics business demands. Trafficking would unnecessarily expose al Qaeda operatives to risks of detection or arrest. Moreover, established traffickers have no reason to involve al Qaeda in their lucrative businesses; associating with the world's most hunted men would attract unwanted attention to their activities and exponentially increase the resources devoted to catching them. Furthermore, Al Qaeda neither controls territory nor brings needed skills and therefore has no leverage to break into the sector.

Allegations that al Qaeda has used the trade in conflict diamonds to fund itself similarly have not been substantiated. Commission staff has evaluated the sources of information for these various public reports raising the diamond allegations. These include reports of journalists, the United Nations, and certain nongovernmental organizations investigating this issue. The FBI conducted an intensive international investigation of the conflict diamond issue, including interviews of key witnesses with direct knowledge of the relevant facts, and found no evidence of any substantial al Qaeda involvement; the CIA has come to the same judgment. Additionally, detained operatives have since reported that al Qaeda was not involved in legal or illegal trading in diamonds or precious stones during its Afghan years. We have evaluated the U.S. government investigations in light of the public reports to the contrary, the relative veracity of the sources of information, and the best available intelligence on the subject, and see no basis to dispute these conclusions. There is some evidence that specific al Qaeda operatives may have either dabbled in trading precious stones at some point, or expressed an interest in doing so, but that evidence cannot be extrapolated to conclude that al Qaeda has funded itself in that manner.

---

[13] We are aware of the December 2003 seizure of two tons of hashish from a ship in the Persian Gulf, and of the initial press reports that three individuals on board had purported al Qaeda links. Both the CIA and the DEA discount the significance of those links, and neither agency believes that this seizure is evidence that al Qaeda is financing itself through narcotics trafficking. We have seen no evidence to the contrary.

Other than support provided by the Taliban in Afghanistan, there is no persuasive evidence of systematic government financial sponsorship of al Qaeda by any country either before or after 9/11. While there have been numerous allegations about Saudi government complicity in al Qaeda, the Commission staff has found no persuasive evidence that the Saudi government as an institution or as individual senior officials knowingly support or supported al Qaeda.[14]

Al Qaeda fund-raising in the United States

The United States is not, and has not been, a substantial source of al Qaeda funding, but some funds raised in the United States may have made their way to al Qaeda and its affiliated groups. A murky U.S. network of jihadist supporters has plainly provided funds to foreign mujahideen with al Qaeda links. Still, there is little hard evidence of substantial funds from the United States actually going to al Qaeda. A CIA expert on al Qaeda financing believes that any money coming out of the United States for al Qaeda is "minuscule." Domestic law enforcement officials, acknowledging the possibility of schemes that they have not identified, generally state it is impossible to know how much, if any, funding al Qaeda receives out of the United States. These officials agree that any funds al Qaeda raises in the United States amount to much less than is raised by other terrorist groups, such as Hamas and Hezbollah, and that the United States is not a primary source of al Qaeda funding.

Finally, contrary to some public reports, we have not seen substantial evidence that al Qaeda shares a fund-raising infrastructure in the United States with Hamas, Hezbollah, or Palestinian Islamic Jihad. None of the witnesses we interviewed, including the FBI's leading authorities on terrorist financing generally and its expert on Palestinian extremist fund-raising specifically, reported evidence of this overlap, although supporters of Palestinian extremist groups travel in the same general circles as suspected al Qaeda supporters and have some contact with them.[15] In fact, there is far more evidence of fund-raising collaboration between Hamas and Hezbollah than between either of these groups and al Qaeda, according to the FBI official responsible for tracking these groups' funding.

How did al Qaeda move its money?

---

[14] The Saudi government turned a blind eye to the financing of al Qaeda by prominent religious and business leaders and organizations, at least before 9/11, and the Saudis did not begin to crack down hard on al Qaeda financing in the Kingdom until after the May 2003 al Qaeda attacks in Riyadh. See chapter 3, "Government Efforts Before and After the September 11 Attacks," and chapter 7 on al Haramain and Saudi Arabia.

[15] In addition, individuals may have made donations both to suspected Hamas front groups and to other organizations believed to be somehow affiliated with al Qaeda. Such overlap does not establish any organizational coordination or cooperation, however.

Before 9/11 al Qaeda appears to have relied primarily on hawala[16] and couriers to move substantial amounts of money for its activities in Afghanistan. Charities were also used as conduits to transfer funds from donors to al Qaeda leaders. At times al Qaeda operatives and supporters in the West and other banking centers freely used the international financing system.

Hawala

Al Qaeda moved much of its money by hawala before 9/11. In some ways, al Qaeda had no choice after its move to Afghanistan in 1996; the banking system there was antiquated and undependable. Hawala became particularly important after the August 1998 East Africa bombings increased worldwide scrutiny of the formal financial system. Bin Ladin turned to an established hawala network operating in Pakistan, in Dubai, and throughout the Middle East to transfer funds efficiently. Hawalas were attractive to al Qaeda because they, unlike formal financial institutions, were not subject to potential government oversight and did not keep detailed records in standard form. Although hawaladars do keep ledgers, their records are often written in idiosyncratic shorthand and maintained only briefly. Al Qaeda used about a dozen trusted hawaladars, who almost certainly knew of the source and purpose of the money. Al Qaeda also used both unwitting hawaladars and hawaladars who probably strongly suspected that they were dealing with al Qaeda but were nevertheless willing to deal with anyone.

Financial institutions

Al Qaeda itself probably did not use the formal financial system to store or transfer funds internally after Bin Ladin moved to Afghanistan. Bin Ladin's finances were initially in dire straits; al Qaeda was living hand to mouth and did not have any funds to store. Additionally, the Afghan banking system was rudimentary at best, and the increased scrutiny after the East Africa bombings and the UN resolutions against Bin Ladin and the Taliban made the use of such institutions problematic.

Al Qaeda's extended network of supporters and operatives did use the formal financial system before 9/11. Hawaladars associated with al Qaeda (like hawaladars generally) relied on banks as part of their hawala operations. One bank, for example, had 1,800 to 2,000 branches in Pakistan, making it relatively easy for a hawaladar to use the bank to move funds.[17] In addition to hawaladars, charities such as Wafa Humanitarian

---

[16] A definition of *hawala* is contained in the case study of the al-Barakaat network. Additionally, a good discussion of hawala is found in U.S. Department of Treasury, *A Report to Congress in Accordance with Section 359 of the USA PATRIOT Act,* November 2002 (online at www.fincen.gov.hawalarptfinal11222002.pdf).

[17] Hawala was frequently combined with other means of moving money. For a single transaction, the hawaladars sometimes used both hawala and the formal banking system or money remitters; the senders and receivers of the funds also often used couriers to transfer the funds to and from their respective hawaladars. Hawala also enabled operatives to access the banking system without having to open an account.

Organization had accounts at banks, which served as a means to move money for terrorists.

Fund-raisers for al Qaeda also used banks to store and move their money. Most banks probably did not know their institutions were being used to facilitate the flow of funds to al Qaeda, although some may have. Corrupt individuals on the inside of these banks may have facilitated the transactions. There is little question that the near-total lack of regulation and oversight of the financial industry in the UAE and Pakistan before 9/11 allowed these activities to flourish.

Al Qaeda operational cells outside Afghanistan made extensive use of the formal financial system. As discussed in appendix A, the September 11 hijackers and their co-conspirators had bank accounts and credit cards, made extensive use of ATM cards, and sent and received international wire and bank-to-bank transfers. Those al Qaeda operatives and supporters who were relatively anonymous could more easily risk using the formal financial system than could al Qaeda's core leadership.

Couriers

Al Qaeda used couriers because they provided a secure way to move funds. Couriers were typically recruited from within al Qaeda and could maintain a low profile—perhaps because of their background, language skills, ethnicity, or documentation—and so, ideally, no outsiders were involved or had knowledge of the transaction. They usually did not know the exact purpose of the funds. A single courier or several couriers might be used, depending on the route and the amount of money involved. They picked up money from a hawaladar, financial facilitator, or donor, and took it to its destination. For example, al Qaeda reportedly used a Pakistani-based money changer to move $1 million from the UAE to Pakistan, at which point the money was couriered across the border into Afghanistan. The 9/11 transaction provides a good example of al Qaeda's use of couriers. As discussed in appendix A, the plot leader Khalid Sheikh Mohammad delivered a large amount of cash, perhaps $120,000, to the plot facilitator Abdul Aziz Ali in Dubai; Ali then used the cash to wire funds to the hijackers in the United States.

Since 9/11

Since 9/11 the core al Qaeda operatives have relied on cash transactions involving trusted hawaladars and couriers. The hawala network that existed prior to 9/11 seems to have been largely destroyed. Several of the main hawaladars who were moving money for al Qaeda before 9/11 have been detained, and the identities of others have been revealed in seized records. Al Qaeda may have developed relationships with other hawaladars, and it most likely uses them to move some of its money. However, major cash transfers apparently are done by trusted couriers or, for added security, by the main operatives themselves. Some couriers may be carrying information (although not specific operational details) as well as cash.

Using couriers has slowed down al Qaeda's movement of money, as physically transporting money over large distances necessarily takes much longer than using electronic means such as wire transfer. In addition, there is evidence that significant delays in moving money, especially to al Qaeda operatives in far-flung parts of the world, have been caused by the limited supply of trusted couriers. Moreover, transferring funds by courier requires planning, coordination, and communication, all of which take time. Al Qaeda's use of couriers presents challenges and opportunities for the intelligence and law enforcement communities. Couriers can be vulnerable to certain forms of enforcement, however.

How did al Qaeda spend its money?

Before 9/11 al Qaeda's expenses included funding operations, maintaining its training and military apparatus, contributing to the Taliban and their high-level officials, and sporadically contributing to related terrorist organizations. The CIA estimates that prior to 9/11 it cost al Qaeda about $30 million per year to sustain these activities.

Al Qaeda's expenses

Once in Afghanistan, Bin Ladin focused on building al Qaeda into a fully operating organization. Al Qaeda spent money on military training and support, including salaries for jihadists, training camps, and related expenses. Reportedly there were also propaganda and proselytizing-related expenses and costs to support al Qaeda outside Afghanistan.

Before 9/11 al Qaeda was reportedly highly organized, with a committee structure that included the Finance Committee. Credible evidence indicates that Bin Ladin played a significant role in planning each operation and was very attentive to financial matters. Other than Bin Ladin, the person with the most important role in al Qaeda financing was reportedly Sheikh Qari Sa'id. Sa'id, a trained accountant, had worked with Bin Ladin in the late 1980s when they fought together in Afghanistan and then for one of Bin Ladin's companies in Sudan in the early to mid-1990s. Sa'id was apparently notoriously tightfisted with al Qaeda's money.[18] Operational leaders may have occasionally bypassed Sa'id and the Finance Committee and requested funds directly from Bin Ladin. Al Qaeda members apparently financed themselves for day-to-day expenses and relied on the central organization only for operational expenses.

Al Qaeda funded a number of terrorist operations, including the 1998 U.S. embassy bombings in East Africa (which cost approximately $10,000), the 9/11 attacks (approximately $400,000–500,000), the October 18, 2002, Bali bombings (approximately

---

[18] Sa'id reportedly vetoed a $1500 expense for travel to Saudi Arabia to get visas for the 9/11 attacks until Bin Ladin overruled him (although there is no reason to believe that Sa'id knew the reason for the travel at that time).

$20,000), and potential maritime operations against oil tankers in the Strait of Hormuz (approximately $130,000). The actual operations themselves were relatively cheap, although these figures do not include such "overhead" as training at camps, evaluation of trainees, and recruitment. Although the cyclical nature of fund-raising may have created periodic cash shortfalls, we are not aware of any evidence indicating that terrorist acts were interrupted as a result.

Money for the Taliban

Once Bin Ladin revitalized his fund-raising after moving to Afghanistan, he provided funds to the Taliban in return for safe haven. Al Qaeda probably paid between $10 to 20 million per year to the Taliban. As time passed, it appeared that the Taliban relied on al Qaeda for an ever-greater share of their needs, such as arms, goods, and vehicles, and even social projects. In return, the Taliban resisted international pressure to expel Bin Ladin or turn him over to a third country.

Money to other terrorist groups

Before 9/11 Bin Ladin appears to have used money to create alliances with other Islamic terrorist organizations. Al Qaeda's cash contributions helped establish connections with these groups and encouraged them to share members, contacts, and facilities. It appears that al Qaeda was not funding an overall jihad program but was selectively providing start-up funds to new groups or money for specific operations. Generally, however, al Qaeda was more likely to provide logistical support and cover and to assist with terrorist operations than to provide money.

Since 9/11

Al Qaeda's expenditures have decreased significantly since the 9/11 attacks and the defeat of the Taliban, although it is impossible to determine to what extent. Al Qaeda has become decentralized and it is unlikely that the Finance Committee still exists. Sa'id continues to operate, but given the difficulties of communication, it is doubtful that he exerts much control. The direction and financing of operations are now based more on personal relationships with operatives than on a management structure.

Al Qaeda no longer pays money to the Taliban (for safe haven or otherwise) and no longer operates extensive training camps in Afghanistan or elsewhere. It still provides operatives and their families with modest support. Al Qaeda occasionally provides funds to other terrorist organizations, especially those in Southeast Asia. Intelligence analysts estimate that al Qaeda's operating budget may be only a few million dollars per year, although such estimates are only tentative.

We have learned much since 9/11 about how al Qaeda raises, moves, and stores money, but our understanding is still somewhat speculative. The U.S. intelligence community is forced to extrapolate from current information to fill in the gaps in our knowledge. Detainees have confirmed the basic sources of al Qaeda funding and methods of moving money, and have provided insights into changes in al Qaeda's financing since 9/11. Moreover, al Qaeda adapts quickly and effectively, creating new difficulties in understanding its financial picture. Intelligence challenges remain and are likely to continue, although the picture is clearer today than ever before. As al Qaeda becomes more diffuse—or becomes essentially indistinguishable from a larger global jihadist movement—the very concept of al Qaeda financing may have to be reconsidered. Rather than the al Qaeda model of a single organization raising money that is then funneled through a central source, we may find we are contending with an array of loosely affiliated groups, each raising funds on its own initiative.

Chapter 3

Government Efforts Before and After the September 11 Attacks

This chapter discusses the U.S. government terrorist financing efforts before September 11, and describes and assesses our current efforts. As in other areas of counterterrorism, the government has poured vastly more resources and attention to combating terrorist financing since the attacks, and has made great strides in a difficult area.

Before the September 11 Attacks

Notwithstanding the government's efforts to choke off Bin Ladin's finances before 9/11, on the eve of the September 11 attacks the CIA judged that Bin Ladin's cash flow was "steady and secure."[19] Although fund-raising was somewhat cyclical, al Qaeda had enough money to operate its network of Afghan training camps, support the families of its members, pay an estimated $10–20 million to the Taliban and its officials, and fund terrorist operations.[20]

Domestic intelligence and law enforcement

Before September 11, FBI street agents in a number of field offices gathered intelligence on a significant number of suspect terrorist-financing organizations. These FBI offices, despite setbacks and bureaucratic inefficiencies, had been able to gain a basic understanding of some of the largest and most problematic terrorist-financing conspiracies that have since been identified. The agents understood that there were extremist organizations operating within the United States supporting a global Islamic jihad movement. They did not know the degree to which these extremist groups were associated with al Qaeda, and it was unclear whether any of these groups were sending money to al Qaeda. The FBI operated a web of informants, conducted electronic surveillance, and engaged in other investigative activities. Numerous field offices, including New York, Chicago, Detroit, San Diego, and Minneapolis, had significant intelligence investigations into groups that appeared to be raising money for foreign jihadists or other radical Islamist groups. Many of these groups appeared to the FBI to have had some connections either to al Qaeda or to Usama Bin Ladin.

The FBI was hampered by an inability to develop an endgame; its agents continued to gather intelligence with little hope that they would be able to make a criminal case or otherwise disrupt an operation. Making a case in terrorist financing was certainly as if not

---

[19] Intelligence report, 29 August 2001. Commission staff has seen no evidence that would contradict the CIA's assessment.

[20] Commission staff, in researching this chapter, conducted a comprehensive review of government materials on terrorist financing from essentially every law enforcement, intelligence and policy agency involved in the effort. This review included interviews of current and former government personnel, from intelligence analysts and street agents, up to and including members of the cabinet.

more difficult than in other similarly complex international financial criminal investigations. The money inevitably moved overseas—and once that occurred, the agents were at a dead end. Financial investigations depend on access to financial records. This usually requires a formal legal request, typically through a previously negotiated mutual legal assistance treaty (MLAT), or an informal request to a foreign government security service through the FBI's legal attaché (Legat) responsible for the relevant country. The United States rarely had mutual legal assistance treaties with the countries holding the most important evidence; and when agents could make an MLAT request, the process was slow and sometimes took years to get results. In addition, an MLAT request required the existence of a criminal investigation. Because the vast majority of FBI terrorist-financing investigations involved intelligence, not crimes, agents could not avail themselves of even this imperfect vehicle for accessing critical foreign information. Informal requests were frequently ignored, even when made of U.S. allies in important cases. Moreover, simply to make a request required that the agents disclose the target and the nature of the evidence. The risk of potential compromise was great, and most agents were not willing to take the risk against such a speculative outcome. Obtaining foreign financial records thus was often a practical impossibility.

As was true in other areas of counterterrorism, agents perceived themselves as being stymied by rules regarding the commingling of intelligence and criminal cases. Chicago intelligence investigators looking at a Hamas subject thought, for example, that opening a criminal case precluded their ability to obtain approvals from the Justice Department for a FISA (Foreign Intelligence Surveillance Act) warrant to tap telephones. The agents believed that the Justice Department would think that the request under FISA would appear to be simply a pretext to further the criminal case.[21] No agents wanted to block themselves from using what could be the most productive investigative tool they had—FISA—so criminal investigations were not opened and potential criminal charges were not seriously contemplated.

Some agents also hesitated because of the nature of the cases. Indicting or even investigating an Islamic charity or group of high-profile Middle Easterners required special sensitivity. Fears of selective prosecution or inappropriate ethnic profiling were always a consideration in going after a high-profile and sensitive target. Certainly, the evidence had to be strong before a prosecution would be considered. As one highly experienced prosecutor told the Commission staff, if the FBI had aggressively targeted religious charities before 9/11, it would have ultimately had to explain its actions before a Senate committee.

Lastly, the legal tools in terrorist financing were largely new, untested, and unfamiliar to field agents and prosecutors in U.S. Attorney's offices. Congress in 1996 had made it a crime to provide "material support" to foreign terrorist organizations.[22] Before the

---

[21] The actual procedures were somewhat different that the agent's perceptions, however. See the 9/11 Commission, Final Report, at 78 to 80, and accompanying footnotes, for a discussion of the issue.

[22] 18 U.S.C. Section 2339B makes it a crime to provide "material support or resources to a foreign terrorist organization." The secretary of state designates foreign terrorist organizations in consultation with the secretary of the treasury and the attorney general.

enactment of this statute, prosecuting a financial supporter of terrorism required tracing donor funds to a particular act of terrorism—a practical impossibility. Under the 1996 law, the prosecutor had only to prove that the defendant had contributed something of value to an organization that had been named by the secretary of state, after a formal process, as a foreign terrorist organization (FTO). Unfortunately, al Qaeda was not named an FTO until 1999, so criminal prosecution could not be considered earlier. Even then, there was little impetus to focus on prosecuting material support cases or committing resources to train prosecutors and agents to use the new statutory powers. As a result, the prospect of bringing a criminal case charging terrorist financing seemed unrealistic to field agents.

It was far easier for agents to find a minor charge on which to convict a suspect, thereby ultimately immobilizing and disrupting the operation. This strategy was used in San Diego in 1999, for example; knowing that individuals may have been supporting a specific terrorist group, the FBI and the U.S. Attorney's Office for the Southern District of California developed a case charging the individuals with relatively low-level fraud. This prosecution effectively disrupted the operation. More often, however, agents knew that it would have been hard to persuade a busy prosecutor to bring a case on low-level fraud or minor money-laundering crimes. If the prosecutors knew the classified intelligence underlying the case, the agents might have had a better shot at convincing them. But sharing that intelligence was difficult, and required approval from FBI headquarters and notice to OIPR. Additionally, some of these low-level crimes carried no jail time, and most agents did not think prosecution for a crime ultimately ending in a probationary sentence would have been sufficient to disrupt an ongoing funding operation.

On a national level, the FBI never gained a systematic or strategic understanding of the nature and extent of the jihadist or al Qaeda fund-raising problem within the United States. The FBI did not understand its role in assisting national policy coordination and failed to provide intelligence to government policymakers. For example, shortly after the East Africa embassy bombings in 1998, a staff member of the National Security Council was assigned the task of coordinating government resources in the hunt for Bin Ladin's finances and ensuring effective interagency coordination of the issue. The NSC wanted the FBI to produce an assessment of possible al Qaeda fund-raising in the United States by al Qaeda supporters, but the FBI shared little information regarding Usama Bin Ladin or al Qaeda. The NSC therefore concluded that the FBI did not have relevant information.

The problem stemmed in part from the FBI's failure to create high-quality analytic products on al Qaeda financing or an effective system for storing, searching, or retrieving information of intelligence value contained in the investigative files of various field offices.[23] There was very little finished intelligence that FBI program managers could use to show trends, estimate the extent of the problem, or distribute to policymakers or other agencies.

---

[23] The Commission staff, in interviews with field agents and in searching the FBI's automated case-tracking system, found a treasure trove of information regarding suspected terrorist fund-raising organizations in the United States, yet none of this information was readily accessible.

The FBI lacked a headquarters unit focused on terrorist financing. According to the then-head of its Counterterrorism Division, the FBI considered setting up such a unit prior to 9/11. However, the FBI viewed terrorist-financing cases as too difficult to make. It also believed that fighting terrorist financing would have little impact, since most terrorist acts were cheap. As a result, the issue was left to the FBI's general counterterrorism program office. Those agents, overworked and focusing on the day-to-day approvals and oversight of the entire FBI counterterrorism program, had neither the time nor the expertise to wade through reports, talk to case agents, or focus on the terrorist-financing problem.

For its part, the Criminal Division of the Department of Justice also lacked a national program for prosecuting terrorist-financing cases, under the 1996 "material support" statute or otherwise. The DOJ's Terrorism and Violent Crime Section (TVCS) had played a role in drafting the material support statute and took the lead in developing the administrative record to support the first round of FTO designations in 1997. After such designations began to be made, TVCS worked on developing a program to use the 1996 statute, but it had little practical success before 9/11.

The fundamental problem that doomed efforts to develop a program to prosecute terrorist fund-raising cases was that DOJ prosecutors lacked a systematic way to learn of evidence of prosecutable crimes in the FBI's intelligence files. The prosecutors simply did not have access to these files because of "the wall." Although the attorney general's 1995 guidelines required the FBI to pass to the Criminal Division intelligence information indicating potential past, current, or future violations of federal law, the FBI almost never did so with respect to terrorist fund-raising matters. Lacking access to the relevant FBI investigations, the TVCS made some efforts to investigate cases on its own, including a cooperative effort with a foreign service to probe potential Hamas fund-raising in the United States. These initiatives took a great deal of time and effort and did not produce any solid criminal leads. As a small section with many responsibilities, the TVCS had insufficient personnel for the resource-intensive task of investigating terrorist financing.

The wall may, in fact, have created a disincentive for FBI intelligence agents to share evidence of prosecutable crimes with criminal prosecutors. One experienced prosecutor believed that it would have violated every bone in their bodies for these agents—who were evaluated in large part on the number and quality of their FISA investigations—to share information with the Criminal Division and thereby jeopardize the continuing viability of a successful intelligence investigation. Another experienced prosecutor expressed the view that FBI agents were focused on potential violent threats and did not think the uncertain prospect of bringing a fund-raising case justified the risk of losing a FISA investigation that might locate terrorist operatives. In any event, the FBI and DOJ's relationship regarding terrorist financing was dysfunctional; FBI agents rarely shared information of potentially prosecutable crimes with DOJ prosecutors, who, therefore, could play no role in trying to develop a strategy to disrupt the fund-raising operations.[24]

---

[24] Richard Clarke of the NSC, who was interested in terrorist fund-raising in the United States, expressed concern about the lack of terrorist fund-raising prosecutions to the chief of the TVCS. Clarke actually brought to a meeting material he had printed off the Internet indicating extremists were soliciting support in

In early May 2000, in response to an inquiry from the NSC's Richard Clarke, a TVCS attorney drew up a detailed proposal for developing a program to prosecute terrorist-financing cases, providing a sophisticated analysis of the relevant legal and practical considerations. The memorandum pointed out that the "vast majority" of the FBI's terrorist-financing investigations were being run as intelligence investigations, and contended that the FBI gave preference to intelligence equities at the expense of the criminal when the two overlapped. To circumvent this problem, the memo proposed the creation of a unit to identify and pursue potential fund-raising matters as criminal rather than intelligence investigations, and described a systematic methodology to investigate and prosecute domestic fund-raisers for foreign terrorist organizations.

The memorandum had no effect; no resources were allocated to pursue the proposal, and it was not implemented. The FBI continued its intelligence investigations, and the criminal prosecutors largely sat on the sidelines.

Most fundamentally, the domestic strategy for combating terrorist financing within the United States never had any sense of urgency. The FBI investigations lacked an endgame. FBI agents in the field had no strategic intelligence that would have led them to believe that any of the fund-raising groups posed a direct domestic threat, so there was no push to disrupt their activities. Without access to the intelligence files, prosecutors had no ability to build criminal cases, and the DOJ was doing little on a practical level to change the situation. As a result, FBI intelligence agents merely kept tabs on the activities of suspected jihadist fund-raisers, even as millions of dollars flowed overseas.

U.S. foreign intelligence collection and analysis

As we note in chapter 2, the CIA's understanding of Usama Bin Ladin and al Qaeda before the September 11 attacks was incomplete. The intelligence reporting on the nature of his wealth was largely speculative, and sourced to general opinion in the Saudi business community.[25]

The intelligence community learned the reality only after White House–level prodding. In 1999 Vice President Al Gore spoke to Saudi Crown Prince Abdullah during a visit to Washington, DC about isolating and disrupting Bin Ladin's financial network. The two leaders agreed to set up a meeting on this issue between U.S. counterterrorism experts and high-ranking Saudi officials. As a result there were two NSC-initiated trips to Saudi Arabia, in 1999 and 2000. During these trips NSC, Treasury, and intelligence representatives spoke with Saudi officials, and later interviewed members of the Bin Ladin family, about Usama's inheritance. They learned that the Bin Ladin family had sold Usama's share of the inheritance and, at the direction of the Saudi government, placed the money into a specified account, which was then frozen by the Saudi

---

the United States and asked the TVCS chief what the DOJ was doing about the problem. The answer was, unfortunately, not much.

[25] For example, a 1998 intelligence report acknowledges that the CIA did not know the exact state of Bin Ladin's personal wealth, although it cited his inheritance as $300 million.

government in 1994. The urban legend that Bin Ladin was a financier with a fortune of several hundred million dollars was nevertheless hard to shake, and U.S. government intelligence documents even after the September 11 attacks sometimes referred to him as such.

The lack of specific intelligence was a source of frustration to policymakers. As the NSC's Richard Clarke testified to the Senate Banking Committee in 2003:

> The questions we asked then [in 1995] of the CIA were never answered—and we asked them for six years: how much money does it cost to be al Qaeda? What's their annual operating budget? Where do they get their money? Where do they stash their money? Where do they move their money? How? Those questions we asked from the White House at high levels for five or six years were never answered because, according to the intelligence community, it was too hard.[26]

The CIA's response to Clarke's criticism was that terrorist financing was an extraordinarily hard target and that, given the legal and policy limitations on covert action against banks during this period, there was little utility in simply collecting intelligence on terrorist financing.

The CIA obtained a very general understanding of how al Qaeda raised money. It knew relatively early on, for example, about the loose affiliation of financial institutions, businesses, and wealthy individuals who supported extremist Islamic activities. It also understood that nongovernmental agencies (NGOs) and Saudi-based charities played a role in funding al Qaeda and moving terrorist-related money. The problem, however, was that the government could not disrupt funding flows, through either covert action or economic sanctions, because the information was not specific enough. The CIA had intelligence reporting on Sudan and the purported businesses Bin Ladin owned there, but by the time of the East Africa embassy bombings this information was dated and not useful. Much of the early reporting on al Qaeda's financial situation and structure came from a single source, a former al Qaeda operative, who walked into the U.S. Embassy in Eritrea in 1996.

CIA devoted few resources to collecting the types of strategic financial intelligence that policymakers were looking for, or that would have informed the larger counterterrorism strategy. The CIA's virtual station—ALEC station—was originally named CTC-TFL (Counter Terrorism Center - Terrorist Financial Links), reflecting the CIA's early belief that Bin Ladin was simply a terrorist financier, as opposed to someone who actually planned and conducted operations. However, the intelligence reporting was so limited that one CIA intelligence analyst told Commission staff that, unassisted, he could read

---

[26] Clarke testimony before the Senate Banking Committee, Oct. 22, 2003; see also Clarke testimony to the Congressional Joint Inquiry. Contemporaneous documents support Clarke's recollection concerning his frustration. For example in November 1998, Clark wrote that four years after the NSC first asked the CIA to track down UBL's finances, the CIA can only guess at the main sources of Bin Ladin's budget, where he parks his money, and how he moves it.

and digest the universe of intelligence reporting on al Qaeda financial issues in the three years prior to the September 11 attacks. Another person assigned to ALEC station told the Commission staff that while its original name may have been Terrorist Financial Links, the station appeared to him to do everything but terrorist financing. Any intelligence it had on terrorist financing appeared to have been collected collaterally, as a consequence of gathering other intelligence. According to one witness, this approach stemmed in large part from the chief of ALEC station, who did not believe that simply following the money from point A to point B revealed much about the terrorists' plans and intentions. As a result, terrorist financing received very little emphasis. Another witness recalled that ALEC station made some effort to gather intelligence on al Qaeda financing, but it proved to be too hard a target, the CIA had too few sources, and, as a result, little quality intelligence was produced.

Some attributed the problem to the CIA's separation of terrorist-financing analysis from other counterterrorism activities. Within the Directorate of Intelligence, a group was devoted to the analysis of all financial issues, including terrorist financing. Called the Office of Transnational Issues (OTI), Illicit Transaction Groups (ITG), it dealt with an array of issues besides terrorist financing, including drug trafficking, drug money laundering, alien smuggling, sanctions, and corruption. The ITG was not part of the CTC, and rotated only a single analyst to the CTC. Moreover, ITG analysts were separated from the operational side of terrorist financing at the CTC, which planned operations against banks and financial facilitators. Members of the NSC staff stressed that this structure was defective because there was almost no intersection between those who understood financial issues and those who understood terrorism. As a result, the NSC was forced to try to educate two different groups on the issues. Inevitable turf wars also resulted.

Before 9/11, the National Security Agency had a handful of people working on terrorist-financing issues. The terrorist-financing group had no foreign-language capability. As a result, its collection had to focus on targets most likely to use the English language. The NSA's effectiveness was limited by sparse lead information from other elements of the intelligence community on financing and, like the rest of the intelligence community, by the wall between intelligence and law enforcement that gave it only limited access to law enforcement information.

One possible solution to these weaknesses in the intelligence community was the proposed all-source terrorist financing intelligence analysis center at Treasury's Office of Foreign Assets Control (OFAC), called the Foreign Terrorist Asset Tracking Center (FTATC), which had been recommended in 2000 by the National Commission on Terrorism (the so-called Bremer Commission). The NSC spearheaded efforts to create the FTATC, but bureaucratic delays and resistance by Treasury and CIA officials delayed its implementation until after the September 11 attacks. The delays resulted from the CIA's belief that the FTATC would duplicate some of its functions, the CIA's unwillingness to host the center temporarily until OFAC could accommodate it, and Treasury's reluctance to create a secure facility to host the center and allow OFAC direct access to intelligence.

The government also considered possible economic disruption, to be effected by targeting Bin Ladin's financial resources or by intercepting money couriers or hawaladars who handled Bin Ladin's money.

There is little doubt that the CIA had the authority to use methods of covert disruption to go after cash couriers or hawaladars. Ultimately it was unsuccessful in doing so, either because it was unable to identify specific useful targets or because such disruption was judged to be too dangerous.

Economic and diplomatic efforts

Treasury's Office of Foreign Assets Control had an early interest in searching out and freezing Bin Ladin assets. Its primary tool, the International Emergency Economic Powers Act (IEEPA), allows the president to designate individuals and entities as a threat to the United States and thereby freeze their assets and block their transactions. OFAC, for example, had long experience in freezing assets associated with Libya and Cuba. In the 1990s the government began to use these powers in a different, more innovative way, to go after nonstate actors. It first imposed sanctions against persons and entities interfering with the Middle East peace process (MEPP) and then against other nonstate threats, such as the Cali, Colombia, narcotics-trafficking cartel. OFAC personnel were interested in trying to find and freeze Bin Ladin's assets, but to do so required either a presidential designation of Bin Ladin or the discovery of a link between Bin Ladin and someone named for disrupting the MEPP. Efforts were made before the East Africa bombings to link Bin Ladin to the names on the MEPP list, but their lack of usable intelligence on the issue hampered OFAC analysts. OFAC did not collect its own intelligence; rather, it relied on the intelligence community to collect and often analyze the evidence, which it then used to make designations.

After the East Africa bombings in August 1998, President Clinton formally designated Usama Bin Ladin and al Qaeda as subject to the sanctions available under the IEEPA program, giving OFAC the ability to search for and freeze any of their assets within the U.S. or in the possession or control of U.S. persons. OFAC had little specific information to go on, however, and few funds were frozen.[27] The futility of this effort is attributed to the lack of usable intelligence, OFAC's reluctance to rely on what classified information there was, and Bin Ladin's transfer of most of his assets out of the formal financial system by that time. Even if OFAC had received better intelligence from the intelligence community, it could have taken little effective action. OFAC has authority over only U.S. persons (individuals and entities), wherever located. Because Al Qaeda money flows depended on an informal network of hawalas and Islamic institutions moving money from Gulf supporters to Afghanistan, these funds would stayed outside the U.S. formal financial system.

---

[27] OFAC did freeze accounts belonging to Salah Idris, the owner of the Al-Shifa facility bombed in response to the East Africa embassy bombings. Idris filed suit against his bank and OFAC, and OFAC subsequently authorized the unfreezing of those accounts.

The Taliban was designated by the president under the IEEPA in July 1999 for harboring Usama Bin Ladin and al Qaeda. Here, OFAC experienced better success against a more stationary target: it blocked more than $34 million in Taliban assets held in U.S. banks, mostly consisting of assets of Afghanistan's central bank and national airline. The Federal Reserve Bank of New York's holdings of more than $215 million in gold and $2 million in demand deposits from the Afghan central bank were also blocked.

With the exception of some limited attempts by Treasury's Financial Crimes Enforcement Network (FinCEN) to match classified information with reports filed by banks, U.S. financial institutions and Treasury regulators focused on finding and deterring or disrupting the vast flows of U.S. currency generated by drug trafficking and by high-level international fraud. Large-scale scandals, such the use of the Bank of New York by Russian money launderers to move millions of dollars out of Russia, captured the attention of the Department of the Treasury and Congress. As a result, little attention was paid to terrorist financing.[28]

A number of significant anti-money-laundering initiatives failed to gain traction during this time. One, the Money Laundering Control Act of 2000, championed by Treasury at the close of the Clinton administration, proposed controls on foreign banks with accounts in the United States. These accounts had been shown to be significant unregulated gateways into the U.S. financial system. The legislation had broad bipartisan support in the House of Representatives but foundered in the Senate Banking Committee, whose chair opposed further regulation of banks.

Additionally, the Treasury Department and the financial regulators had proposed draft regulations in 1999, under the rubric of "know your customer" requirements. Broadly, these regulations required a bank to know the beneficial owner of the money and the sources of the money flowing through the owner's accounts, and to take reasonable steps to determine this information. This proposal caused such a storm of controversy— Treasury received more than 200,000 negative comments and fierce resistance from the financial services industry—that it was abandoned. Congress even considered rolling back the money-laundering controls then in place. As a result, Treasury regulators hesitated to move forward with future directives.

Another foundering financial regulation involved "money services businesses" (MSBs) loosely defined as check cashers, businesses involved in wiring money, and those selling money orders and traveler's checks. It would also have covered informal movers of money, such as hawaladars and other neighborhood shops that could wire money to a foreign country for a fee. These businesses were unregulated for money laundering and posed a huge vulnerability: criminals shut out of the banking system by regulatory controls could easily turn to these industries to move and launder criminal proceeds. Investigators had seen a significant increase in the use of these casual money remitters. Drug traffickers in particular took advantage of this relatively inexpensive and risk-free method of moving money. A study commissioned by FinCEN in 1997 recognized the

---

[28] The 2001 National Money Laundering Strategy, for example, issued by Treasury in September 2001, does not discuss terrorist financing in any of its 50 pages.

vulnerability of MSBs to money laundering. In 1994 Congress directed Treasury to regulate these businesses to discourage money laundering, but Treasury failed until after 9/11 to implement regulations that would have required the businesses to register with the government and report activity judged to be suspicious.[29]

On the diplomatic front, the State Department formally designated al Qaeda in October 1999 as a "foreign terrorist organization." This designation allowed the criminal prosecution of any U.S. person proven to be materially supporting the organization, required U.S. banks to block its funds, and denied U.S. visas to aliens associated with it. Additionally, the United Nations Security Council passed UNSCR 1267 on October 15, 1999, calling for the Taliban to surrender Bin Ladin or face a U.S.-style international freeze of assets and transactions. The resolution provided a 30-day period before sanctions would take effect, however, allowing al Qaeda operatives to repatriate funds from banks in the United Kingdom and Germany to Afghanistan. The United Nations adopted a second resolution, UNSCR 1333, against the Taliban and Usama Bin Ladin on December 19, 2000. These sanctions brought official international censure, but were easily circumvented. Other than this UN action, there was no multilateral mechanism to encourage countries to outlaw terrorist financing or ensure that their financial systems were not being used as conduits for terrorists.[30] The effect, according to a State Department assessment, was to leave the Middle East vulnerable to the exploitation of its financial systems because of generally weak or nonexistent financial controls.

Before the September 11 attacks, the Saudi government resisted cooperating with the United States on the al Qaeda financing problem, although the U.S. government did not make this issue a priority or provide the Saudis with actionable intelligence about al Qaeda fund-raising in the Kingdom. Despite high-level intervention by the U.S. government in early 1997, the Saudis universally refused to allow U.S. personnel access to al Qaeda's senior financial figure, al-Ghazi Madani al Tayyib, who had turned himself in to Saudi authorities. Two NSC-led trips to Saudi Arabia, while producing useful intelligence about Bin Ladin's personal finances, failed to gain any traction on the larger question of al Qaeda's fund-raising or any commitment to cooperate on terrorist financing. However, the United States did little to prod the Saudis into action; the generalized and nonactionable nature of the existing intelligence made a confrontation

---

[29] Draft regulations did not come out until 1997; a final rule was not issued until 1999, setting the implementation date for December 31, 2001. In the summer of 2001, Treasury announced that it would push back the requirement for registration an additional six months and the requirement for reporting nine months. After the September 11 attacks, Treasury decided to maintain the earlier implementation date.

[30] The Financial Action Task Force (FATF), a multilateral government organization dedicated to setting standards, focused on money laundering, particularly as it related to crimes involving vast amounts of illegally gotten money, such as drug trafficking and large-scale fraud. As part of the setting of standards, FATF engaged in a concentrated effort to assess the world's anti-money-laundering efforts and "named and shamed" jurisdictions that failed to establish minimum safeguards by publicly listing them and instituting economic sanctions against them. Although in December 1999 the United Nations General Assembly adopted the International Convention for the Suppression of Financing Terrorism, which had been proposed by the French and drafted by the G-8 members, the convention did not enter into force until April 2002.

difficult.[31] Moreover, other issues, such as supporting the Middle East peace process, ensuring the steady flow of oil, cutting off support to the Taliban, and assisting in the containment of Iraq, took primacy on the U.S.-Saudi bilateral agenda.

Saudi Arabia had not enforced its professed money-laundering regulations and, like most of the countries in the Middle East, it had enacted no other controls on the movement of money. Moreover, it had delegated the regulation of charities to the government's religious establishment and did little to address the problem of al Qaeda fund-raising in the Kingdom.

The United Arab Emirates, the financial center for the Gulf area, also had a reputation for being "wide open," with few regulations on the control of money and a woefully inadequate anti-money-laundering program.[32] The UAE system had been a concern of U.S. policymakers long before the 9/11 attacks, and they directly raised their concerns with UAE officials. The UAE had no money-laundering law, although at U.S. urging in 1999 it started drafting one, which was not finalized until after 9/11. Although the UAE was aware that terrorists and other international criminals had laundered money through the UAE, and that it was the center for hawala and courier operations, it did little to address the problem. Additionally, the United States expressed its concern about UAE support for Ariana Airlines and the movement of Bin Ladin funds through Dubai. Shortly before the September 11 attacks, the departing U.S. ambassador to the UAE warned senior officials in the Emirates that they needed to move forward on money-laundering legislation, so as not to be placed on the Financial Action Task Force (FATF) "blacklist" of countries not fully complying with international standards in this area. These warnings had no discernible effect.

Intergovernmental coordination and policy development

NSC Senior Director Richard Clarke considered terrorist financing important, and he established an NSC-led interagency group on terrorist financing after the East Africa embassy bombings. This group consisted of representatives from the NSC, Treasury, the CIA, the FBI, and State and was initially focused on determining and locating Bin Ladin's purported wealth. After interagency visits to Saudi Arabia in 1999 and 2000, the group succeeded in dispelling the myth that Bin Ladin was funding al Qaeda from his personal fortune. The group also focused on trying to figure out how to stop the flow of funds to Bin Ladin and was concerned about Bin Ladin's apparent ability to raise funds from charities. While the CIA paid more attention to terrorist financing during the interagency group's life span, Clarke was unable to get the FBI to participate

---

[31] State Department memorandum, Nov. 24, 1998 ("We are still far, however, from possessing detailed information that would enable us to approach key Middle Eastern and European government with specific action requests concerning Bin Ladin's financial network").

[32] The vast majority of the money funding the September 11 attacks flowed through the UAE. The fact that Ali Abdul Aziz Ali was able to use an alias or partial name, and show no identification, for five of the six wire transfers from the UAE should come as a surprise to no one.

meaningfully in the interagency process. Responsibility for the problem was dispersed among a myriad of agencies, each working independently and cooperating, if at all, on an ad hoc and episodic basis.

Where Are We Now?

Since September 11 the world has indeed changed, and nowhere more than in the area of countering terrorist financing. The attacks galvanized the world community and an international sanctions regime against terrorists and their supporters was established, with the United States leading the way with a vigorous effort to freeze their assets. With an understanding of the nature of the threat, both the intelligence and law enforcement communities established significant entities to focus on and bring expertise to this area. These new entities are led by experienced individuals committed to the issue who know how to use money flows to identify and locate unknown associates of known terrorists. They are supported by the leadership within their respective agencies, who have provided them significant resources and authority to do the job. A broad and active interagency mechanism was established and new legal provisions against terrorist financing were enacted, while many of the legal obstacles hampering terrorist-financing investigations were stripped away.

Domestic intelligence and law enforcement

In the days after the September 11 attacks, the FBI set up the Financial Review Group (FRG) to bring order to a chaotic financial analysis of the attacks, in which every FBI field office conducted its own investigation as though it were the originating office. The initial goals of the FRG were to investigate the September 11 plot and look for an al Qaeda support mechanism that could sustain a second attack. All relevant federal agencies, including Customs, the Internal Revenue Service, the banking regulators, FinCEN, and OFAC, agreed to staff the FRG and work together. The FRG brought in agents with financial investigative expertise from around the country. The local field offices continued their investigations, but provided everything they learned to the FRG for coordination.

The FRG, ultimately renamed the Terrorist Financing Operations Section (TFOS) and located in the FBI's counterterrorism division, is the FBI's national program office for terrorist financing. The FBI believes that TFOS allows for (1) consistency of financial investigations and the assurance that every major terrorism case will have a financial investigative component; (2) the establishment of effective working relationships with international banking, law enforcement, and intelligence communities;[33] (3) the development of a real-time financial tracking capability, resting in large part on the FBI's extensive relationships with the financial community, which has transformed financial investigations from the traditional, methodical, slow-paced analysis to a tool that can

---

[33] In this regard, one experienced criminal prosecutor said TFOS does a very good job at outreach to the financial community because its agents "speak the language" of accountants and auditors.

provide near real-time information in urgent situations;[34] and (4) the formation of teams that can be sent to field offices to bolster document-intensive financial investigations and provide guidance and leadership on conducting financial investigations. Significantly, it is the first time a single office has been given responsibility for coordinating the FBI's terrorist-financing efforts.

TFOS and the FBI still need to improve their abilities to systematically gather and analyze the information developed in their investigations and create high-quality analytic products and finished intelligence. As of spring 2004, the FBI has generated very little quality finished intelligence in the area of al Qaeda financing. The FBI's well-documented efforts to create an analytical career track and enhance its analytical capabilities are sorely needed in this area.[35] TFOS must also establish its own formal system for tracking and evaluating the extent of terrorist fund-raising by various groups in the United States. TFOS has created a program management unit responsible for, among other things, evaluating the extent and scope of the terrorist-financing problem in the United States. Such an effort is plainly needed to help guide the allocation of law enforcement resources and to help inform policymakers.

The individual FBI field offices retain primary responsibility for conducting terrorist-financing investigations, but TFOS provides field agents with resources not previously available as well as coherent programmatic leadership. To help integrate the field offices' efforts with TFOS, each field office has a terrorist-financing coordinator who serves as a liaison with headquarters and a resource to fellow field agents. As of spring 2004, this program is in its early stages, but it is a positive step toward a truly national effort.

The Department of Justice also has dramatically increased its focused efforts to investigate and disrupt terrorist financing in the United States. The Terrorism and Violent Crimes Section, using resources from various parts of the DOJ (including prosecutors from U.S. Attorney's offices, the Criminal Tax Section, and other sections of the Criminal Division), formed a unit to implement an aggressive program of prosecuting terrorist-financing cases. That unit ultimately evolved into a distinct Terrorist Financing Unit within the DOJ's Counterterrorism Section (CTS). The Terrorist Financing Unit coordinates and pursues terrorist-financing criminal investigations around the country and provides support and guidance to U.S. Attorney's offices on terrorist-financing issues.

---

[34] TFOS has made extraordinary strides in this area, including a great leap forward in the use of sophisticated software to help locate terrorist suspects in urgent situations.

[35] Some of the FBI's post-9/11 efforts in this area have been disappointing, in part because of a disconnect between the FBI's new analytical operation and TFOS. For example, a December 2002 analytical document titled "Al-Qaida's US Financial Network Broad and Adaptable" was distributed to FBI field offices and Legats worldwide. The then-head of TFOS told Commission staff that this piece was prepared by FBI analysts entirely without any involvement of TFOS and that its conclusion, as reflected in the title, was dramatically overstated and did not reflect a law enforcement judgment about what the evidence actually showed concerning any Al Qaeda financing network in the United States. Since December 2002, the FBI has taken steps to ensure analytical product about terrorist financing not be distributed without TFOS involvement.

In stark contrast to the dysfunctional relationship between the FBI and DOJ that plagued them before 9/11, the two entities now seem to be working cooperatively. The leadership of TFOS praises the CTS Terrorist Financing Unit for its unwavering support. TFOS leadership also believes that the U.S. Attorney's offices have been supportive and that the CTS Terrorist Financing Unit has been helpful in resolving any issues that have arisen between FBI field offices and U.S. Attorney's offices. The head of the CTS Terrorist Financing Unit identifies TFOS, as well as the FBI's post-9/11 International Terrorism Operating Section, as valuable allies, and describes the enthusiasm of these sections for criminal prosecutions as a "sea change" from the FBI's recalcitrance before 9/11.

Fundamentally, the FBI now understands that its terrorist fund-raising investigations must have an endgame. TFOS, in particular, with its financial investigative skills and prosecutorial mind-set, is a strong ally of the DOJ's terrorist-financing prosecutors. Generally, the demise of "the wall" has facilitated the flow of terrorist-financing information between the FBI and the DOJ's criminal prosecutors. This sharing of information has addressed the problems that stymied the DOJ before 9/11. Still, information-sharing problems arise in the field, and the DOJ must at times encourage its prosecutors to fight for access to classified FBI information.

Despite these improvements, prosecuting terrorist-financing cases continues to present vexing problems for prosecutors and agents. Although some within the DOJ argue that the average terrorist fund-raising case is no harder to investigate and prosecute than any complex white-collar criminal case,[36] sophisticated jihadist fund-raising operations, especially those involving international NGOs that support both humanitarian and militant causes, are generally very difficult to penetrate and prosecute. Investigating a material support case usually requires obtaining records from another country to show the destination of the money, which itself is often very difficult, as discussed above. Even with access to the relevant records, tying the funds to a specific criminal act or a designated terrorist group is extraordinarily difficult. Funds are often dispersed overseas in cash, making them virtually impossible to trace.

Unraveling terrorist-financing schemes can be even more complicated because the same groups that finance terror and jihad often provide real humanitarian relief as well. The people running these groups believe in charity, practice it, and keep voluminous records of it, thereby serving to conceal their illicit fund-raising activities more effectively. Prosecutors who fail to acknowledge that the corrupt NGOs do provide charity will likely be confronted with the beneficiaries of the charity lining up in the courtroom to testify for the defendant.

Even if money can be traced to an illicit activity or a designated group, proving the U.S. donors or NGOs knew where the money was going can also be extraordinarily difficult.

---

[36] It may well be that cases involving Hamas or certain other terrorist groups are easier to prosecute because the fund-raisers are more open about supporting causes that have legitimacy in certain circles and, therefore, are more likely to make incriminating comments on wiretaps or to informants. Anyone raising money in the United States for al Qaeda or groups affiliated with al Qaeda is likely to be extremely secretive and do everything possible to ensure the funds cannot be traced back to him or her.

Although there may be substantial grounds for suspicion, proving the level of knowledge required in a criminal case poses significant problems. Notwithstanding this difficulty, the DOJ appears to be committed to aggressive prosecution of terrorist fund-raisers in the United States, believing that such prosecutions can deter more fund-raising and disrupt ongoing fund-raising operations. The best cases may well require luck, fruitful electronic surveillance or a well-placed informant, or even the prosecution of the suspect organization for a non-terrorism-related charge such as fraud or tax evasion. This strategy can be effective in disrupting suspected terrorist fund-raisers, but can also lead to accusations of selective prosecution and oppression of Muslim charities.[37]

In addition to the FBI, other agencies, including the Department of Homeland Security's Immigration and Customs Enforcement (ICE) and the IRS's Criminal Investigative Division, play a role in investigating terrorist financing through their participation in the Joint Terrorism Task Force (JTTF). The FBI is the lead agency on terrorist-financing investigations through the FBI-led JTTF structure.[38] Commission staff believes this is appropriate. Terrorist-financing investigations are inextricably intertwined with overall terrorism enforcement; a fund-raising investigation may give rise to evidence of a group poised to commit a terrorist act, or the investigation of a terrorist group will necessarily use financial leads to further its investigation. One agency needs to be in charge of the entire counterterrorism effort and other agencies can still contribute expertise in particular cases through the JTTF. Of course, giving the FBI the lead requires continuing vigilance to ensure that the FBI properly shares information and willingly coordinates with its JTTF partners.

U.S. foreign intelligence collection and analysis

The day after the September 11 attacks, the CIA began beefing up its effort on terrorist financing and by mid-month had created a new section dedicated to terrorist financing, whose purpose was to create long-term intelligence capacity in this area. It is staffed with personnel from the FBI, NSA, and DoD and it absorbed the CIA intelligence analysts working on terrorist-financing issues in the Office of Transnational Issues, thereby correcting the perceived structural defect previously identified. This new section's mission is to use information about terrorist money to understand their networks, search them out, and disrupt their operations. The CIA has devoted considerable resources to the task, and the effort is led by individuals with extensive expertise in the clandestine movement of money. It appears that the CIA is devoted to developing an institutional and long-term expertise in this area.

---

[37] See chapter 6 (discussing reaction to non-terrorism conviction of the executive director of the Benevolence International Foundation).

[38] This designation occurred in a May 2003 memorandum of understanding (MOU) between the secretary of the DHS and the attorney general. The MOU became necessary to resolve turf battles between the FBI and ICE, largely resulting from Operation Green Quest, which began as a U.S. Customs–led initiative to investigate terrorist financing after 9/11 and followed Customs when it moved from Treasury to become part of DHS/ICE. For a report on the success of the MOU, see GAO Report 04-464R, *Investigations of Terrorist Financing, Money Laundering and Other Financial Crimes* (Feb. 20, 2004).

The FBI and CIA report that the information sharing between the FBI and the CIA is excellent, and that FBI personnel assigned to the CTC's new unit have duties indistinguishable from those of the CIA personnel and have complete access to all CIA data systems, subject to a need-to-know requirement. The CIA has access to FBI data as well. The CIA distributes its information to the FBI through criminal information referrals, liaisons at the field-level JTTFs, and interactions between their respective headquarters units.

Economic and diplomatic efforts

On September 23, 2001, President Bush signed Executive Order 13224 against al Qaeda, Bin Ladin, and associated terrorist groups, freezing any assets belonging to the listed terrorists or their supporters and blocking any economic transactions with them. Thereafter, the U.S. government embarked on a public course of issuing additional lists of designated terrorist supporters—a pattern that continued into the winter of 2002. The goal was to try to deprive the terrorists of money, but this approach also served to assure the general public that action was being taken in the area of terrorist financing and to keep the intelligence and world communities focused on identifying terrorist financiers.

The United States, understanding that an executive order covered only U.S. persons and transactions, pushed at the United Nations for a near-universal system of laws to freeze terrorist assets worldwide. The United Nations Security Council, galvanized into action as a result of the attacks, passed Resolution 1373 on September 28, mandating member nations formulate laws to designate individuals and entities as supporters of terrorism and freeze their assets. In the weeks after 9/11, in an intense effort around the world, more than 100 nations drafted and passed laws addressing terrorist financing or money laundering. Worldwide, more than $136 million, including $36 million in the United States, has been frozen. Currently, approximately 170 nations have the legal ability to freeze terrorist assets. Moreover, the United States engaged in a broad diplomatic and educational offensive to make other countries aware of some of the basic methods of raising and moving money in support of terrorist activities.

There are significant multilateral norms now in place to set standards for ensuring that terrorists do not use the formal financial system. Chief among these are the efforts of the Financial Action Task Force (FATF), which, prior to 9/11, had been the multilateral body responsible for setting international standards for the detection and prosecution of money laundering. In the months after 9/11, the FATF expanded its remit to include setting standards for terrorist financing, and made eight recommendations to prevent terrorist financing. These recommendations included, for example, creating the ability to freeze terrorist assets, licensing informal money remitters, and regulating nongovernmental organizations.[39] While setting standards is a necessary exercise, far more will depend on each country's diligently implementing and enforcing these standards.

---

[39] FATF, "Special Recommendations on Terrorist Financing," Oct. 31, 2001 (online at http://www1.oecd.org/fatf/pdf/SRecTF_en/pdf); FATF, "Guidance for Financial Institutions in Detecting

As part of the USA PATRIOT Act, Congress enacted financial institution regulations that had been largely rejected before the attacks; many were only tangentially related to terrorist financing. In part, they give the Secretary of the Treasury the power to name countries, institutions, or transactions found to be of primary money-laundering or terrorist-financing concern and implement new requirements that banks more closely scrutinize their relationships with foreign persons and banks. A broader range of industries—insurance companies, money services businesses, broker-dealers, and credit card companies, for example—were potentially subject to a host of new requirements, including reporting suspicious financial activity on the part of their customers to the Treasury Department. Federal Reserve examiners now inspect banks for compliance with antiterrorism directives. As noted in chapter 4, private financial institutions provided, and continue to provide, significant assistance in investigating terrorist groups.

Although Saudi Arabia's cooperation on al Qaeda financing was limited and inconsistent in the first year and a half after the September 11 attacks, the situation changed dramatically after the May 12, 2003, al Qaeda attacks in Riyadh. Saudi leadership, now finally understanding the al Qaeda threat, is by all accounts providing significantly higher levels of cooperation. Much of the Saudi government's efforts understandably focus on killing or capturing terrorist operatives, but the Saudis also have moved against fund-raisers and facilitators, shared intelligence, and enacted financial controls, such as requiring that all charitable donations destined for overseas be administered by the government and banning cash donations in mosques. They have taken significant action against al Haramain, for example, a charity suspected of funneling money to terrorist organizations, and seem prepared to go further. In addition, the Saudis are participating in a joint task force on terrorist financing with the United States, in which U.S. law enforcement agents are working side by side with Saudi security personnel to combat terrorist financing. To further this effort, the Saudis have accepted substantial—and much needed—U.S. training in conducting financial investigations and identifying suspicious financial transactions, help that the Saudis had long refused. Although Saudi Arabia likely remains the best and easiest place for al Qaeda to raise money, the Saudi crackdown appears to have had a real impact in reducing its funding. In addition, the Saudi population may feel that as a result of the attacks against their own people, they should be more cautious in their giving.[40]

The Saudis have demonstrated they can and will act against Saudi financiers of al Qaeda when the United States provides them with actionable intelligence and consistently applies high-level pressure on them to take action. At least until recently, as noted in chapter 7, the Saudis have generally moved slowly, and only after considerable U.S. prodding. Because Saudi Arabia remains the primary source for al Qaeda fund-raising, it is in a better position than the United States to identify the fund-raisers and collect intelligence about their activities. Apparently the Saudis may now be willing to take the

---

Terrorist Financing," Apr. 24, 2002 (online at http://www1.oecd.org/fatf/pdf/GuidFIT01_en/pdf); Jaime Caruana and Claes Norgren, "Wipe Out the Treasuries of Terror," *Financial Times*, Apr. 7, 2004, p.17.
[40] See chapter 7, the case study on al Haramain, and chapter 2, on al Qaeda financing, for more on these issues.

initiative. Certainly, the joint task force, their willingness to accept U.S. training in conducting financial investigations, and their recent successful actions against key facilitators are significant steps in the right direction. Time will tell whether the Saudis follow through on these efforts and accept their responsibility to lead the fight against al Qaeda fund-raising by Saudi sources.

Intergovernmental coordination and policy development

Terrorist financing is now, and has been since the attacks, the subject of extensive interagency coordination mechanisms involving the intelligence community, law enforcement, Treasury, and State. An NSC-level Policy Coordinating Committee (PCC) on Terrorist Financing was established in March 2002 to replace the ad hoc structure that had arisen in the immediate aftermath of the attacks. The PCC was chaired by the General Counsel of the Department of the Treasury until he left government service in November 2003. The process, often driven by force of personality rather than by any structural mechanism, appears to have worked well in resolving differing points of view on terrorist-financing policy and operational differences. The key participants in the interagency process, especially the leaders of the CIA and FBI terrorist-financing units, have lavishly praised each other's commitment to cooperation and information sharing. The PCC often was not fully integrated into the United States' broader counterterrorism policy and Saudi relations, however.

An Assessment

After 9/11, the government, in an attempt to "starve the terrorists of money," engaged in a series of aggressive and high-profile actions to designate terrorist financiers and freeze their money, both in the United States and through the United Nations. Donors and al Qaeda sympathizers, wary of being publicly named and having their assets frozen, may have become more reluctant to provide overt support. The overall or long-term effect of these actions, however, is not clear.

Moreover, these initial designations were undertaken with limited evidence, and some were overbroad, resulting in legal challenges. Faced with having to defend actions in courts that required a higher standard of evidence than was provided by the intelligence that supported the designations in the first place, the United States and the United Nations were forced to "unfreeze" assets (see, generally, chapter 5).

The difficulty, not completely understood by the policymakers when they instituted the freezes, was that the intelligence community "linked" certain entities or individuals to known terrorist groups primarily through common acquaintances, group affiliations, historic relationships, phone communications, and other such contacts. It proved far more difficult to actually trace the money from a suspected entity or individual to the terrorist group, or to otherwise show complicity, as required in defending the designations in court. Intelligence agents, long accustomed to the Cold War reality of collecting intelligence for extended periods of time before public action was necessary, were now faced with a new demand for intelligence that needed not only to be immediately and publicly acted on but to be defended in court as well. Policymakers, many newly thrust into the world of intelligence, were sometimes surprised to find that intelligence assessments were often supported by information far less reliable than they had presumed.[41]

These early missteps have made other countries unwilling to freeze assets or otherwise act merely on the basis of a U.S. action. Multilateral freezing mechanisms now require waiting periods before money can be frozen, a change that has eliminated the element of surprise and virtually ensured that little money is actually frozen. The worldwide asset freezes have not been adequately enforced and have been easily circumvented, often within weeks, by simple methods.

Treasury officials were forthright in recognizing the difficulty in stopping enough of the money flow to stop terrorist attacks, but argue that such freezes and the prohibition of transactions have other benefits. Designations prevent open fund-raising and assist, for example, in preventing al Qaeda from raising the amounts of money necessary to create the kind of refuge it had in Afghanistan, or from expending the sums necessary to buy or develop a weapon of mass destruction. Moreover, freezing groups or individuals out of the world's financial systems forces them into slow, expensive, and less reliable methods of storing and moving money. Additionally, there is significant diplomatic utility in having the world governments join together to condemn named individuals and groups as terrorists.

A far more nuanced and integrated strategy has since evolved. As the government's understanding of the methods al Qaeda uses to raise, move, and spend money has sharpened, the United States has recognized that measures to counter terrorist financing are among the many tools for understanding terrorist networks, to be used in conjunction with and in close proximity to other types of intelligence. Moreover, these measures, again when closely coordinated with the overall counterterrorism effort, can be used to disrupt terrorist operations and support systems. Intelligence and law enforcement agencies have targeted the relatively small number of financial facilitators—individuals al Qaeda relied on for their ability to raise and deliver money—at the core of al Qaeda's revenue stream (see chapter 2), and appear to have reaped benefits as a result. The death and capture of several important facilitators have decreased the amount of money al Qaeda has raised and have increased the costs and difficulty of raising and moving that money. These captures have additionally provided a windfall of intelligence, which can then be used to continue the disruption.

Some entirely corrupt charities are now completely out of business, with many of their principals killed or captured. Charities that have been identified as likely avenues for

---

[41] Compare Tenet's speech at Georgetown University, Feb. 5, 2004 ("In the intelligence business, you are almost never completely wrong or completely right") with Mueller's testimony to the 9/11 Commission, April 14, 2004, p. 126 ("If there's one concern I have about intelligence, it is that often there are statements made about an uncorroborated source with indirect access and then there is a stating of a particular fact....I think there has to be a balance between the information we get and the foundation of that information").

terrorist financing have seen their donations diminish and their activities come under more scrutiny. Controlling overseas branches of Gulf-area charities remains a complex task, however. The sheer volume of charitable dollars originating in the Gulf region, the nature of charitable giving in the Islamic world, and the austere and uncompromising version of Islam practiced by many Saudis pose a daunting challenge.[42] U.S. efforts have shown that detecting and disrupting the terrorist money among the billions is extremely difficult, even with the best capabilities and intentions.[43]

The May 2003 terrorist attacks in Riyadh, moreover, apparently have contributed to a reduction of funds available to al Qaeda. Increased public scrutiny and public designations of high-profile Gulf-area donors have made other donors cautious. The fight has come to the Saudi homeland, and Saudis and their government (as well as other Gulf-area governments) have come to realize the problems that unfettered financial flows may bring.[44] Although Saudi Arabia has by most accounts become more fully engaged in stopping al Qaeda financial flows, the Kingdom requires considerable technical assistance and must take the initiative in combating terrorist financing, as opposed to merely responding to U.S. requests. The Saudi regime must balance its terrorist-financing efforts, the legitimate charitable relief Saudi charities provide, and the need to maintain its own stability. A critical part of the U.S. strategy to combat terrorist financing must be to monitor, encourage, and nurture Saudi cooperation while simultaneously recognizing that terrorist financing is only one of a number of crucial issues that the U.S. and Saudi governments must address together. Managing this nuanced and complicated relationship will play a critical part in determining the success of U.S. counterterrorism policy for the foreseeable future.

While overall al Qaeda funding has apparently been reduced, it is nevertheless relatively easy to fund terrorist operations. When investigators do not know where to look, the tiny amounts of money needed for deadly operations are impossible to find and stop in a multi-trillion-dollar global economy. The U.S. intelligence community has attacked the problem with imagination and vigor, and cooperation among the world's security services seems to be at unprecedented levels, but terrorist financing remains a notoriously hard target. The small sums involved, al Qaeda's use of decentralized and informal methods of moving funds (including trusted hawaladars and relatively anonymous couriers), and the existence of a cadre of dedicated financial facilitators who raise money from potentially unwitting sources all contribute to a significant and ongoing challenge for the intelligence community for the foreseeable future.

---

[42] See chapters 2 and 7 for a discussion of the role of charities in Saudi Arabia.

[43] The United States perhaps leads the world in its ability to conduct financial investigations, yet often finds itself stymied in doing the financial tracing and analysis necessary to detect terrorist money flows. See generally chapter 6.

[44] As noted in chapter 2, despite numerous allegations about Saudi government complicity in al Qaeda, the Commission has found no persuasive evidence that the Saudi government as an institution or senior officials within the Saudi government knowingly support or supported al Qaeda. A lack of awareness of the problem and failure to conduct oversight over institutions, however, probably created an environment in which such activity has flourished.

The U.S. financial community and some international financial institutions have generally provided law enforcement and intelligence agencies with extraordinary cooperation, particularly in furnishing information to support quickly developing investigations. Obvious vulnerabilities in the U.S. financial system, such as the largely unchecked use of correspondent or private banking accounts by foreign banks or other high-risk customers, have been corrected. However, no valid financial profile of terrorist financing exists (despite efforts to create one), and the ability of financial institutions to detect terrorist financing without receiving more information from the government remains limited.

Law enforcement investigations often fail to prove the destination and purpose of money transferred across continents in complex transactions, and transactions recorded in a bank statement or a wire transfer say nothing about their source or purpose. Funds are sent overseas through a charity; a fraction of these funds may then be diverted for terrorist or jihadist purposes, often through additional charities and cash transactions. The investigations of the Benevolence International Foundation (BIF) and the Global Relief Foundation (GRF) vividly illustrate that even substantial intelligence of ties to terrorist groups can be insufficient to prove a criminal case beyond a reasonable doubt (see chapter 6). When terrorism charges are not possible, the government has brought nonterrorist criminal charges against those suspected of terrorist financing. Such an approach, while perhaps necessary, leaves the government susceptible to accusations of ethnic or religious profiling that can undermine support in the very communities where the government needs it most. Moreover, ethnic or geographic generalizations, unsupported even by intelligence, can both divert scarce resources away from the real threats and violate the Constitution.

Because prosecuting criminal terrorist fund-raising cases can be difficult and time-consuming, the government has at times used administrative orders under the IEEPA to block transactions and freeze assets even against U.S. citizens and entities, as we show in the case studies of the al-Barakaat money remitters and the Chicago charities (in chapters 5 and 6). In some cases, there may be little alternative. But the use of administrative orders with few due process protections, particularly against our own citizens, raises significant civil liberty concerns and risks a substantial backlash. The government ought to exercise great caution in using these powers, as officials who have participated in the process have acknowledged,[45] particularly when the entities and individuals involved have not been convicted of terrorism offenses.

The designated person or entity in such a situation does not have certain rights that might be available in a civil forfeiture action, when the government in most circumstances must file a lawsuit and bear the burden of proof by a preponderance of the evidence. As in any other lawsuit, the owner of the property has the right to conduct discovery of the government's evidence, such as taking sworn depositions and obtaining documents. Moreover, the defendant has the right to avoid forfeiture by demonstrating that he or she

---

[45]*See, e.g.,* Treasury Memorandum, Apr. 12, 2002. The memorandum proposed a six-month limit for discussion purposes, and offered a "clear recommendation" that "temporary blocking orders be pursued with due diligence and an anticipated end date."

is an innocent owner—that is, obtained or possessed the property in question without knowing its illegal character or nature. The difference between an IEEPA freeze and a civil forfeiture is that a freeze does not technically divest title. But when a freeze separates the owner from his or her money for dozens of years, as it has in other IEEPA contexts, that is a distinction without a difference.

Even more controversial is the government's use of the provisions to block assets "during the pendency of an investigation," codified in the USA PATRIOT Act. The government is able to (and has, on at least three occasions) shut down U.S. entities without developing even the administrative record necessary for a designation. Such action requires only the signature of a midlevel government official. The "pending investigation" provision may be necessary in true emergency situations, when there is not time to marshal the evidence to support a formal designation before a terrorist financier must be shut down. But when the interim blocking lasts 10 or 11 months, as it did in the Illinois charities cases (as we note in chapter 6), real issues of administrative due process and fundamental fairness arise.

The premise behind the government's efforts here—that terrorist operations need a financial support network—may itself be outdated. The effort to find, track, and stop money presumes that it is being sent from a central source or group of identifiable sources. As al Qaeda is further disrupted and its members are killed and dispersed, it loses the central command and control structure it had before. Some terrorist operations do not rely on outside sources of money, and cells may now be self-funding, either through legitimate employment or through low-level criminal activity. Terrorist groups only remotely affiliated with al Qaeda—and dependent on al Qaeda as a source of inspiration rather than operational funding—pose a significant threat of mass casualty attacks. Our terrorist-financing efforts can do little to stop them, as there is no "central command" from which the money flowed, as in the 9/11 attacks. Terrorist operations cost next to nothing. It is to our advantage to ensure that operational cells receive as little money as possible from established terrorist organizations, but our success in doing so will not guarantee our safety.

Chapter 4

Combating Terrorist Financing in the United States: The Role of Financial Institutions

Since the 9/11 terrorist attacks, U.S. financial institutions have, almost uniformly, wanted to do everything in their power to prevent their use by terrorist operatives and fund-raisers. Indeed, law enforcement and intelligence officials have praised the private financial services sector for its willingness to assist in terrorist-related investigations. The effort is clearly there, but what about the results?

The current regulatory regime was designed primarily for discovering and reporting money laundering—the efforts of criminals, such as drug traffickers, to filter huge amounts of cash through the financial system. Only banks have the information needed to discover and report those kinds of transactions. A regulatory regime in which valuable data are passed from the banks to the government, in that context, makes sense.

For terrorist financial transactions, the amount of money is often small or consistent with the customer's profile (such as a charity raising money for humanitarian aid) and the transactions seemingly innocuous. As a consequence, banks generally are unable to separate suspicious from legitimate transactions. The government, however, may have information that would enable banks to stop or track suspicious transactions. As a result, financial institutions can be most useful in the fight against terrorist financing by collecting accurate information about their customers and providing this information—pursuant to legal process—to aid in terrorism investigations. At the same time, the government should strive to provide as much unclassified information to financial institutions as possible.

Terrorist Financing in the United States

The term "terrorist financing" is commonly used to describe two distinct types of activity. First, it can consist of the financing of operational terrorist cells, like the 19 hijackers who conducted the 9/11 attacks. This financing consists of the funds the cell needs to live and to plan, train for, and commit the terrorist act. The second type of terrorist financing is fund-raising—the process by which an organized terrorist group, such as al Qaeda or Hamas, raises money to fund its activities. Such fund-raising often takes place through nongovernmental organizations, which may raise money for legitimate humanitarian purposes and divert a fraction of their total funds for illicit purposes.

The funding of terrorist operations involves relatively small dollar amounts, from the estimated $10,000 cost of the 1998 U.S. embassy bombings in East Africa, to the estimated $400,000–500,000 for the 9/11 attacks themselves (of which roughly $300,000 passed through U.S. bank accounts over a period of nearly two years). The 9/11 attack provides a good case study of how a large terrorist cell can be financed in the United States. The hijackers moved money into the United States in three ways. They received wires totaling approximately $130,000 from overseas facilitators in the United Arab Emirates and Germany; they physically carried large amounts of cash and traveler's checks with them; and some of them set up accounts overseas, which they accessed in the United States with credit or ATM cards. Once here, the hijackers opened bank accounts in their real names at U.S. banks, which they used just as millions of other people do to conduct the routine transactions necessary to their plan. The hijackers used branches of both large national banks and smaller regional banks.[46]

Nothing the hijackers did would have alerted any bank personnel to their being criminals, let alone terrorists bent on mass murder. Their transactions were routine and caused no alarm. Their wire transfers, in amounts from $5,000 to $70,000, were utterly anonymous in the billions of dollars moving through the international financial system on a daily basis. Their bank transactions, typically large deposits followed by many small ATM or credit card withdrawals, were entirely normal, especially for foreign students living in the United States. No financial institution filed a suspicious activity report (SAR) and, even with benefit of hindsight, none of them should have.[47] Contrary to numerous published reports, there is no evidence the hijackers ever used false Social Security numbers to open any bank accounts. In some cases, bank employees completed the Social Security number fields on the new account application with a hijacker's date of birth or visa control number, but did soon their own to complete the form.[48]

The use of a financial institution for a fund-raising operation looks entirely different from the use of an institution by a terrorist cell, like the 9/11 plotters. The transactions are often much larger. For example, the Benevolence International Foundation (BIF), an Illinois charity designated a terrorist supporter by the U.S. government in 2002, received more than $15 million in donations between 1995 and 2000.[49] Funds are likely pooled from multiple small donors and then sent overseas, frequently to troubled places in the world under the auspices of a charity. For example, the Global Relief Foundation (GRF), another Illinois charity designated a terrorist supporter by the U.S. government in 2002, annually sent millions of dollars overseas, especially to such strife-torn regions as Bosnia, Kashmir, Afghanistan, Lebanon, and Chechnya. According to its IRS filings, GRF sent $3.2 million overseas in 1999 and $3.7 million in 2000. Like the financing of a cell such as the 9/11 hijackers, however, a competent terrorist fund-raising operation will not be apparent to bank personnel. The money sent overseas will not go to al Qaeda or any designated terrorist group. Instead, the money will go to an overseas office of the charity or an affiliated charity, and the diversions to terrorist facilitators or operatives will likely

---

[46] See appendix A (discussing 9/11 transactions in detail).

[47] As discussed later, U.S. law requires banks to report potentially criminal financial activity by filing SARs with the Financial Crimes Enforcement Network (FinCEN) within 30 days of the suspicious transaction.

[48] This is not to say that the hijackers were experts in the use of the U.S. financial system. For example, the teller who opened an account for plot leaders Atta and al Shehhi spent an hour with them, explaining the procedures for ATM transactions and wire transfers, and one branch refused to cash a check for al Shehhi on one occasion because he presented IDs with different addresses. This incident led the bank to issue a routine, internal security alert to watch the account for possible fraud, but provided no basis for concern about serious criminality—let alone terrorism. These minor blips provided no clue to the financial institution about the hijackers' murderous purpose.

[49] Whether BIF actually funded al Qaeda remains an open question. See chapter 6.

take place overseas. In the current environment, the donors presumably will not include pro-Jihad comments on the memo line of their checks, as did pre-9/11 donors to one suspect charity the FBI investigated. The fund-raising operation will look to the bank like a charity sending money to troubled parts of the world—which it is doing, at least in part.

Why Suspicious Activity Reporting Works for Money Laundering But Is Less Useful for Terrorist Financing

The Bank Secrecy Act (BSA) regime, described below, was designed to combat money laundering and related offenses and, assuming that it is well-implemented and well-enforced, it is reasonably effective for this purpose. However, the requirement that financial institutions file SARs does not work very well to detect or prevent terrorist financing, for there is a fundamental distinction between money laundering and terrorist financing. Financial institutions have the information and expertise to detect the one but not the other.

The Bank Secrecy Act—what it is and what it does

The premise behind the money-laundering laws and regulations was that because the underlying crimes generate enormous amounts of cash, criminal enterprises need to convert that cash into something less traceable and more usable. In perhaps the best-known example of money laundering, Russian and U.S. shell corporations were able to move billions of dollars through correspondent accounts owned by foreign banks at the Bank of New York and Citibank. Likewise, Raul Salinas, the former president of Mexico, was found to have laundered millions of dollars in alleged public corruption money through Citibank accounts. The role of Mexican banks was highlighted in a U.S. law enforcement investigation known as Operation Casablanca, which found that millions of drug-tainted dollars had been laundered through Mexican banks.

The United States' method to prevent criminals from taking advantage of the financial system relies on the basic premise that financial institutions—not the government—are in the best position to detect money laundering and related illicit transactions. Thus, the law imposes on financial institutions the obligation to report suspicious activity that involves their use. This law and related regulations, generically referred to as the "Bank Secrecy Act," require banks (and now a host of other financial institutions, including broker-dealers, credit card companies, insurance companies, and money service businesses)[50] to understand, control, and report transactions that may have a questionable origin or purpose. Specifically, banks are required to report cash transactions in excess of $10,000, as well as any other transactions they deem "suspicious."[51]

---

[50] For purposes of this discussion, we use the term *bank*, although in most respects the obligations extend to other financial institutions.

[51] Additionally, banks must ensure that they do not unwittingly engage in transactions with individuals listed on Treasury's list of prohibited persons, maintained by the Office of Foreign Assets Control (OFAC). Such transactions are prohibited by a number of statutes tied to the president's ability to bar U.S. persons

The SAR requirement is at the core of the government's anti-money-laundering effort. Inherent in a bank's responsibility to report (or refuse to conduct) a suspicious transaction is an obligation to have sufficient knowledge of its own transactions and customers to understand what is suspicious. This requires a bank to "know" its customer—who the beneficial owner of an account is, what the customer's likely transactions should be, and what, in general, is the source of the customer's money. Once it understands its customer and the customer's likely transactions, the bank is able to determine whether the customer is conducting transactions out of character for that profile. Additionally, understanding the customer's probable transactions enables the bank to assess the risk that the account will be used to launder money, and will in some respects determine how closely the institution monitors the customer's account. A bank's failure to report suspicious activities, or to have a system in place that could reasonably detect suspicious financial transactions, is punishable by some combination of administrative sanctions, civil fines, and criminal penalties.

A bank can best detect suspicious transactions at one of two points. The "front end" of a transaction involves the tellers and other individuals who may have face-to-face contact with the customer and can often determine if a specific transaction is worth a second look. A bank will typically train tellers and other such individuals to look for specific "red flags" to determine if a transaction is suspicious. The second likely point of detection occurs in the "back office"—an analysis of financial transactions, which takes place in a specialized unit, for example, or in particularly high-risk areas such as the bank's wire transfer operations. Money-laundering analysts look at the bank's transactions to determine if they can conclude, by examining patterns of transactions, whether those patterns are suspicious.

Analysts are aided significantly by software that is programmed to catch "anomalies" (i.e., unusual financial transactions) that are indicative of money laundering. The key is to find those transactions that would be out of character for the customer's purported business activity. A large cash deposit would not be suspicious for a customer like Wal-Mart, but it would be for a customer whose only reported source of income is a Social Security check. Sophisticated software should be able to distinguish between such transactions and alert the money-laundering compliance analyst at the bank to investigate further. This software, however, is not self-executing. It must be set up and fine-tuned. Such adjustments can only be done by the bank itself; they require a deep and thorough understanding both of the bank's ordinary business and of its potential high-risk product lines and high-risk customers. Additionally, the bank typically has specialists with a fairly sophisticated understanding of money laundering. Because money laundering must involve large transactions, banks are able to safely ignore a significant percentage of their transactions that fall below specific thresholds.

---

from trading with an enemy of the state. Violations of these prohibitions are enforced by criminal penalties or by civil fines, depending on the seriousness of the offense, among other factors. The listing process, described elsewhere, is generally considered to be too cumbersome to be of use in detecting operational elements of terrorist organizations.

If further review does not dispel suspicions, the bank is required to file a SAR within 30 days from the discovery of the suspicious conduct. (When a bank cannot identify a suspect, it has an additional 30 days to try to do so.) The bank must also monitor the account and should refuse to engage in future transactions it deems to be suspicious. In some cases, it may terminate the relationship with the customer.

The BSA regime also reflects sensitivities concerning financial privacy. A system requiring bank reporting was thought to be less intrusive than allowing unfettered government surveillance of bank records. The specter of a bank "knowing its customer" is somewhat less threatening than the idea that the government ought to understand and know all of a citizen's probable financial transactions.

As a result of the BSA regime, most money launderers, drug dealers, and high-level fraudsters understand that trying to pump massive amounts of cash through a U.S. bank is fraught with peril. As a result, they generally prefer instead to use other, less risky, methods to move money—sending it in bulk across our porous borders, for example, or through a less-regulated industry like money-transmitting services. If they do use banks, they take care to structure smaller transactions among dozens of different accounts—less risky, to be sure, but considerably slower and more costly.

The terrorist-financing model

The model of banks having superior knowledge to detect illicit activity may not apply to terrorist financing. Although the U.S. government may possess the intelligence that could reveal terrorist operatives and fund-raisers, financial institutions generally do not. The 9/11 operation provides a perfect example. The 19 hijackers hid in plain sight: none of their transactions could have revealed their murderous purpose, no matter how hard the banks looked at them (see appendix A). Intelligence the government had, however, could have been critical to identify the terrorists among us. For example, the U.S. government had reason to believe that future hijackers Khalid al Mihdhar and Nawaf al Hazmi were al Qaeda operatives in the United States. Both these terrorists had U.S. bank accounts, but bank personnel never could have suspected that their customers were terrorists no matter how diligently they studied the transactions, which were utterly routine.

Since September 11, financial institutions and the government have made efforts to create a financial profile of terrorist operatives. The FBI examined the financial transactions of the 9/11 hijackers and came up with some distinguishing features: they arrived at banks in groups; they listed their occupation as students; they spent a large percentage of their income on flight schools and airfare, particularly first-class airfare; and they were funded in large part through wire transfers from the UAE. This profile might help detect another plot exactly like 9/11, but we can expect that the next plot will look entirely different. As a result, this profile does not especially help banks find future terrorist operatives, who we can expect will make different, although equally routine, use of the financial system. In fact, no effective financial profile for operational terrorists located in the United States exists. The New York Clearinghouse, a private consortium of the largest money-center banks, attempted to put together such a profile in partnership with government investigators. After two years, they concluded it could not be done.

Creating a profile for terrorist fund-raising groups is not necessarily any easier. An Islamic organization that collects funds from small donors, pools the funds, and then sends large monthly wire transfers to Chechnya, Afghanistan, Kashmir, or the West Bank could be a jihadist or terrorist fund-raising operation, or an entirely legitimate humanitarian operation devoted to serving civilians in impoverished and war-torn regions of the world. The government may have information (derived from sources such as electronic surveillance or human intelligence) from which it can distinguish between the two rationales for the transactions, but it is unlikely that banks will be able to tell the difference from the transactions themselves.

The government has also tried to describe suspicious activity indicative of terrorist fund-raising. The Financial Crimes Enforcement Network (FinCEN) conducted a comprehensive analysis of potential terrorist-financing patterns, which it published in January 2002. Drawing on actual SARs filed by banks, it described five cases that might have been examples of terrorist fund-raising. Ultimately, these cases centered on financial transactions indicative of money laundering that involved, as FinCEN delicately put it, "nationals of countries associated with terrorist activity."[52] This analysis appears to be of little use in ferreting out a sophisticated terrorist fund-raising operation, which will likely look to the bank identical to a legitimate Islamic charity.

Although FinCEN took great pains to caution that country of origin or ethnicity should not, absent other factors, be taken to indicate potential criminal activity, the report highlights a problem with applying the BSA regime to terrorist financing. The inability to develop meaningful indicia of a terrorist cell or terrorist fund-raising operation creates a risk that financial institutions could rely primarily on religious, geographic, or ethnic profiling in an attempt to find some criteria helpful for identifying terrorist financing. Such profiling raises a number of problems. Fundamentally, it will not be an effective means to combat terrorist financing. The vast majority of Islamic or Arab bank customers are not terrorists or terrorist supporters, so indiscriminately filing SARs on them will do nothing but waste resources and cause bad will. Similarly, reporting that an Islamic charity is sending money to Afghanistan will not be particularly effective in finding terrorist financiers; there are certainly many legitimate humanitarian needs there. In addition to doing little good, this type of profiling may subject customers to heightened scrutiny without legitimate basis, and could even extend to refusing to service customers meeting a certain profile. Of course, religion, nation of origin, or ethnicity can and should be taken into consideration, along with many other factors, in the subjective judgment as to whether a certain transaction or account is suspicious. Our point is that profiling—by itself—is both an unfair and an ineffective way for financial institutions to attack terrorist financing.

---

[52] FinCEN, *SAR Bulletin*, no. 4 (Jan. 2002). Typically, they included structuring multiple deposits or other transactions to be below the $10,000 reporting threshold, collecting funds through a variety of financial channels then funneling them to a small number of foreign beneficiaries, or a volume of financial activity inconsistent with the stated purpose of the account.

That being said, there may be utility in having financial institutions examine transactions for indicia of terrorist financing. It certainly assists in preventing open and notorious fund-raising and forces terrorists and their sympathizers to raise and move money clandestinely, thereby raising the costs and risks involved. The deterrent value in such activity is significant and, while it cannot be measured in any meaningful way, ought not to be discounted.

Financial Institutions Have a Role in Combating Terrorist Financing in the United States

The inability of financial institutions to detect terrorist operatives or terrorist fund-raising does not relegate the private sector to the sidelines in the fight against terrorism. To the contrary, there are a number of things that financial institutions can do right now. There also are a number of things that could be done in the future, if current law or government policies are changed. This section addresses what can be done now and assesses some possibilities for the future.

Now: Helping the government find the terrorists

Financial tracking

Although financial institutions lack information that can enable them to identify terrorists, they have information that can be absolutely vital in finding terrorists. If the government can determine where a terrorist suspect banks, his account opening documents can provide his address, and his ATM and credit card usage can show where he is and what he is doing. Again, the 9/11 plot provides a good example. Had the U.S. government been able in August 2001 to learn that hijackers Nawaf al Hazmi and Khalid al Mihdhar had accounts in their names at small New Jersey banks, it could have found them. The hijackers actively used these accounts, through ATM, debit card, and cash transactions, until September 10. Among other things, they used the debit cards to pay for hotel rooms—activity that would have enabled the FBI to locate them, had the FBI been able to get the transaction records fast enough. Moreover, al Hazmi used his debit card on August 27 to buy tickets on Flight 77 for himself, his brother, and fellow Flight 77 hijacker Salem al Hazmi.

If the FBI had found either al Mihdhar or Nawaf al Hazmi, it could have found the other. They not only shared a common bank but frequently were together when conducting transactions. After locating al Mihdhar and al Hazmi, the FBI could have potentially linked them through financial records to the other Flight 77 hijackers. For example, as noted, Nawaf al Hazmi used his debit card on August 27 to buy plane tickets for himself and his brother, linking those two hijackers. Nawaf al Hazmi and Flight 77 pilot Hani Hanjour had opened separate savings accounts at the same small New Jersey bank at the same time and both gave the same address. On July 9, 2001, the other Flight 77 muscle hijacker, Majed Moqed, opened an account at another small New Jersey bank at the same time as Nawaf al Hazmi, and used the same address. Given timely access to the relevant records and sufficient time to conduct a follow-up investigation, the FBI could have shown that Hani Hanjour, Majed Moqed, and Salem al Hazmi were connected to potential terrorist operatives al Mihdhar and Nawaf al Hazmi. No one can say where the investigation would have gone from there, but financial records could potentially have been used, along with other information—including perhaps information found in the possession of or provided by the Flight 77 hijackers—to link the Flight 77 hijackers to the others and, perhaps, disrupt the plot.

Unfortunately, this theoretical investigation would not have worked quite as smoothly in the world that existed before September 11. First, an agent attempting to locate the hijackers would have needed to know where to look. There are thousands of financial institutions in the United States, and making an inquiry of each one of them, regardless of the exigency of the situation, would not have been a realistic enterprise. Even an experienced agent tasked to find al Mihdhar or al Hazmi would have been unlikely to think to use financial tracking; and an agent who did probably would have first called those institutions with which he or she had some personal relationship—probably big banks.

Moreover, before 9/11 financial investigations almost always moved at a slow, methodical pace. In a typical investigation, a financial institution received a grand jury subpoena or a National Security Letter (NSL) from a federal prosecutor or agent. The subpoena had a return date—the date by which the bank was required to produce the records requested. In a typical investigation, the bank searched its records and produced hard copies of the material requested. Banks and other financial institutions then needed substantial time to locate and produce records, even in response to a lawful subpoena. Financial institutions had been prohibited from giving law enforcement certain records absent compulsory legal process.

Before 9/11, the U.S government did not think in terms of financial tracking, certainly not systematically and on an urgent basis. The terrorist attacks changed this thinking. Since 9/11, the government uses financial information to search out terrorist networks so that a known suspect like al Mihdhar could be quickly located. There are now two primary approaches for doing this: FBI outreach that has enhanced private sector cooperation and Section 314(a) of the USA PATRIOT Act.

The FBI's Terrorist Financing Operations Section (TFOS) has taken the existing legal rules, which were developed within the context of traditional after-the-fact investigation of financial crimes, and created a systematic approach to gain expedited access to financial data in emergencies. To facilitate emerging situations, the FBI has compiled a list of high-level contacts within the financial community—banks, brokerage houses, credit card vendors, and money services businesses—to whom it can turn to get financial information on an expedited basis at any time, including nights, weekends, and holidays. The FBI serves them on an expedited basis with a subpoena or other legal process to get the relevant data. In true emergencies, the FBI can get information quickly to locate an individual or find links among co-conspirators.

Applying the post-9/11 FBI approach to the pre-9/11 search for al Mihdhar and al Hazmi strongly suggests the current system would have enabled the hijackers to be quickly located. Indeed, the recently retired founder and chief of TFOS stated that given the same circumstances today, the FBI would find al Mihdhar "in a heartbeat."[53] Corroborating this contention, FBI has successfully used its system a number of times to locate terrorist suspects and prevent terrorist attacks. For example, after the FBI received information that certain potential terrorists had infiltrated the United States, TFOS put into practice the process it had developed to track the suspects through their financial transactions. The TFOS process proved successful in obtaining useful data in a very compressed time frame. Although the subjects proved not to be terrorists, the system demonstrated its capability. The FBI's ability to do near real-time financial tracking has enabled it to locate terrorist operatives in a foreign country and prevent terrorist attacks there on several occasions. The system also helped crack a major criminal case, played a role in clearing certain persons wrongly accused of terrorism, and has proved very valuable in vetting potential threats.

The second approach to obtaining basic financial information on an expedited basis is through a regulation issued under Section 314(a) of the USA PATRIOT Act. By this regulation, the Department of Treasury requires financial institutions upon the government's request to search their records and determine if they have any information involving specific individuals. Financial institutions must report any positive matches to law enforcement within two weeks after the request for information. If there are matches, law enforcement must follow up with a subpoena to obtain the actual transaction records as discussed above. In an emergency, law enforcement can ask Treasury to require banks to respond more quickly to the request, sometimes in two days, a procedure that they have used on several occasions thus far.

In practice, this process enables law enforcement to find out if an individual of interest has accounts or has conducted transactions in any one of thousands of financial institutions across the country. It saves an investigator hundreds of hours that would have otherwise been spent on a bank-by-bank inquiry—an inquiry that would not have been done under the old system owing to time and resource constraints. One agent told the Commission staff that the new procedure so far has produced "tremendous results." She cited an instance in which a terrorism investigation resulted in the discovery of two bank accounts using conventional investigative techniques. Then, as a result of the Section 314 process, investigators were able to identify 19 other accounts across the country— accounts that they would have never been able to find otherwise.[54]

---

[53] By contrast, he said that while it would have been theoretically possible to use financial tracking to find the hijackers before 9/11, the probability of doing so in a timely fashion would have been extremely low.

[54] One concern about the Section 314 process is the possibility that a request to thousands of financial institutions will cause the information to be leaked. In a Las Vegas criminal investigation in October 2002 and a New York terrorism case in March 2003, the media published the fact of the law enforcement requests. In the New York case, the *New York Post* even called the subjects to ask them why the FBI was making the request. As a result, the FBI conducts a risk-benefit analysis before making each request. There are civil and criminal penalties in the event of a disclosure, and Treasury includes a warning with every request. There is no guarantee, however, that such warnings will be sufficient to deter leaks.

Account opening and customer identification procedures/data retention

Financial institutions play a critical role in any effort to find terrorists under either the FBI's system or Section 314. To fulfill this role properly in the life-and-death emergencies that can arise, financial institutions must (1) know their customers by their real names and possess other essential identifying information, (2) have the ability to access this information in a timely fashion, and (3) quickly provide this information to the government in a format in which it can be effectively used.

Section 326 of the USA PATRIOT Act requires that financial institutions "enhance the financial footprint" of their customers by ensuring effective measures for verifying their identity. Section 326 recognized that effective customer identification may deter the use of financial institutions by terrorist financiers and money launderers and also assist in leaving an audit trail that law enforcement can use to identify and track terrorist suspects when they conduct financial transactions. In May 2003 the Department of the Treasury issued regulations implementing the statute, setting forth the type of information that must be collected as well as the acceptable methods for verifying identity.

The need for accurate identifying information puts a premium on financial institutions having effective account opening procedures that vet the true identify of each customer, to the extent possible. A name search for Khalid al Mihdhar will not find him if he is banking under another name. Obviously, banks cannot be expected to detect perfectly forged passports and other identification documents; but terrorists rarely are perfect, and training in spotting false identification documents could help bank personnel catch the most egregious examples. In addition, bank personnel must ensure that account documents reflect the full and accurate name of the customer, even if that name is long.[55] Equally important, banks must obtain and accurately record key identifying information about their customers, including date of birth, Social Security number, and passport number. Many names are so common that nationwide searches for them would generate so many false positives as to be useless in an emergency. At times, however, the FBI can obtain and provide other identifying information, such as a passport number, which can be crucial in narrowing the search—provided that the institution where the subject is a customer has that information.

The need to locate terrorist operatives in the most exigent circumstances means that financial institutions must be able to access their data quickly. Quick retrieval can be a problem for some financial institutions, where years of piecemeal information-system upgrades have created a dysfunctional structure that greatly complicates the task of determining if a particular person is a customer. For example, an official of one midsize

---

[55] Shortening the name could mean that the account will be missed if the FBI is seeking a permutation different than the one used. For example, Ali Abdul Aziz Ali, a.k.a. Ammar al Baluchi, a key facilitator of the 9/11 attacks, would not be found if a bank listed him only as Abdul Aziz Ali and the FBI was looking for Ammar al Baluchi.

regional bank told Commission staff that his institution must email 28 different people to respond to a Section 314(a) request. Some banks simply lack electronic searching capability altogether. An FBI agent with a leading role in the Bureau's financial-tracking effort said that many financial institutions can search their data only manually, which is both resource-intensive and painfully slow in an emergency. Ideally, financial institutions should be able to do quick electronic searches by customer name, by other identifying information such as Social Security number or date of birth, or even by address or employment. Many financial institutions lack this ability today.

Once a financial institution has informed the government that a suspect is a customer and has received appropriate legal process, it can assist law enforcement greatly by providing continuous updates about the suspect's transactions. For example, the information that the suspect just used his credit card to rent a hotel room, book an airline flight, or rent a Ryder truck can be essential in an emergency. Many sophisticated financial institutions can provide the FBI with near "real-time" information on a suspect's activities, but other institutions entirely lack this capability, owing to technical limitations.

Finally, upon receipt of legal process, financial institutions must be able to communicate the relevant account information to the government officials quickly and efficiently. For many types of information, this means in electronic format. Although the FBI has long lagged behind the rest of the country in information systems technology, it has made tremendous strides since 9/11 in using available technology to find terrorists suspects, especially through TFOS's financial-tracking efforts. In many cases, emergency tracking can be streamlined if information is provided to TFOS in electronic format. Many financial institutions lack this capability, however.

The FBI's ability to find terrorist suspects in an emergency through financial tracking depends in large part on the private sector's voluntary cooperation. By all reports, the financial sector's cooperation has been immense since 9/11, but there is a risk that cooperation will decrease as the terrorist attacks fade into history and antiterrorism efforts become just another cost center for financial institutions. Government misuse of emergency procedures in non-emergency situations could also substantially reduce the likelihood that the private sector will respond when its help is truly needed to save lives. To avoid this problem, it is critical that law enforcement and the financial community maintain good lines of communication. This communication is important at all levels. Industry groups and major national institutions must meet regularly with national law enforcement leaders, such as the senior agents running FBI TFOS and the director of FinCEN, to focus on larger strategic issues. At the same time, FBI field offices need to reach out to smaller regional financial institutions, which they may need to contact in an emergency.

This is not to say that financial institutions should become simply another appendage of law enforcement. To the contrary, under either the FBI approach or Section 314(a), without legal process financial institutions can answer only one basic question: does X have an account at your bank? Everything beyond this question requires legal process under current law. It is hard to see why any privacy or liberty concerns should be raised about the private sector and financial institutions working together to develop streamlined procedures for providing critical data quickly in an emergency—pursuant to a lawful subpoena or other process.

The future: What more can be done?

A number of proposals have been made in recognition that the traditional BSA approach is inadequate to address the challenges of terrorist financing.

Sharing classified information with bank personnel: A bad idea

The BSA model fails with respect to terrorist financing because the government—not the financial institutions—has the information that can best identify the terrorist operatives or fund-raisers. Some have proposed correcting that problem by providing security clearances to financial institution personnel and then providing these cleared officials with classified intelligence about terrorist financing. The idea is that the cleared bank personnel, armed with intelligence to give them a better idea of what they are looking for, will be able to ferret out the terrorists among their customers.[56]

The idea of clearing financial institution personnel may be attractive on its face, particularly to those unfamiliar with the nature of financial intelligence. The proposal would likely do little, however, to help banks combat terrorist financing and creates a number of serious privacy and civil liberty concerns. Most intelligence on terrorist financing is not actionable—it does not identify specific terrorist financiers and their accounts with sufficient precision to allow actions to disrupt the activity. The intelligence tends to be limited and speculative, and it frequently relies on dubious sources of information. It can be valuable to trained intelligence experts, who can evaluate it in the context of the broad spectrum of available information, but not to bank compliance directors, who will necessarily lack the time and current knowledge to properly evaluate it. Even if bank personnel have time and expertise, the intelligence rarely will yield information that they would find useful, such as names of specific account holders.

To the extent that the intelligence community can generate specific names or accounts, such information can usually be shared with banks in an unclassified way. Banks can be told to be aware of person X from country Y without needing to know how that information was obtained. If the intelligence community develops patterns or trends, this information presumably also can be shared with financial institutions without need for security clearances.

---

[56] See, e.g., testimony of former National Security Council official Richard A. Clarke, Senate Banking, Housing and Urban Development Committee (October 22, 2003) (clearing bank compliance personnel will "bring us back great benefits because then they'll know what to look for"). Representatives of financial institutions made similar recommendations to Commission staff.

Providing intelligence about terrorist financing to bank personnel raises serious privacy and civil liberty issues. People may be named in intelligence reports, but many of the allegations within these reports are unproven. Some reports prove to be entirely baseless. Turning these reports over to private citizens like bank personnel runs the risk that entirely unsubstantiated allegations may lead banks to shut customer accounts or take other adverse action. Even assuming that the classified information itself is never leaked, the names of people identified in the intelligence cannot be kept secret. When the bank compliance officer who receives the secret intelligence asks for scrutiny of a customer's accounts for no apparent reason, other bank personnel will likely surmise that classified information drove this request.

Supporters of giving security clearances to bank personnel point out that the U.S. government regularly clears private citizens, such as employees of defense contractors. There are, however, few if any instances in which the U.S. government provides classified information potentially adverse to U.S. citizens to private actors for the specific purpose of causing those private actors to subject the U.S. citizens to greater scrutiny.[57] Creating such an unusual and potentially dangerous situation cannot be justified by the minimal benefits that sharing classified information might produce.

Broad government access to private data: Perhaps someday

A more radical, but perhaps far more effective, proposal would give government authorities direct unfettered access to private financial data for the limited purpose of finding or detecting terrorist operatives or fund-raisers.[58] Under this approach, counterterrorist officials would be able to access privately held data by using computer technology to search for known terrorist suspects by name, data of birth, Social Security number, or other identifying information, which would find terrorist suspects living under their own name and also help identify others living under assumed names. The government could also use privately held financial data in conjunction with a wide variety of other data to link a suspect to his or her associates. As one former government official testified to the Commission: "Counterterrorism officers should be able to identify known associates of the terrorist suspect within 30 seconds, using shared addresses, records of phone calls to and from the suspect's phone, emails to and from the suspect's accounts, financial transactions, travel history and reservations, and common memberships in organizations, including (with appropriate safeguards) religious and expressive organizations."[59] The government is currently far from these capabilities, and

---

[57] The commonality of many names, especially Arabic names, compounds the potential for mayhem. For example, an official of one major financial institution told Commission staff that there were 85 Mohamed Attas in New York City alone. Intelligence reports of varying quality may provide the basis for bank action against not only the persons alleged to be involved in terrorist financing but innumerable people with the same or similar names.

[58] See, e.g, *Creating a Trusted Network for Homeland Security*, Second Report of the Markle Foundation Task Force (Dec. 2003), appendix F ("Within 30 seconds [of learning the identify of a terrorist suspect], the counterterrorism agency should be able to access U.S. and international financial records associated with the suspect").

[59] Prepared testimony of Stewart Baker, Dec. 8, 2003.

significant technical, legal and privacy hurdles would need to be crossed before it would have anything remotely approaching this ability.

Supporters of this approach contend that privacy would be protected through anonymity and technology. The data of millions of people could be electronically searched but all individuals would remain anonymous except those identified as terrorist suspects, who would then be subjected to further scrutiny. Sophisticated technology would control access to the data, electronically audit the data and keep a detailed record of exactly who accessed it for what purpose, and ensure the anonymity of persons whose data are searched.

If such a system existed, it would be tremendously useful in looking for known terrorist operatives living under their own name, such as al Mihdhar or al Hazmi, or future hijackers living under false identities. Technology could be imagined that would scan masses of financial data looking for terrorist fund-raising operations as well, while preserving the anonymity of the data belonging to persons whom it does not identify as potential terrorist fund-raisers.

Of course, major technological improvements would be required to implement this kind of a system. Currently, financial records are spread out across the country in thousands of financial institutions, each with its own data collection and retrieval system and level of technological sophistication.[60] There is no single database that the government can tap even in an emergency.

Even if such a database could be created, sweeping legal changes would be required to use it. The government does not have unfettered access to this financial information under current laws. Although the Supreme Court has stated that an account holder does not have an expectation of privacy in information he or she gives to another, such as a bank, there are a number of restrictions on the government's right to obtain such data. Most fundamentally, the government can obtain financial information or data only by lawful process, such as a grand jury subpoena or an NSL, for a particular case or investigation. The government has no general authority to access the entire country's financial records en masse, so that it can scan them to find potential terrorists or criminal suspects. Instead, an inquiry has to be made of each financial institution for each investigation.

Pushing the technological and legal limits even further is the idea that the government could develop the technology to sift through all the financial data that exists and create a program able to single out those financial transactions that are inherently suspicious.

---

[60] Banks and other financial institutions keep records as a part of the operation of their ongoing businesses. Financial institutions are generally required to keep financial information on hand, in a retrievable form, for five years. In contrast, other industries whose records would also be of use to counterterrorism investigators, such as Internet service providers, are not required to keep transaction records for any length of time and can (and do) regularly destroy them unless law enforcement requests that they be maintained. This has often been a source of frustration to law enforcement and intelligence agents, whose investigations are often hampered in the digital age by lack of a uniform and mandated record retention policy for internet service providers.

These ideas have been discussed in the open literature and have triggered major controversy and speculation. The Department of Defense's "Total Information Awareness" program, complete with its logo of an all-seeing eye, was a prime example of this type of technology. This research program sought to use sophisticated technologies to detect terrorist planning activities from the vast data in cyberspace; in other words, it sought to "pick the signal out of the noise." Congress has prohibited the funding of such a program, largely because of privacy concerns. Despite 9/11, it seems that privacy concerns will prevent anything remotely like these ideas from becoming reality in the foreseeable future.

That is not to say research should not go forward. Government and the private sector can, and should, continue to work on technology that could scan vast amounts of financial data to find known terrorist suspects, while protecting the privacy of the innocent persons whose data are searched. Perhaps sophisticated technology can be developed that would even be able to pick out unknown terrorist operatives or fund-raisers by their financial transactions—currently a near impossibility. Legitimate concerns about privacy should not retard research that might someday make us safer and, at the same time, actually not infringe on privacy rights. Ideally, the research efforts should draw on both the law enforcement and intelligence expertise of the government and the sophisticated technology and data management expertise of the private sector. Obviously, no such technology should ever be implemented on real data without public acceptance that the technological and legal safeguards in place will be sufficient to ensure privacy. The development of such technology and any public acceptance of it remain, at this point, pure speculation.

Chapter 5

Al-Barakaat Case Study

The Somali Community and al-Barakaat

In about 1991, the East African country of Somalia became embroiled in turbulent civil unrest that wreaked devastation on its people and institutions. Already destitute, the government collapsed and basic services withered. Famine and violence in the country were the norm, and a diaspora of Somalis began. Many arrived in the United States. In one of those strange flukes sometimes found in patterns of migration, cold and snowy Minneapolis has the largest concentration of Somali immigrants in the United States.

Somali immigrants, like individuals in immigrant communities throughout the United States, sought a safe, quick, and effective way to move money earned in the United States back to their families and homes. The need was even more dire for Somalia, as this was one of the only sources of hard currency available to the country. Many foreign workers in the United States have a number of different options to move money internationally. The most formal and obvious way is to use the established backbone of the international wire transfer system to shift funds between a bank account in the United States and one in the destination country. This method has several significant advantages. It is safe and convenient, particularly when large amounts of money are being sent between commercial customers. There are drawbacks to wiring money, however: it can be expensive; banks can hold the money for extended periods before sending it; it requires a bank account in the United States; and the banks are required to use the official exchange rate and in some countries levy a tax on foreign exchange, which often makes the effective rate of exchange punitively high. Indeed, other countries often restrict the export of foreign currency and foreign exchange.

However, for Somalis living in the United States, the question was moot. Somalia simply had no banking system and no central bank by which foreign exchange could be made. Thus, a different way had to be found to get money to Somalia. The al-Barakaat network of money remitters was set up to address this need. Founded by Ahmed Nur Ali Jumale in 1985, al-Barakaat at the time of 9/11 had more than 180 offices in 40 countries, all existing primarily to transfer money to Somalia. The financial headquarters for al-Barakaat was in the United Arab Emirates, where Jumale had opened a number of accounts at the Emirates Bank International (EBI) to facilitate the transmission of money. At the time of the terrorist attacks, al-Barakaat was considered the largest money remittance system operating in Somalia; in addition to being used by a significant number of Somalis who had fled the anarchy in their home country, it was the primary means that the United Nations used to transmit money in support of its relief operations there.

A money remitter, described most simply, collects money from an individual at one point and pays it to another in another location, charging a fee for the service. The money itself does not actually move; rather, the originating office simply sends a message to the destination office, informing it of the amount of money and the identity of the sender and of the recipient. The destination office then pays the ultimate recipient. To settle, money is periodically wired in aggregate amounts from the originating office's bank account either to a central clearing account owned by the money-remitting company or through correspondent bank accounts. The central office, in turn, settles with the destination office. Each office is typically an agent or licensee of the main office, and its relationships are usually arm's-length and governed by a written contract. The main office is responsible for keeping track of the settling transactions with all of the other offices. Most money remitters in the United States belong to large franchise, such as Western Union or MoneyGram. They effectively operate along the same principles as al-Barakaat, albeit more formally. Additionally, the absence of any agents for large, Western-based money remitters in Somalia forced Somalis to use smaller, ethnically based ones.

Al-Barakaat has been commonly called a hawala, but it is not one.[61] There are similarities between the two systems. In both, there is a need to compensate the agent who has paid out money pursuant to a money transfer. In both, the money is not sent for each individual transaction; rather, there is a larger settling transaction conducted periodically to adjust for the differences in what each office took in and what it had to pay out.

The key difference is in how the money or value moves between the office obtaining the money from the customer and the office paying the money out to the ultimate beneficiary. In transferring value between the sending and the receiving offices, a money remitter uses the formal financial system, typically relying on wire transfers or a correspondent banking relationship. A hawala, at least in its "pure" form, does not use a negotiable instrument or other commonly recognized method for the exchange of money. Hawaladars instead employ a variety of means, often in combination, to settle with each other: they can settle preexisting debt, pay to or receive from the accounts of third parties within the same country, import or export goods (both legal goods, with false invoicing, or illegal commerce, such as drug trafficking) to satisfy the accounts, or physically move currency or precious metal or stones.

There are other distinguishing characteristics of a hawala. Many hawalas operate between specific areas of the world, or even specific areas within a specific country. An individual wanting to send money from Canada to one area in Pakistan, for example, might use one hawaladar; to move money to a different part of Pakistan, it may be necessary to use a different one. Hawalas typically do not maintain a large central control office for settling transactions. Instead, a loose association of hawaladars conduct business with each other, typically without any formal or legally binding agreements. Hawaladars often keep few formal records; those that do exist are usually handwritten in idiosyncratic shorthand and are typically destroyed once the transaction is completed.

As noted in chapter 2, Usama Bin Ladin and al Qaeda made significant use of hawalas to move money in the Middle East—particularly in Pakistan, the UAE, and Afghanistan—in

---

[61] The following discussion is aided by two reports, both produced by FinCEN: *A Report to Congress in Accordance with Section 359 of the USA PATRIOT Act,* (2002) and *Hawala: the Hawala Alternate Remittance System and its Role in Money Laundering,* (undated, probably 1996)

the period before 9/11. This does not make the use of hawalas inherently criminal, although it has been recognized that some of their characteristics allow criminal activity to flourish: little formal record keeping, lack of government controls, and settling transactions that do not go through formal financial channels.

The Somali money remitters in Minneapolis had attracted official attention for some time. There were three primary remitters in Minneapolis in the late 1990s: al-Barakaat, Dahb Shiil, and Shirkadda Xawilada Amal. Al-Barakaat had by far attracted the most attention. A local bank had filed Suspicious Activity Reports (SARs)[62] as early as the summer of 1996 with the Treasury Department regarding what they believed to be suspicious financial activity: large amounts of cash and other instruments were being deposited and then immediately wire transferred to a single account in the UAE the next day. The SARs did not describe what the bank thought the nature of the activity was, just that it seemed inconsistent with normal banking activity. By 9/11, these reports numbered in the hundreds.

The FBI, which received a regular summary of these reports, opened a criminal money-laundering case file on al-Barakaat in May 1997.[63] In a typical money-laundering investigation, an investigative agent tries to develop evidence that the money was derived from a crime that was statutorily described as a "specified unlawful activity" (SUA), and that the purpose of the transaction was either to disguise the nature, source, ownership, or control of the money or to further the criminal activities. The difficulty here, which would plague both the intelligence and criminal investigators for the rest of the investigation into al-Barakaat, was that the transactions themselves revealed neither who the recipient of the money was nor what happened to the money once it arrived in the UAE. The source of the money or purpose behind the transaction could be legitimate or nefarious: in the absence of further information, it was impossible to know which. After a preliminary investigation, the FBI closed its criminal investigation of al-Barakaat in August 1998, unable to find an SUA or gain an understanding of the purpose of the transactions. More SARs continued to pour in, however, and U.S. Customs and Internal Revenue Service agents in Minneapolis, who had opened a separate investigation into al-Barakaat, continued to investigate.

---

[62] Suspicious Activity Reports and their role in the overall scheme of anti-money laundering regulation of banks and other financial institutions are discussed in chapter 4.

[63] The description of the FBI intelligence and multi-agency law enforcement investigation against al-Barakaat was derived from a review of FBI case reports and source reporting, as well as face to face interviews with the agents and FBI officials. The description of the government's understanding of al-Barakaat prior to 9/11 was derived from a review of intelligence agency reporting. The description of the foreign government participation in the al-Barakaat action is derived from State Department cables and Treasury memoranda. The discussion of OFAC is derived from review of internal Treasury documents and from interviews of Treasury and OFAC officials.

The Early Intelligence Case

The primary domestic investigation of potential Somali-based terrorist activities occurred in Minneapolis.[64] The lead case agent was able to develop intelligence both from his own investigative efforts and from his review of the materials in the possession of the CIA. In December 1998, a case agent in the intelligence squad in Minneapolis developed a source of information on the activities of the Somali community. The source indicated that the terrorist group Al-Itihaad Al-Islamiya (AIAI) had a cell in Minneapolis, and that it supported radical Islamic activities against the United States. The investigation focused on a specific individual within the United States, who was alleged to have plotted to bomb U.S. embassies in Uganda and Ethiopia and to have been engaged in fund-raising in Minneapolis to support AIAI activities overseas. Additionally, the source provided information regarding about 15 Somali immigrants. After further inquiry, including searches and an interview, the investigations were closed when it was found that the FBI's original source lacked credibility regarding this specific threat and that other reliable sources had no knowledge of the suspected plotter.

While the original source did not pan out, the agent was able to learn from his contacts in the intelligence community, particularly the CIA, a great deal about AIAI. The agent learned that AIAI operated primarily in East Africa and was considered a loose affiliation of Islamists. AIAI was considered a significant threat by the Defense Intelligence Agency, which had experience in Somalia during the early 1990s, and intelligence suggested that AIAI had links to Usama Bin Ladin. For example, there were indications that Usama Bin Ladin had visited Somalia and visited an AIAI stronghold in southern Somalia to look for a new base of operations when his stay in Sudan ended. Bin Ladin purportedly met with the leaders of AIAI as well, and was said to have given AIAI $400,000 in 1997 to support attacks on Ethiopia. Some of this intelligence was reinforced after 9/11, when it was reported that AIAI discussed hiding Bin Ladin in the event he needed to leave Afghanistan.

Despite these troubling links, the State Department thought AIAI did not meet the standard for designation as a Foreign Terrorist Organization (FTO), which would have the effect, among other things, of criminalizing support of it. Additionally, there was a concern on the part of the State Department that some of the reporting involving AIAI was simply not credible. State said that multiple reports from the CIA discredited its earlier sources.

In the late 1990s, the intelligence community also began to draw links between AIAI, al-Barakaat (particularly its founder, Ahmed Nur Ali Jumale) and Usama Bin Ladin. The reporting centered on a few key facts. First, it alleged that Usama Bin Ladin not only assisted Jumale in establishing al-Barakaat in about 1992 but was in fact a silent partner, and that Jumale managed Bin Ladin's finances as well. This was consistent with other information that indicated a prior relationship between Jumale and Bin Ladin. Second,

---

[64] The first FBI investigation on AIAI and al-Barakaat was started in San Diego in October 1996, on an individual investigated as a result of his connection with HAMAS.

the reporting indicated that al-Barakaat was associated with AIAI, in that al-Barakaat managed the finances of AIAI, and AIAI used al-Barakaat to send money to operatives. Variations of that reporting stated that the head of al-Barakaat, Jumale, was part of the AIAI leadership, or that Usama Bin Ladin used al-Barakaat to fund AIAI. Third, there were allegations that al-Barakaat actually assisted in procuring weapons for AIAI or sold weapons to AIAI. There were specific reports, for example, of al-Barakaat's supplying Somalia's Sharia court with 175 "technicals" and 33 machine guns between January and mid-July 2000, and AIAI with 780 machine guns, which it had procured from sources in China and Chechnya. Other reporting indicated that al-Barakaat was founded by members of the Muslim Brotherhood in order to facilitate the transfer of money to terrorist organizations, including Hamas and AIAI.

Lastly, there was fairly detailed information from a U.S. embassy in Africa in July 1999. Two sources known to the embassy claimed that Usama Bin Ladin was a silent partner and frequent customer of al-Barakaat. One of the sources further related that Bin Ladin gave Jumale $1 million of venture capital to start al-Barakaat, and that terrorist funds were intermingled with the funds sent by NGOs. A third source told the embassy that al-Barakaat did not practice any kind of due diligence in making financial transactions. Both sources claimed that al-Barakaat security forces supported Usama Bin Ladin by providing protection for Bin Ladin operatives when they visited Mogadishu. The embassy cautioned that the allegations could not be confirmed and noted the risk that the sources may simply be spreading negative information about their rivals.

The Minneapolis FBI intelligence agent continued to develop sources and investigate the activities of the Somali community. By July 1999, he was able to open a "full field investigation" (FFI) into AIAI as a group. All FBI FFIs require predication: that is, some evidence must already exist to give the FBI reason to believe that an individual is involved in activities on behalf of a foreign government or terrorist organization, which would justify further surveillance or intelligence collection. This requirement, which prevents the FBI from undertaking random domestic intelligence collection on individuals, was introduced as a way to protect civil liberties. An FFI can be instituted after a preliminary investigation (PI), which is opened to determine whether an FFI is justified. A PI can be opened only for a limited time, and agents in a PI are restricted in their methods of collecting intelligence.

When they opened the AIAI investigation, the Minneapolis agents saw it as "purely intelligence gathering." They simply wanted to learn whether AIAI was operating in the United States and, if so, determine the nature of its activities (such as fund-raising, logistics, or operations). There was no attempt to build a criminal case in the traditional sense, nor was any effort given to developing probable cause, the standard that criminal case agents typically work toward. They were interested in developing probable cause that specific individuals were agents of a foreign power or the particular communications were to be used in the furtherance of terrorist activities, the standard used to obtain a FISA warrant.

Considering a Criminal Case

The intelligence agent knew of the SARs and knew that al-Barakaat was closely tied into the Somali network in Minneapolis. Moreover, the intelligence agent knew what the federal criminal agents investigating the money-laundering claims did not: intelligence reports tied the al-Barakaat network to AIAI and Usama Bin Ladin. As a result, the intelligence agent thought that it would be useful to open a criminal case on al-Barakaat. This was a matter of some controversy, as there was a fairly rigid rule within the FBI and Department of Justice against mingling intelligence cases and law enforcement cases. In the jargon of the day, this prohibition was known as "the wall," and it was the source of considerable confusion among agents in the field. Working-level agents understood that headquarters frowned on having simultaneous criminal and intelligence cases, although it was hard for them to articulate why.

Opening a criminal case to complement the intelligence case would have several advantages, however, if the agent could get the approvals. First, criminal charges could be threatened against subjects, providing motivation for them to cooperate in furthering the intelligence investigations. Equally important, a criminal case would give the intelligence agent far better tools to investigate al-Barakaat and the suspected AIAI members in Minneapolis. These tools included grand jury subpoenas to obtain bank records. Grand jury subpoenas were far preferable to National Security Letters (NSLs), the method for obtaining documents in intelligence investigations, because the FBI could obtain subpoenas almost instantly, whereas NSLs took 6 to 12 months to be issued.[65] Outside of the New York Field Office, which had its own procedures, NSLs could be approved only at FBI headquarters and had to be signed by a supervisor.

Additionally, the intelligence agent wanted to brief the Assistant U.S. Attorney (AUSA), the local federal prosecutor in Minneapolis, on the intelligence investigation. He thought that it would be useful for the prosecutor to obtain an understanding of the context and motivation for the criminal case. From past experience the agent believed that the U.S. Attorney's Office would not get involved in a criminal spin-off of an intelligence case unless FBI headquarters approved the transfer. And he also knew from past experience that because the potential criminal charges evident at that time were relatively minor, the U.S. Attorney's Office would not be interested unless the prosecutors were briefed on al-Barakaat's terrorist connections.[66] As a result, the agent applied for permission to brief the AUSA on the case. He did not receive this approval for 13 months—many months after the FBI Director himself took a personal interest in the case.

The FBI Radical Fundamentalist Unit (RFU) at headquarters, responsible for approving this briefing, initially opposed it. The RFU did not see it as necessary and questioned whether the evidence was strong enough to justify breaching the wall between criminal

---

[65] According to the intelligence agent doing these types of investigations, this delay no longer exists, and NSLs can be obtained just as fast as grand jury subpoenas.

[66] The most obvious crime was "structuring financial transactions." The crime consists of breaking apart cash bank deposits into increments of less than $10,000, so that the bank does not file a form identifying such depositors to the Department of the Treasury.

and intelligence cases. At the time, FBI headquarters required greater evidence to brief the U.S. Attorney's Office on an intelligence case than it did to open an intelligence full field investigation, and headquarters did not think the evidence regarding the AIAI case had reached the requisite level. In the Minneapolis intelligence agent's view, headquarters viewed Minneapolis as excessively aggressive in pushing the limits of the wall and may have been more cautious in this case as a result.

According to the Minneapolis intelligence agent, the RFU thought the case was not strong for a number of reasons. First, the RFU supervisor did not believe AIAI was a threat to the United States and questioned whether AIAI, with its decentralized command structure, was really a group at all. Moreover, AIAI had not been designated a foreign terrorist organization by the Secretary of State. This was a significant point because without that designation, it was not a crime to give AIAI material support (absent evidence that the support went to carrying out a specific terrorist attack). As for al-Barakaat, the RFU thought that the information about connections with al Qaeda was dated; also, it pointed out, there was no evidence that any of the Somalis who used al-Barakaat to remit funds did so with the intention of supporting terrorism. The agent agreed that all of these allegations remained unproven and required further investigation, but he wanted to brief the AUSA to obtain better tools to find out the truth.

While waiting for the approval to brief the AUSA, the Minneapolis intelligence agent came to learn of the IRS and U.S. Customs investigation, and in October 1999 he met with those involved. The FBI opened a criminal investigation in November 1999. The agents agreed to work together, along with the Immigration and Naturalization Service, to see whether they could make a criminal case. Multiagency cooperation has become common in large criminal investigations, as each agency brings its unique skills to bear: the FBI provides resources and investigative experience, the IRS has a reputation for very well trained and skilled financial investigators, Customs has the ability to control the borders, and INS brings to bear its authorities to enforce the immigration laws (critical to developing witnesses in investigations of this type). Moreover, a joint case makes possible information sharing, as each agent can search his or her own agency's database and communicate the results to the group.

Ultimately, following several meetings by officials in Washington, the Minneapolis FBI received approval to brief the AUSA in December 2000 on the connections between the criminal violations and the larger intelligence issues, which it did. It thereafter enjoyed an excellent relationship with the U.S. Attorney's Office in Minneapolis.

The strategy in the criminal case was to try to gather evidence and gain an understanding of where the money was going once al-Barakaat sent it, and thus to determine whether it was being used to support terrorism. The focus was on the employees and owners of the three al-Barakaat outlets in Minneapolis. Part of the mission of the criminal case would be to support the intelligence case. At the time, the investigators were "still trying to find out what we had." The criminal FBI agent (the criminal case had to have a separate investigator because of "wall" issues, although both agents worked in the same intelligence squad) was looking more toward a "nickel-and-dime fraud case." There did not seem to be enough evidence to make a pure terrorist-financing case.[67]

One difficulty was that it was almost impossible to follow the money once it left the United States. All of the transfers went to the UAE, and there the investigators lost the trail. To pick it up again, they would have to get records from the bank the money was being wired to—the Emirates Bank International in Dubai. But U.S. law enforcement could not simply ask the EBI for the records. Rather, the agents would have to ask the government of the UAE to ask the EBI for the records. Then, the UAE could turn the records over to the United States. Obtaining records from a foreign government is a long and cumbersome process, filled with potential pitfalls. To begin with, there is no guarantee that the foreign country will even consider the request, particularly in the absence of a treaty requiring such cooperation. Each country has its own notions about bank secrecy and many jurisdictions resist opening up their records to another country. Even if the foreign jurisdiction agrees in principle to the request, it must be persuaded that the United States has a legitimate need for the records and is not merely undertaking a fishing expedition. This showing may require the disclosure of sensitive information to a foreign government, and the United States may not necessarily be able to trust that government or have confidence in its control over the further dissemination of the information. Thus, an agent conducting such an investigation has to balance the need for the records against the possibility of disclosure.

Al-Barakaat was moving significant amounts of money overseas, and to the Minneapolis criminal case agent, it seemed improbable that the relatively low-skilled Somali community in Minneapolis, although large, could have amassed so much money through legitimate wages. In early 2001, al-Barakaat was transferring as much as $1,000,000 through its Minneapolis facilities. The agent believed that some of that money *must* have been derived from fraud.

The Other Field Offices Pick Up the Investigation

In the meantime, other FBI field offices were finding similar al-Barakaat activity. By the summer of 1999, the FBI knew that there were al-Barakaat offices in San Diego, Washington, D.C., and Minneapolis, and Minneapolis was actively polling other cities to determine the links. Seattle opened a case in December 1999, and by February 2001 had developed a source who reported that "apparently" al-Barakaat fees were used to fund AIAI.[68] The FBI field offices coordinated with each other, and ultimately held

---

[67] The central terrorist financing crime is called "material support," in violation of 18 U.S.C. 2339B. This requires the knowing contribution of something of value (it need not be money) to an organization that has been listed as a Foreign Terrorist Organization by the Secretary of State. It is an extraordinarily broad statue, in that prosecutors need not trace specific money to a terrorist act.

[68] A review of the FBI files in the case revealed a substantial amount of secondary reporting. The most valuable intelligence is from first hand witnesses: individuals who can report something based on personal experience. There were few sources who could do this regarding al-Barakaat. Rather, most of what was collected was information that others had heard. The line between intelligence and rumor mongering can be quite thin, and great care needed to be taken to evaluate that information for what it was.

multidistrict meetings in April 2000 and May and June 2001. Unlike in other cases, however, there was very little to coordinate: each al-Barakaat office appeared to be operating independently, with the EBI account in the UAE serving as the only link between them. By 9/11, there were FBI investigations in Charlotte, Cincinnati, New York, Seattle, San Diego, and Washington, D.C.

Al-Barakaat also had attracted the attention of the Financial Crimes Enforcement Network (FinCEN), the Treasury agency established to review and disseminate suspicious activity reports submitted by banks and other financial institutions. In December 1999 (about four months after the FBI was reporting that al-Barakaat had ties to Bin Ladin and offices in at least three U.S. cities), a FinCEN analyst reviewing intelligence community cables noted a reference to al-Barakaat along with the identification of a specific account in the UAE. The analyst recalled that a co-worker the previous month had noted an anomaly in reviewing al-Barakaat SARs. FinCEN analyzed the al-Barakaat SARs and, in February 2000, briefed FBI headquarters concerning the results. By March 2000, FinCEN had prepared a report and link-analysis chart highlighting the connections between the al-Barakaat entities and the UAE accounts. Still, no one knew the purpose behind the money transfers, the source of the money, or the ultimate destination. To get to the source, the agents would have to locate informants in the community who could tell them; to understand the ultimate destination of the money, they would need access to the records within the UAE.

The FBI had a number of informants who could tell them about al-Barakaat. The criminal case agent, in the course of the criminal investigation, had found two confidential sources who were reporting that al-Barakaat was siphoning money to AIAI. The sources also indicated that to be an al-Barakaat representative, one also had to be a member of AIAI. But the criminal case agent's sources had no direct knowledge of these claims; they were simply repeating what was purportedly common knowledge within the Somali community.

In conjunction with members of the intelligence community, the intelligence agent also worked two sources who could speak out of personal knowledge. These sources were able to travel and provide intelligence on AIAI and the situation in East Africa. His sources claimed direct contact with senior al-Barakaat management. Much of the reporting, however, concerned AIAI in Somalia; there was less on the local AIAI cells within the United States, or on the relationship of al-Barakaat to either AIAI or Usama Bin Ladin.

Nevertheless, the statements of these two sources did corroborate information regarding the relationship between al-Barakaat, al Qaeda, and AIAI. The sources contended that at the direction of senior management, al-Barakaat funneled a percentage of its profits to terrorist groups and that UBL had provided venture capital to al-Barakaat founder Ahmed Jumale to start the company. The agent believed these sources, because they had been vetted and the information they were providing was consistent with intelligence he had previously received. Moreover, the intelligence agent believed that relationship of these sources to al-Barakaat management was such that the sources would have firsthand knowledge of al-Barakaat's activities.

The September 11 attacks

After the attacks, "all bets were off." The al-Barakaat criminal team—the FBI, U.S. Customs, and the IRS—which had been working in separate offices received space to work together. More agents were assigned. Moreover, they contemplated bringing criminal charges, and considered getting criminal search warrants on the al-Barakaat businesses. The headquarters of both FBI and Customs, too, started to take a special interest in the case. FBI headquarters had set up a "financial review group" to sift through the financial transactions of the 9/11 hijackers. It started to look at the al-Barakaat case, as did "Operation Green Quest," a newly formed Treasury task force with essentially the same mission as the FBI's group.

Moreover, within the upper levels of the National Security Council (NSC) and State, attention turned to al-Barakaat, and specifically to the EBI as a facilitator of terrorist finance. According to State Department cables at the time, the U.S. government had "strong evidence" that the EBI was used as a facilitator of terrorist financing. An obvious option would be to designate the bank as a supporter of terrorism and block its assets from coming into the country, a move that would send a message to the world financial community. The UAE agreed to act against al-Barakaat and allowed a U.S. law enforcement team to take a look at the EBI records—something none of the agents in either the intelligence or the law enforcement investigations had been able to access previously.[69]

Designation by the Office of Foreign Asset Control

On September 23, 2001, the President signed Executive Order 13224, which expanded the list of terrorist organizations subject to freezing and blocking.

Pre-9/11 designation efforts

The mission and authorities of the Office of Foreign Asset Control (OFAC) deserve a brief discussion here. In implementing sanctions programs aimed at combating global terrorism, OFAC derives its authority from delegations under the President's powers pursuant to the International Emergency Economic Powers Act (IEEPA) and other Presidential authorities. IEEPA grants the President broad powers to deal with any unusual and extraordinary threat to the national security, foreign policy, or the economy of the United States if the President declares a national emergency with respect to such threat. The source of the threat must be in whole or substantial part outside the United

---

[69] As we note in chapter 3, the UAE had been a source of concern before 9/11 for their largely unregulated financial system.

States. The President may also designate specific entities or individuals who pose or contribute to the threat and set forth the standards for identifying more such entities and individuals. The President delegates to the Executive Branch, generally the Department of Treasury or State, the task of finding those who meet that criteria and "designating" them as subject to the Executive order.

President Bill Clinton signed Executive Order 12947 in January 1995, blocking the assets in the United States of specific terrorists and terrorist groups who threatened to use force to disrupt the Middle East peace process and prohibiting U.S. persons from engaging in transactions with these groups. The groups were named as a result of a presidential judgment that they stood in the way of peace in the Middle East and, because peace in the Middle East is deemed to be vital to our own national security, posed a national security threat to the United States. The authority was not limited to those named in the executive order; those supporting or associated with those named could also be listed by an administrative designation authorized by the director of OFAC (a "secondary designation"). Usama Bin Ladin was not named on this 1995 list. However, beginning in approximately 1995 until the East Africa embassy bombings in the summer of 1998, OFAC attempted to discover a link between Usama Bin Ladin and those named on the list. This effort was not successful, both because the links between Usama Bin Ladin and such groups were tenuous and because OFAC did not have the ability to undertake any significant classified research or analysis.[70] In the late 1990s, there was no thought given to issuing a new executive order naming Bin Ladin, because of what one participant in the process described as "sanctions fatigue" and a general reluctance by Treasury policymakers to impose additional sanctions.

The NSC had a long and deep interest in trying to provide OFAC with sufficient resources to conduct classified all-source analysis on terrorist financing. At the direction of Richard Clarke, the Office of Management and Budget requested, and Congress appropriated, $6.4 million dollars for a center to conduct such analysis, dubbed the Foreign Terrorist Asset Tracking Center (FTATC), beginning in fiscal year 2001 (nominally October 2000). By November 2000, Clarke had suggested a two-week pilot program, which would use CIA facilities to test if the FTATC concept was workable. On the eve of 9/11, FTATC was little more than a plan on paper and an unspent budget authorization.

After the East Africa bombings, President Clinton amended E.O. 12947 to name Usama Bin Ladin and his key aides, thereby prohibiting any U.S. persons from financial dealings with any of them. But the OFAC's success in blocking terrorist assets under this order was limited, for it covers only property or interests in of U.S. persons or within the United States. Moreover, because it named individuals, not groups, OFAC could not build on it with secondary designations—a listing by the head of OFAC of individuals

---

[70] This was a significant problem both before and after the September 11 attacks. OFAC line level analysts were nearly universal in their frustration in not being able to engage in the type of all source analysis that would be required to understand the financial links involved. One analyst with a background in intelligence described the process by which OFAC obtained classified documents as 20 years behind the procedure used by the CIA.

supporting the group named in the executive order. In addition, there was little intelligence on assets to block. These limitations were sources of frustration for the NSC, which wanted action on the financial front of the government's war on Bin Ladin. In retrospect, one OFAC official thought that the reason it was unable to freeze Bin Ladin assets is because none existed within OFAC's jurisdiction.

The United Nations Security Council passed UNSCR 1267 on October 15, 1999, calling for the Taliban to surrender Bin Ladin or face a U.S.-style international freeze of its assets and transactions. The resolution gave a 30-day period before sanctions took effect, however, allowing the Taliban and al Qaeda to repatriate funds from banks in the United Kingdom and Germany to Afghanistan. As a result, these sanctions brought official international censure but were easily circumvented.

Post-9/11 designation efforts

After the 9/11 attacks, the President signed Executive Order 13224 with great fanfare (the White House described it as the "first strike in the war on terror"), but since OFAC already had the ability to go after Bin Ladin and Taliban assets from the prior executive orders, it did little to change OFAC's authorities to name, block, and freeze assets associated with Usama Bin Ladin or the Taliban. After the attacks, OFAC accelerated the search for entities to name by either a presidential declaration (by amending the list attached to E.O. 13224) or a secondary administrative designation, working off a CIA-supplied list of entities and persons. OFAC analysts and attorneys, like everyone in the government engaged in counterterrorism at the time, were working nights and weekends to evaluate and put together administrative records sufficient to freeze the assets of these entities. A significant number of these individuals needed access to classified information, but they had virtually no facilities in which to handle it. As a result, a number of them crammed into the secure FinCEN facility in Northern Virginia that, unlike OFAC's downtown offices, could handle the most highly sensitive materials.

OFAC analysts started working on the designation of al-Barakaat about two weeks after the attacks. This effort won preliminary approval almost immediately from Treasury officials, on the basis of a one-page memo. Thereafter, OFAC officials began a two-pronged approach to supporting the designation: gathering information informally through an OFAC analyst's contacts with U.S. law enforcement, and conducting research on classified documents at FinCEN's secure facility. The informal method for gathering law enforcement data was necessary because of the weaknesses of the FBI's data system. The FBI, unlike the foreign intelligence agencies, wrote very few finished intelligence reports. The only way to find out what was happening domestically was either to troll the FBI's data system, ACS (Automated Case Support), for periodic reports (a hit-or-miss proposition at best) or call field agents and ask them what was going on (if you knew whom to call). The analysts' efforts to survey the foreign intelligence were easier because the reports were more centralized, but had other frustrations: because of Treasury's archaic method of retrieving intelligence, the analysts received only about half of the relevant intelligence on Jumale and al-Barakaat, and the omitted material included some of the best, most useful reports (a fact that was not known to the analysts until after the designation).

Nevertheless, the OFAC analysts plowed forward and put together a package on al-Barakaat. They were greatly helped by a list of worldwide al-Barakaat offices seized during a raid of an al-Barakaat office in Norway and shared with the United States. The analysts were told that they did not need to have evidence that each al-Barakaat entity took part in terrorist financing; it was sufficient to show only that the main entity itself was involved to be able to close all of the branches and freeze all of the money. Thus, the analysts needed only to refer to the seized telephone lists or a commercial index of businesses such as Dun & Bradstreet to justify the closing of each al-Barakaat branch office. The Justice Department, which would have to defend any action should there be a legal challenge, blessed the sufficiency of this tactic.

More nationwide coordination took place, including meetings at the NSC, the FBI, and Customs. As people within the law enforcement community came to understand what OFAC was planning, they asked it to hold off for 60 or 90 days so they could continue their investigations. A number of field offices made this request, as did the Office of Naval Intelligence, which was in the midst of a major intelligence operation on al-Barakaat. OFAC, however, was under substantial pressure to proceed with the designation as rapidly as possible. The analysts also wanted more time to make their evidentiary package more complete and robust, but the OFAC management, apparently reacting to external demands, told them they could not have it. Moreover, the head of the FBI's terrorist-financing effort ultimately concurred in the action.

The post-9/11 period at OFAC was "chaos." The goal set at the policy levels of the White House and Treasury was to conduct a public and aggressive series of designations to show the world community and our allies that the United States was serious about pursuing the financial targets. It entailed a major designation every four weeks, accompanied by derivative designations throughout the month. As a result, Treasury officials acknowledged that some of the evidentiary foundations for the early designations were quite weak. One participant (and an advocate of the designation process generally) stated that "we were so forward leaning we almost fell on our face." The rush to designate came primarily from the NSC and gave pause to many in the government. Some believed that the government's haste in this area, and its preference for IEEPA sanctions, might result in a high level of false designations that would ultimately jeopardize the United States' ability to persuade other countries to designate groups as terrorist organizations. Ultimately, as we discuss later, this proved to be the case with the al-Barakaat designations, mainly because they relied on a derivative designation theory, in which no direct proof of culpability was needed.

A range of key countries were notified several days in advance of the planned U.S. designation of the al-Barakaat entities, and were urged to freeze related assets pursuant to the own authorities.

The November Raids

On November 7, 2001, federal agents entered eight al-Barakaat offices in Minneapolis; Columbus, Ohio; Alexandria, Virginia; Seattle, Washington; and Boston, Massachusetts. Using Treasury Department private contractors who handle asset forfeiture, OFAC and federal agents seized everything with the businesses. In the UAE, about $1 million was seized from the UAE EBI accounts, four offices were raided and their records seized, and Jumale was ordered not to leave the UAE. The U.S. actions resulted in the freezing of approximately $1.1 million, and Treasury claimed that the actions disrupted approximately $65 million in annual remittances from the United States alone.

The President of the United States traveled to FinCEN's offices and, with the Secretary of the Treasury and Attorney General, announced the action in a press event, describing Jumale as a "friend and supporter of Usama Bin Ladin." Secretary of the Treasury Paul O'Neill described al-Barakaat offices as "the money movers, the quartermasters of terror . . . a principal source of funding, intelligence and money transfers for Bin Ladin." He later announced that "we estimate that $25 million was skimmed from the al-Barakaat network of companies each year, and re-directed toward terrorist operations."

Abdullahi Farah was the owner of Global Services, one of the Minneapolis wire remittance companies named in the November 7, 2001 blocking order. He is a naturalized U.S. citizen, having emigrated from Somalia in 1992. Although there already were money remitters in Minneapolis at the time, Farah believed that there was still a need for his services in the Somali community. Farah previously had been a customer of al-Barakaat and had dealt with the al-Barakaat business representative for North America. After having applied for a license and after establishing a formal business relationship with al-Barakaat, Farah opened his operation. He claims that he never met Jumale and had only an arm's-length business relationship with al-Barakaat. While the business was cyclical, with more money being transmitted during Ramadan, Farah generally transmitted about $200,000 per month. He banked at the local Norwest Bank, where he would deposit cash from his customers and then wire aggregate amounts to al-Barakaat's central office in the UAE. Farah made approximately $1,200 per month from this business, and paid another employee about the same.

Farah's first interaction with the federal government with regard to his business occurred on November 7, 2001, when armed agents entered and seized his business, confiscated all his records and his office equipment, and put a seal on the door preventing reentry. His three business accounts, containing approximately $298,000 of his customers' money, were frozen, making it impossible for him to send that money forward on their behalf. The name of his company was placed on the U.S. and UN lists as a supporter of terrorism.

The money that his customers, primarily Somali immigrants, had entrusted to Farah was not delivered to the intended recipients; his customers were angry and suspicious and did not accept his explanations as to what had become of it. Most of his customers simply did not believe that the U.S. government could do such a thing. For many Somalis, the blocked money represented their life savings and an economic lifeline to an impoverished country. The United Nations estimated that the freeze cut the remittances to Somalia in half.

Another of the Minneapolis money remitters, Garad Nor (also a U.S. citizen), had a considerably bigger problem. On November 30, 2001, both Nor and his business were publicly designated as a supporter of terrorist as a consequence of running a money-remitting company. The net effect of that designation was that no one in the United States could engage in any financial transactions with him. Not only could he not work but, in the words of his lawyer, "the guy couldn't buy a cup of coffee" without violating the OFAC blocking order. On April 26, 2002, after he filed suit against the United States, OFAC issued a license to Nor to allow him to get sufficient money to live. As a result, for five months Nor, a U.S. citizen, faced the unenviable choice of starving or being in criminal violation of the OFAC blocking order.

The Effect of the al-Barakaat Seizures

Al-Barakaat offices were closed in the United States, the UAE, Djibouti, and Ethiopia. Before the action against al-Barakaat, the CIA surmised that AIAI would easily move to other financial institutions in the event that al-Barakaat was shut down. It also understood that the loss of money from al-Barakaat would only temporarily disrupt AIAI, which had other revenue sources. Early intelligence reporting after the freeze indicated that AIAI came under financial pressure because of the closure of al-Barakaat, but moved quickly to develop alternative funding mechanisms. There was no analysis of whether that pressure was the natural result of the closing of the country's largest conduit of funds or was due particularly to al-Barakaat's alleged complicity in funding AIAI. Al-Barakaat ultimately moved its offices to other locations in Dubai and Somalia and changed its name. Moreover, AIAI was able to move money through alternative means. Even as early as mid-November 2001, the CIA judged the Islamic terrorist-funding networks to be "robust," indicating that most Sunni-based Islamic terrorist funding went through interlocking Islamic NGOs and financial entities in the Gulf region. To this day, the Commission staff has uncovered no evidence that closing the al-Barakaat network hurt al Qaeda financially.

U.S. Investigators Travel to the UAE

As OFAC continued to gather support for designations, or designation packages, plans were made to send a team of investigative agents to the UAE to look at records seized from the al-Barakaat offices as well as the al-Barakaat bank records at the EBI. The investigators moved into the main conference room of the UAE's central bank and were supplied with thousands of pages of documents culled from ten accounts held by al-Barakaat. They were able to take back to the United States for further analysis about 7,000 pages of documents from this trip. The investigators obtained unparalleled access and support (unparalleled even in the United States, where criminal investigators do not typically work closely with the central bank regulators). However, the size and complexity of this investigation of a worldwide financial network, responsible for moving millions of dollars, required a follow-up trip in March 2002. In the United States, a financial investigation can take years before investigators understand the intricate financial transactions involved.

Before the second trip, the agent spearheading the effort for the FBI reviewed the OFAC designation package for al-Barakaat and noticed some discrepancies between it and the evidence obtained on the first UAE trip. His review left him with a number of significant factual questions concerning what he thought to be uncorroborated allegations of al-Barakaat's ties to al Qaeda and AIAI. For example, the designation package described Jumale as an associate of Usama Bin Ladin from the original Afghanistan jihad, who was expelled from Saudi Arabia and then moved to Sudan, and who currently lives in Kenya. However, the documentation obtained from the first UAE trip, including Jumale's passport, did not support that intelligence. In addition, a number of EBI accounts that had been frozen did not appear, from the records obtained and analyzed, to be associated with al-Barakaat at all. Overall, the agent believed that much of the evidence for al-Barakaat's terrorist ties rested on unsubstantiated and uncorroborated statements of domestic FBI sources.

The second U.S. delegation to the UAE enjoyed a level of cooperation similar to that of the first. The UAE Central Bank placed 15 people at the investigative team's beck and call. The UAE government did everything the U.S. team requested, including working all night at times to make copies of documents. Jumale was interviewed by U.S. federal agents twice, the first time for ten hours. The U.S. investigative team interviewed 23 individuals (including Jumale), other top al-Barakaat personnel, its outside accountant, and various UAE banking officials. They also reviewed approximately 2 million pages of records, including the actual EBI bank records.

To review some records, the U.S. government team worked where the records were maintained: in un-air-conditioned warehouses in the desert, in stifling 135-degree heat. The agents found that the bank maintained the same kind of records as one would find in the United States and that they were relatively complete, well-organized, and well-preserved. In fact, it appeared to the agent that the records extended far into the past; UAE banks apparently did not systematically destroy older records, as U.S. financial institutions commonly do. Constraints of time and resources prevented the agents from conducting a comprehensive audit of all the records. Instead, they focused on key persons and entities, looked for suspicious transactions, and selected certain dates as representative samples for detailed analysis. On this second trip, the U.S. team brought copies of about 10,000 pages back to the United States for further analysis. Additionally, the FBI was able to make mirror images of data from dozens of the al-Barakaat and EBI computers for further analysis.

No Direct Evidence That al-Barakaat Funded Terrorism

The FBI agent who led the second U.S. delegation said diligent investigation in the UAE revealed no "smoking gun" evidence—either testimonial or documentary—showing that al-Barakaat was funding AIAI or al Qaeda. In fact, the U.S. team could find no direct evidence at all of any real link between al-Barakaat and terrorism of any type. The two major claims, that Bin Ladin was an early investor in al-Barakaat and that al-Barakaat diverted a certain portion of the money through its system to AIAI or al Qaeda, could not be verified. Jumale and all the al-Barakaat witnesses denied any ties to al Qaeda or AIAI, and none of the financial evidence the investigators examined directly contradicted these claims. Moreover, some of the claims made by the early intelligence, such as the assertion that Jumale and Bin Ladin were in Afghanistan together, proved to be wrong. In additional, it appeared that the volume of money was significantly overstated. Secretary O'Neill, in his announcement of the al-Barakaat action, had estimated that al-Barakaat had skimmed $25 million per year and redirected it toward terrorist operations. The agents found that the profits for all of al-Barakaat (from which this money would have to come) totaled only about $700,000 per year, and could not conclude whether *any* of that money had been skimmed.

Although the U.S. team could not find evidence of terrorist financing, they did identify several inexplicable anomalies in the evidence. For example, the team's review of documents revealed several suspicious transactions that Jumale could not adequately explain. Specifically, two NGOs made a number of unusually large deposits into the account of a Kuwaiti charity official over which Jumale had power of attorney. The funds were then moved out of the account in cash. When asked to explain the transactions, Jumale claimed that the money was deposited for use in Somalia. After the deposit, the charity would direct Jumale to send cash from those accounts to Somalia for charitable or religious purposes, such as building a mosque. Because the funds were sent as cash, no other records existed.

The FBI thought this explanation suspicious, as it was inconsistent with Jumale's normal business practices. Although the cash nature of the transactions may have been necessitated by the state of the financial system in Somalia—given the absence of financial institutions there, sending cash may have been the best way to build a mosque— al-Barakaat had a bank in Somalia to which the funds for charitable use could have been sent. However, the agents could draw only suspicions and no conclusions from these transactions. The money transfers might have involved terrorism, they might have represented the proceeds of another kind of crime, or they might have been nothing at all. There was just no way to tell.

At the conclusion of the trip, the agent spearheading the FBI portion of the trip drafted a memorandum, to be distributed to the UAE officials, describing the conclusion the team had reached:

> It has been alleged that the Barakaat Group of Companies were assisting, sponsoring, or providing financial, material, or other services in support of known terrorist organizations. Media and U.S. law enforcement reports have linked al-Barakaat companies and its principle manager, Ahmed Nur Ali Jumale, to Usama bin Ladin and bin Ladin's efforts to fund terrorist activities. *However, this information is generally not firsthand information or it has not been*

*corroborated by documentary or other circumstantial evidence that
supports the allegation.* For example, it has been reported that it is
common knowledge in the United States–based Somali community
that Al Barakaat is a money laundering operation backed by bin
Ladin. It has also been reported that bin Ladin provided Mr. Jumale
the initial financing to start the Al Barakaat businesses. *At this time,
these items of information have not been substantiated through
investigative means.* (emphasis added)

Thus, notwithstanding the unprecedented cooperation by the UAE, significant FBI
interviews of the principal players involved in al-Barakaat (including its founder), and
complete and unfettered access to al-Barakaat's financial records, the FBI could not
substantiate any links between al-Barakaat and terrorism.

OFAC analysts hotly contest this conclusion, and insist that their designation was based
on solid intelligence. The FBI's conclusions, they argue, reflect a profound
misunderstanding of the case, and ignore certain pieces of intelligence. [71] At the very
least, the OFAC officials contend, there is credible evidence that al-Barakaat was a
money-laundering group, responsible for millions in U.S. currency being laundered
through the United States, to an account in the UAE, and then out to suspect third-party
countries. Additionally, they point to documents yet to be translated, as well as records
from the hard drives of al-Barakaat, in the FBI's possession and yet to be analyzed. At
this writing, neither the FBI nor OFAC is attempting to continue to investigate this case.

Delisting Designated Entities and Concluding the Case

Other countries who had joined in the international designation of al-Barakaat were
voicing real concern by early 2002. Their concern stemmed in part from a difference in
how each country set up its terror-financing designation scheme. In the United States, for
example, the power to designate derives from the executive's power to wage war against
foreign enemies. As a result, the executive may rely on less evidence than is required in a
criminal or even civil trial. The judicial review that is afforded a designation is extremely
deferential to the executive's judgment. In other countries, a designation is viewed as a
judicial or quasi-judicial act, in which the accused is afforded a right to answer the
charges and the standard of evidence is at least as high as would be needed to sustain a
civil lawsuit.

In January 2002, three Swedish citizens of Somali origin who were listed in the original
al-Barakaat designation petitioned OFAC and the United Nations for removal from the
list. Sweden, although not a member of the UN Security Council, sought to have the
Council adopt a criminal evidentiary standard prior to placing anyone on the sanctions
list. The Canadians, similarly, moved to take one of its own citizens off the UN list. All

---

[71] Intelligence community sources have informed Commission staff that the intelligence sources for much
of the reporting regarding al-Barakaat's connection to al Qaeda have since been terminated by the relevant
agency as intelligence sources, based on concerns of fabrication.

of the UN designations to that point had come at the suggestion of the United States, and the Swedish proposal could have required the removal of either most or all of the names on the list. The State Department sent demarches to all Security Council member nations, urging "in the strongest terms" that they oppose Swedish effort.

Meanwhile, in Minneapolis, Abdullahi Farah and Garad Nor were trying to resolve their cases and working toward getting their money unfrozen. They hired a lawyer, who made both men available for interviews with the U.S. Attorney's Office and federal agents concerning their involvement in al-Barakaat.[72] The lawyer contacted OFAC to try to resolve the case; for months the calls were unreturned and neither of his clients was told of the evidentiary basis of the freezing actions. Finally, in April 2002, Farah and Nor filed suit against the government, alleging that the OFAC action deprived them of their constitutional rights.

In response to the lawsuits and the concerns of our allies, and in order to forestall more drastic action, the United States moved to develop a delisting process for those who claimed that they were designated incorrectly. At the time, there was no procedure to delist, either at the United Nations or at OFAC. Ultimately, the Policy Coordinating Committee decided on a set of standards to use. Treasury Under Secretary Jimmy Gurule went to the UN in the spring of 2002 and presented a whitepaper on delisting, which included a requirement for an attestation that the individual had severed the link with the tainted organization and a commitment not to associate with terrorist-related entities again. The goal was to force behavior changes and to have an orderly process based on principles, as opposed to requests for delistings based on the "inconvenience" or dislike of the designations regime.

The OFAC analysts were then required to go back and justify their designations of the three Swedes and the U.S. al-Barakaat entities and individuals. For the original listing, the analysts were required to show only that the individual entities were part of the overall al-Barakaat operation, which they could do through commercial directories such as the Dun & Bradstreet registry, as well as the list that had been seized in Norway. In the spring and summer of 2002, however, the analysts were tasked to show that each al-Barakaat individual was involved in the funding of terrorism, rather than that he or she simply belonged to an entity that, overall, supported terrorism. There was no such evidence, although OFAC analysts complained of not having sufficient access to classified information, as well as being denied information held by the FBI.[73]

---

[72] Farah was interviewed, but the US Attorney's Office never arranged to interview Nor.

[73] The analysts were hampered in the fact that they did not have access to the records seized in the November raids. While those records were seized under OFAC authority, it was limited only to seizing and retaining them. In order to exploit them for evidentiary purposes, the FBI was able to execute a search warrant, which was then served on OFAC as custodian of the records. Those records were imaged and made available to the criminal agents and the U.S. Attorney's Office. According to the OFAC analysts, the FBI, perhaps burned by what they considered a premature designation, never shared a copy of the seized records with them.

On August 27, 2002, OFAC removed the U.S.-based money remitters in Minneapolis and Columbus, Ohio, as well as two of the three[74] Somali Swedes, from its list of designated entities. Abdullahi Farah, the Minneapolis money remitter, signed an affidavit stating that he had severed all ties with al-Barakaat, and received his money back. Throughout the litigation, Nor had maintained that he was unassociated with al-Barakaat, and signed an affidavit to that effect. He, too, received his money back.

The federal agents working on the al-Barakaat criminal investigation in Minneapolis spent hundreds of hours reviewing financial records and interviewing witnesses. Despite this effort, their attempt to make a criminal case simply had no traction. Ultimately, prosecutors were unable to file charges against any of the al-Barakaat participants, with the exception of one of the customers in Minneapolis who was charged with low-level welfare fraud. The FBI supervisor on the criminal case, deciding that their efforts could be better spent elsewhere, closed their investigation.

---

[74] The third was found to have made false statements to the investigating agents and on his application for removal from the list.

Chapter 6

The Illinois Charities Case Study

Two Illinois-based charities, the Global Relief Foundation (GRF) and the Benevolence International Foundation (BIF), were publicly accused by the federal government shortly after 9/11 of providing financial support to al Qaeda and international terrorism. The FBI had already been investigating both GRF and BIF for several years, but only after 9/11 did the government move to shut down these organizations and stop their flow of funds overseas.[75]

Introduction

GRF, a nonprofit organization ostensibly devoted to providing humanitarian aid to the needy, with operations in 25 countries around the world, raised millions of dollars in the United States in support of its mission. U.S. investigators have long believed that GRF was devoting a significant percentage of the funds it raised to support Islamic extremist causes and jihadists with substantial links to international terrorist groups, including al Qaeda, and the FBI had a very active investigation under way by the time of 9/11. BIF, a nonprofit organization with offices in at least 10 countries around the world, raised millions of dollars in the United States, much of which it distributed throughout the world for purposes of humanitarian aid. As in the case of GRF, the U.S. government believed BIF had substantial connections to terrorist groups, including al Qaeda, and was sending a substantial percentage of its funds to support the international jihadist movement. BIF was also the subject of an active investigation by 9/11.

After 9/11, the Office of Foreign Assets Control (OFAC) froze both charities' assets, effectively putting them out of business. The FBI opened a criminal investigation of both charities, ultimately resulting in the conviction of the leader of BIF for non-terrorism-related charges. The Immigration and Naturalization Service (INS) detained and ultimately deported a major GRF fund-raiser. No criminal charges have been filed against GRF or its personnel, as of this writing.

The cases of BIF and GRF illustrate the U.S. government's approach to terrorist fund-raising in the United States before 9/11 and how that approach dramatically changed after the terrorist attacks, moving from a strategy of merely investigating and monitoring terrorist financing to one of active disruption through criminal prosecution and the use of its powers under the International Emergency Economic Powers Act (IEEPA) to block the assets of suspect entities in the United States. Although effective in shutting down its

---

[75] This chapter is based on interviews with many participants, including FBI agents and supervisors, OFAC personnel, representatives of BIF and GRF, as well as other witnesses, extensive review of contemporaneous documents, both classified and unclassified, from a variety of agencies, and the court filings and judicial opinions from litigation concerning BIF and GRF.

targets, this aggressive approach raises potential civil liberties concerns. The BIF and GRF investigations also highlight two fundamental issues that span all aspects of the government's efforts to combat al Qaeda financing: the difference between seeing "links" to terrorists and proving the funding of terrorists, and the problem of defining the threshold of information necessary to take disruptive action.

FBI Investigations of BIF and GRF before 9/11

Contrary to a common misconception, the FBI did not ignore terrorist financing before 9/11. The intelligence side of the FBI gathered extensive information on terrorist fundraising in the United States, although the Bureau lacked any strategy for disrupting the activity. In various field offices around the country, street agents actively investigated groups and individuals, including GRF and BIF, suspected of raising funds for al Qaeda or other extremist groups. Working in the face of many obstacles, including what agents believed to be a dysfunctional FISA (Foreign Intelligence Surveillance Act) process, these agents aggressively gathered information and tried to coordinate with other field offices, the intelligence community, and even foreign governments. The FBI lacked a headquarters unit that focused on terrorist financing before 9/11, however, and also lacked a coherent national approach to tackling the problem. As Assistant Director, Counterterrorism John Pistole testified, "there did not exist within the FBI a mechanism to ensure appropriate focus on terrorist finance issues and provide the necessary expertise and overall coordination to comprehensively address these matters."[76]

Origins of GRF

GRF was incorporated in Bridgeview, Illinois, in 1992. According to the U.S. government, GRF's founders had previously been affiliated with the Mektab al Khidmat (MAK) or "Human Services Office," cofounded by Abdullah Azzam and Usama Bin Ladin in the 1980s to recruit and support mujahideen to fight against the Soviets in Afghanistan. MAK funneled money and fighters to the mujahideen and set up a network of recruiting offices around the world, including in the United States. The U.S. government has called MAK the "precursor organization to al Qaeda."[77] One offshoot of MAK in the United States, the Al Khifa Refugee Center in Brooklyn, facilitated the movement of jihadist fighters in and out of Afghanistan. After the defeat of the Soviets, MAK and Al Kifah continued the mission of supporting jihadist fighters throughout the world. According to the U.S. government, a number of the persons convicted in the first World Trade Center bombing were associated with the Al Khifa Refugee Center, as was Sheikh Omar Abdel Rahman, the "Blind Sheikh," who is now serving a life sentence for his role in the foiled plan to bomb New York City tunnels and landmarks. President

---

[76] J. Pistole, July 31, 2003, Prepared Testimony, Senate Governmental Affairs Committee.

[77] Treasury Department Statement Regarding the Designation of the Global Relief Foundation, October 18, 2002 (Treasury GRF Statement).

George W. Bush designated MAK/Al Khifa a specially designated global terrorist in the original annex to Executive Order 13224 on September 23, 2001.

GRF described itself as a nongovernmental organization (NGO) that provided humanitarian relief aid to Muslims through overseas offices around the world, especially in strife-torn regions such as Bosnia, Kashmir, Afghanistan, Lebanon, and Chechnya. GRF began operating with $700,000 in cash. By 2000, it reported more than $5 million in annual contributions. According to its Internal Revenue Service (IRS) filings, GRF sent 90 percent of its donations abroad between 1994 and 2000.[78] GRF's numerous offices overseas received their own contributions in addition to what they received from the U.S. operation.

The FBI investigation of GRF before 9/11

GRF came to the attention of the FBI's Chicago Division in the mid-1990s, because of GRF's affiliation with Al Khifa and other unsubstantiated allegations about GRF's potential involvement in terrorist activity. After lying dormant for some time, the GRF investigation was assigned to two agents, who began to discover evidence of what they viewed as suspicious conduct. The Chicago office opened a formal full field investigation (FFI)[79] in late 1997, largely on the strength of a series of telephone calls between GRF personnel and others with terrorist affiliations, as well as information from the intelligence community that GRF personnel had undertaken suspicious travel to Afghanistan and Pakistan. The Chicago agents stepped up the investigation of GRF, including physical surveillance, review of GRF's trash, and attempts to get telephone records through a legal request known as a National Security Letter (NSL). Among other things, the trash revealed copies of GRF's newsletter, "Al-Thilal" ("The Shadow"), which openly advocated a militant interpretation of Islam and armed jihad.

The NSLs yielded very useful information, but the process for their internal approval frustrated the Chicago agents, who said that the tremendous delays in getting NSLs authorized by FBI headquarters was the biggest obstacle they had to overcome in their pre-9/11 investigation of GRF. It routinely took six months to a year to get NSLs approved for routine documents, such as telephone or bank records. The Chicago agents believed their contact at the FBI headquarters in the Radical Fundamentalist Unit was very good at his job, but was overwhelmed with work, which caused a major bottleneck in getting the NSLs.

The Chicago agents received substantial information about GRF from foreign government agencies. They worked directly through the relevant FBI legal attaché, or Legat (an FBI agent posted overseas who acts as a liaison with foreign officials), to get foreign information. The process could be very slow and somewhat uncertain, but it often

---

[78] For example, GRF sent $3.2 million overseas in 1999; and $3.7 million overseas in 2000.

[79] Approval to open an FFI requires some predication that the investigation is being conducted for legitimate intelligence purposes. Agents, using limited investigative techniques can open a preliminary investigation (PI) for a limited time to gather evidence to determine whether a FFI is warranted.

yielded helpful information. One European country where GRF had a substantial office provided the most useful information in the early stages of the investigation.

By mid-1998, the Chicago agents had evidence that led them to conclude that GRF was doing much more than providing humanitarian aid. The Chicago office summarized its views in an August 3, 1998, memorandum: "The FBI believes that GRF, through its Bridgeview headquarters and satellite offices around the globe, is actively involved in supplying and raising funds for international terrorism and Islamic militant movements overseas." At the time, the FBI suspected the executive director of being a supporter or member of the Egyptian extremist group Al Gama'a Al Islamiyya (AGAI), which was affiliated with the Blind Sheikh.

The Chicago office submitted a FISA application for GRF in mid-1998; it was not approved until mid-1999. According to the Chicago agents, the application posed no significant problems, although it appeared that the fact that domestic charities were involved may have slowed the process. In any event, it took a year for the application to be approved and authorized. After receiving FISA approval, the agents initiated electronic surveillance, which allowed them to expand the investigation.

By late 1999, the Chicago case agents were comfortable in their conclusion that GRF was a jihadist organization and that its executive director had connections to both AGIA and what they called the "Islamic Army organization of international terrorist financier Usama Bin Ladin."[80] They believed that multiple sources of evidence supported these conclusions. In the agents' view, the phone records they had obtained proved a compelling, although indirect, link between GRF's executive director and Usama Bin Ladin. In reviewing intelligence information and the executive director's phone records, they concluded that the executive director called a phone used by a mujahideen leader who was a close associate of Usama Bin Ladin. Phone records also connected GRF, through its office in Brussels, Belgium, with Bin Ladin's former personal secretary, Wadi al Hage, who is now serving a life sentence in the United States for his role in the 1998 embassy bombings.

The Chicago FBI agents were able to get critical information about the persons associated with international phone numbers because they had a working relationship with the CIA before 9/11. The Chicago agents said the quality of this relationship varied depending on the CIA representatives, who tended to be replaced frequently. Although the relationship was not always smooth, it did succeed in providing important information.

The Chicago agents also conducted "trash covers," virtually every week for years, which provided key intelligence on GRF. In this technique, the agents secretly entered GRF's dumpster late at night and took out its trash for review. Among other things, GRF threw away pictures of communication gear it had shipped overseas, including sophisticated military-style handheld radios that the agents believed were far beyond what relief workers would ever need, but valuable to set up a military communications network. After 9/11, they learned this communication gear was shipped to Chechnya. They also

---

[80] January 20, 1999, FBI Document.

found in GRF's trash pro-jihad books and literature, including the writings of Abdullah Azzam.

The Chicago agents summarized their view of GRF to a foreign government service in a January 6, 2000, memorandum:

> Although the majority of GRF funding goes toward legitimate relief operations, a significant percentage is diverted to fund extremist causes. Among the terrorist groups known to have links to the GRF are the Algerian Armed Islamic Group, the Egyptian Islamic Jihad, Gama'at Al Islamyia, and the Kashmiri Harakat Al-Jihad El-Islam, as well as the Al Qaeda organization of Usama Bin Laden. . . . In the past, GRF support to terrorists and other transnational mujahideen fighters has taken the form of purchase and shipment of large quantities of sophisticated communications equipment, provision of humanitarian cover documentation to suspected terrorists and fund-raising for terrorist groups under the cover of humanitarian relief.[81]

By 9/11, the Chicago agents believed that they had uncovered enough information to conclude that GRF was raising substantial funds in the United States to support international jihad. Bank records obtained through NSLs revealed large transfers of funds to the GRF overseas offices. The agents believed GRF distributed the bulk of funds as humanitarian relief, but also supported armed militants in the strife-torn regions where it was active.

On January 10, 2001, the Chicago agents wrote that "GRF is a highly organized fundraising machine, which raises millions of dollars annually" and that GRF's "operations have extended all over the globe."[82] The executive director, in his capacity as head of the organization, "has been and continues to be a supporter of worldwide Islamic extremist activity" and he "has past and present links and associations with a wide variety of international Muslim extremists," including al Qaeda and Usama Bin Ladin. The agents did not believe GRF was part of the formal al Qaeda network. Instead, they believed it "free-lanced" to support jihadists around the world, including in Europe, Bangladesh, India, and Pakistan. They also knew GRF was underwriting substantial humanitarian aid, which they thought was critical to its pro-jihad mission.[83]

The Chicago agents believed GRF had two types of donors during this period. People not in the know thought they were giving money for humanitarian relief. Others clearly knew the purpose of their donations: When the agents later obtained donors' checks, they saw that some donors had actually written pro-jihad statements on their memo lines.

The money trail generally stopped at the U.S. border, and the agents could never trace it directly to jihadists or terrorists. Before 9/11, they had no means to get foreign bank

---

[81] January 6, 2000 FBI Document.
[82] January 10, 2001 FBI Document.
[83] January 10, 2001 FBI Document.

records. A formal request for records, called a mutual legal assistance treaty (MLAT) request, was impossible because the FBI did not have an open criminal investigation—the GRF inquiry was an intelligence investigation. The agents did ask one European country for help, but were told that that country's restrictive laws prohibited electronic surveillance and obtaining bank records. The Chicago agents wanted to travel to Europe to meet with officials who had investigated GRF, but the Chicago FBI office denied permission because of budgetary constraints.

The Chicago investigation of GRF in turn led to an investigation by the Detroit FBI agents of GRF subjects within its jurisdiction. In early 2000, Chicago informed Detroit that GRF's executive director had been calling two Michigan residents. One of these subjects was considered GRF's spiritual leader and the other, Rabih Haddad, was a major GRF fund-raiser. A Detroit agent went to Chicago and reviewed the extensive investigative file. Upon his return, the agent prepared a request to open FFIs on the two subjects; it was approved in late March 2000. The evidence gathered in Chicago made clear to the Detroit agent that the GRF investigation was potentially "pretty big."[84]

The Detroit agents, however, believed themselves to be stymied by the inability to get FISA coverage. At the same time that the case agent opened the FFIs, he sought FISA coverage of those two subjects. None of these FISA applications was approved until after 9/11, some 18 months later. The Detroit agent was never given even an ostensible reason for the holdup. On the contrary, FBI headquarters told the agent that the applications looked good. These applications were being actively reviewed by both OIPR and FBI headquarters. Still, nothing ever happened. When he called FBI headquarters to check on the status of his applications, the Detroit agent was told only "we're [the FBI] working on it." The Detroit agent was very frustrated and upset by the delay, which he believes caused him to miss a great opportunity to gather critical intelligence and substantially limited the Detroit investigation of GRF before 9/11.

Resource limitations also limited Detroit's role before 9/11. Though many counterterrorism investigations might have been undertaken, Detroit had only 12 agents on these cases; and because each agent was working multiple cases, no case could receive the attention it needed. Because of the lack of FISA coverage, resource limitations, and the apparent focus GRF's activities in Chicago, the Detroit investigation was largely a satellite to the Chicago investigation before 9/11.

The Chicago agents thought that FBI headquarters provided support for their GRF investigation before 9/11, approving the FISA application, for example, and providing analytical support. In addition, one of the analysts at headquarters saw relevant material in a case file from another field office and very helpfully brought it to Chicago's attention. From the Detroit perspective, however, headquarters was interested in the GRF investigation but was swamped with work and itself understaffed.

---

[84] Commission Staff Interview.

No realistic opportunities for disruption before 9/11

The Chicago agents saw no way to make a criminal case against GRF before 9/11, even though the agents thought they had considerable evidence that GRF was a major fund-raising operation for international jihad. The two lead agents thought about and even discussed the possibility of mounting a criminal case, but dismissed it. They had much smoke but no real fire—they had no direct evidence of serious criminal activity. They could not trace the millions of dollars GRF sent overseas to any specific jihadist or terrorist organization, although they had their suspicions. Even the electronic surveillance coverage yielded no evidence that would conclusively prove a criminal offense.

The Chicago agents worked with the INS to pick up several GRF employees on immigration overstays, with the goal of seeing if they would cooperate with the FBI against their employer. This effort proved fruitless, however. They considered doing the same with Rabih Haddad, the Detroit subject and major GRF fund-raiser, but decided it made more sense to continue investigating him; the Detroit agents agreed.[85] The Chicago agents thought that the executive director himself was also technically out of status—he had requested a certain status adjustment from the INS but not yet received it—though an arrest in such a situation would be unusual. In any event, they did not ask the INS to arrest him, preferring to continue to monitor him.

The very concept of a criminal international terrorism case was foreign to the Chicago agents, and they did not think that the U.S. Attorney's Office had sufficient expertise in such cases. In addition, the agents believed that the rules regarding "the wall" between intelligence and criminal cases prevented the case agents from even discussing intelligence information with the U.S. Attorney's Office. Other than in New York, there were few criminal international terrorist (IT) investigations or cases in process. The Chicago office was undertaking only two criminal IT investigations, neither of which focused on al Qaeda suspects. According to the agent who supervised the GRF and BIF cases before 9/11, the case agents had always wanted to open a criminal case, despite the wall; but they thought that doing so would have hurt their ability to get and maintain FISA coverage because of their perception of the Department of Justice's restrictive interpretations of the wall restrictions, which they understood had impaired the Chicago office's ability to get FISA warrants approved in the past. As result, Chicago agents were cautious about pursuing criminal matters pertaining to ongoing intelligence investigations.

The lead Detroit investigator also saw no prospect of a criminal case before 9/11. He said that while working the case as an intelligence investigation he always kept in the back of his mind that possibility, but he knew that he had nowhere near the type of evidence required for criminal prosecution; he had his own concerns about the wall as well. In any event, neither Detroit nor Chicago, which had the lead in formulating an overall strategy, had sufficient evidence to move forward with criminal charges.

---

[85] The Chicago and Detroit agents each attributed to the other the decision to refrain from detaining Haddad, but both agree they concurred with the decision made by the other, without objection.

The Chicago investigation of GRF suffered a major blow in late spring or early summer 2001 when the FISA warrants were not extended. The Chicago agents were now in the same position as those in Detroit—deprived of electronic surveillance, their most potent intelligence-gathering tool.

GRF's status on 9/11

The FBI's investigation over the several years before 9/11 led the investigating agents to believe GRF was an organization dedicated to supporting international jihad and was raising substantial funds in the United States toward that goal. The FBI agents developed what they thought was a good understanding of GRF's activities, despite significant obstacles imposed by a dysfunctional process for obtaining NSLs and FISA warrants. Although the FBI did the bulk of the work investigating GRF, the investigation benefited from contributions by the intelligence community and by foreign law enforcement sources, both of which substantially aided the FBI's understanding of the GRF's overseas activities. Despite the considerable body of knowledge they had, the FBI agents believed they lacked the evidence necessary to bring a criminal prosecution against GRF or its principals. In any event, the perceived restrictions imposed by the wall made such a prosecution extremely difficult, at best, and initiating a criminal investigation could have put the FISA warrants at risk. As a result, the FBI was left with nothing to do but continue to gather intelligence on GRF's activities in the United States. This task was made far more difficult by the inability to renew the FISA warrants in Chicago or obtain FISA coverage in Detroit. The agents did not have any plan to disrupt what they believed to be a major jihadist fund-raising operation, or any endgame for their investigation.

The origin of BIF

BIF was incorporated in Illinois in March 1992 and received tax-exempt status in March 1993. Its origins can be traced to Saudi Arabia, where in 1987 Sheikh Adel Abdul Jalil Batterjee founded Lajnat Al-Birr Al-Islami (LBI), a Jeddah-based NGO. LBI provided support to the mujahideen fighting the Soviets in Afghanistan, as well as humanitarian aid to refugees of the war in Afghanistan. Batterjee, from a merchant family in Saudi Arabia, was affiliated with a group of wealthy donors from the Persian Gulf region known as the "Golden Chain," which provided support to mujahideen, including mujahideen under the leadership of Usama Bin Ladin. The U.S. government has alleged that BIF was incorporated in the United States to attract more donations and deflect scrutiny from LBI.

At BIF's founding in 1992, its three directors were Batterjee and two other Saudis. In March 1993, Batterjee and the two other Saudis were replaced by three new directors, including Enaam Arnaout, who became BIF's executive director, managing its day-to-day operations and reporting to Batterjee. The U.S. government contends the change was made after Batterjee came under scrutiny in Saudi Arabia for financially supporting jihad outside of approved channels. Despite his formal removal, Batterjee continued to play a major role in running BIF and was in frequent contact with Arnaout from his home in Saudi Arabia. The government contends that Arnaout was a longtime jihadist supporter, with personal ties to Usama Bin Ladin dating back to the 1980s. He allegedly provided military and logistical support to the mujahideen in the late 1980s and early 1990s, as an employee of LBI and another Saudi NGO, the Muslim World League. In doing so, he allegedly worked closely with Usama Bin Ladin and other mujahideen who later became significant members or supporters of al Qaeda. According to INS data compiled by the FBI, Arnaout, a native Syrian, lived in Hama, Syria, from his birth in 1962 until 1981, when he went to study in Saudi Arabia. In 1989, Arnaout married an American citizen he met in Peshawar, and he became a naturalized U.S. citizen in March 1994.

BIF publicly described itself as an "organization devoted to relieving the suffering of Muslims around the world." According to its IRS filings, it received more than $15 million in donations between 1995 and 2000.

The FBI investigation of BIF

The FBI started its investigation of BIF in 1998 as a result of a conference that a Chicago agent attended in Washington, D.C., where he learned of foreign intelligence reports indicating that Arnaout was involved in providing logistical support for jihadists. The FBI in Chicago opened an FFI in February 1999, focusing on Arnaout as the key player. The GRF case agents also served as the lead case agents on BIF investigation. Much like the early GRF investigation, BIF investigation featured surveillance and digging through garbage. The FBI also sought to develop sources. The trash covers were fruitful, as BIF "threw out everything"—including telephone bills and detailed and elaborate reports on its activities, which Arnaout demanded from his subordinates on a daily basis. The FBI began to run down some of the names and numbers appearing in the trash. In addition, on April 21, 1999, the agents recovered from BIF's trash a newspaper article on bioterrorism, in which someone had highlighted sections relating to the United States' lack of preparedness for a biological attack.

When it opened the FFI, the FBI in Chicago knew of Adel Batterjee but had little understanding of who he was. They later obtained records showing Batterjee was contributing funds to BIF. In the summer of 1999, they sent what the Bureau calls a lead—relaying information and requesting action—to Saudi Arabia, through the Legat, for information on Batterjee. As of 9/11 they still had received no response.

Chicago submitted a FISA request in April 2000, but it was not approved until after 9/11. Notwithstanding evidence that BIF had significant links to Usama Bin Ladin and was sending significant amounts of money overseas, the Chicago agents could not get an inside look at the organization that a FISA could provide. As we will later show, after 9/11 it was simply too late.

After opening the FFI, FBI Chicago obtained NSLs for phone and bank records. The bank records gave a good indication of the scope of BIF's fund-raising activities. According to contemporaneous documents, the FBI believed based on its yet to be completed investigation that BIF was receiving approximately forty to sixty thousand dollars a week, and that between 1997 and 1998, BIF sent more than $2.5 million to its overseas offices in Bosnia, Azerbaijan, Pakistan, and Tajikistan.

FBI Chicago had cultivated a good human source who provided useful information on BIF, though never any smoking guns. The Chicago agents had a much closer relationship with the CIA on BIF than they did on GRF, because they cooperated on certain international matters in the BIF investigation. They regularly met with the CIA concerning BIF, received some useful information, and shared much of their information. For example, the Chicago agents learned from the CIA important information about BIF's founding and the sources of its funding. Still, the CIA and the FBI did not have a perfect relationship, and the CIA held back some information. The Chicago agents believed the CIA wanted to shield certain information from the FBI because of fears of revealing sources and methods in any potential criminal litigation in the United States.

The Chicago agents obtained all the bank account numbers for the BIF's overseas offices, which BIF had typed up and later thrown out in the trash. They provided this information to the intelligence community, which they hoped could trace the money overseas. They never heard anything back about such a trace, however.

The BIF investigation revealed the difficulties in securing foreign cooperation in terrorism investigations. FBI Chicago submitted a lead to a European ally, through the Legat, for information about European intelligence reports concerning a BIF official's purported involvement in the kidnapping of Americans in Kashmir. The U.S. ally never even acknowledged the request, let alone replied. The FBI did not submit MLAT requests for foreign records because, again, it had no criminal case.

The FBI's New York Field Office, which ran the primary FBI investigation of Bin Ladin, was a key source of information for Chicago. But the New York agents were overwhelmed with work, and did not always coordinate well with their Chicago counterparts. Although the New York agents were aware of the BIF/GRF investigations, they sent out their own leads relevant to these investigations, annoying the Chicago agents. The agents in New York did not have time to share information proactively, although those in Chicago were welcome to look through New York's files for relevant information—which they did, gaining helpful information.[86]

GRF's bank filed a money-laundering Suspicious Activity Report with the Treasury Department's Financial Crimes Enforcement Network (FinCEN) regarding BIF's large transfers of money to the Republic of Georgia. It was apparently concerned that BIF was involved with Russian organized crime. The Chicago agents said they did not make any requests of FinCEN before 9/11, explaining that FinCEN would not have been useful to

---

[86] According to the BIF's attorney, the bank actually closed the BIF's accounts just before 9/11, forcing BIF to find another bank in the Chicago area, which it was able to do.

them because it could not help them trace the money once it got overseas. They knew that BIF was sending big money overseas, and even knew the account numbers and office directors of the BIF overseas offices that were receiving the money. Their problem was tracing the money once it got there, and the believed FinCEN could provide no help in this regard because, like the FBI agents, it had no access to the relevant foreign records.

Inability to bring a criminal case to disrupt BIF

Overall, BIF investigation was in the same position as the GRF investigation on 9/11: the agents believed BIF had substantial ties to al Qaeda, was supporting jihad, and was sending a great deal of money overseas, but they could not trace the money directly to its ultimate destination overseas. Although they had access to considerable information, the agents believed they still could not come close to proving a criminal case against Arnaout or BIF. The BIF investigation was actually in worse shape because, unlike in the GRF investigation, the agents could not get approval for electronic surveillance. The agents tried to understand what was going on overseas, and a European agency had invited the Chicago agents to a meeting to share information. The agents tried to go but, as had happened with the GRF investigation, the Chicago FBI could not afford to send them. The misunderstanding of the wall also created the same problems in the BIF investigation as it did in that of the GRF. For all of these reasons, the FBI could not take any action against BIF, despite what the agents considered extensive knowledge of BIF's malfeasance.

Like the GRF investigation, the BIF investigation lacked an endgame. Believing themselves unable to initiate a criminal investigation and lacking any other means to disrupt what they thought to be a major jihadist fund-raising operation with substantial links to Bin Ladin and al Qaeda, the Chicago agents saw no options other than continued monitoring of BIF's activities. In this respect, the BIF and GRF investigations typified the FBI's pre-9/11 approach to terrorist financing. The FBI had numerous terrorist-financing investigations under way, but the vast majority of them were pursued as intelligence-gathering exercises by FBI intelligence agents, with little or no thought of disrupting the fund-raising through criminal prosecution or otherwise.

Post-9/11 Developments

FBI investigations of BIF and GRF after 9/11

Everything changed almost immediately after 9/11 with respect to the BIF and GRF investigations. Major obstacles to the investigation dropped away, more resources became available, and the issue of terrorist financing gained new prominence among national policymakers in Washington.

As a result, the course of the BIF and GRF investigations dramatically changed and led to a series of events unimaginable on 9/10: the long-delayed FISA warrants were instantaneously approved; the FBI opened a major criminal investigation of GRF and BIF; FBI agents raided the Illinois headquarters of both organizations in an unprecedented overt FISA search; OFAC—an entity entirely unknown to the FBI case agents before 9/11—froze the assets of GRF and BIF; NATO troops kicked in doors of the charities' overseas offices and carted away all their contents; and Bosnian criminal investigators raided BIF's office in Bosnia, seizing a treasure trove of documents directly concerning BIF's relationship with Bin Ladin that dated to the origins of al Qaeda.

In the immediate wake of 9/11, the Chicago FISA warrant for GRF was reinstated, and that for BIF was finally approved. The previously moribund FISA applications from Detroit for GRF were approved as well, as the agent was informed by an emergency call from FBI headquarters.

But after the events of 9/11, electronic surveillance was not very useful, even though the FBI assigned a significant number of translators to the cases. The agents believed that the GRF subjects feared electronic monitoring in the wake of the attacks; they were extremely cautious about their communications. The GRF FISA warrants proved unproductive. On the other hand, electronic surveillance of BIF yielded some useful information, including the fact that Arnaout was passing messages to Batterjee. In addition to electronic surveillance, the agents continued other investigative techniques, including trash covers and physical surveillance.

Coincidentally, the U.S. Attorney for Chicago, Patrick Fitzgerald, on the job for only a couple of weeks, had extensive experience as a terrorism prosecutor and immediately became involved in the investigation of BIF and GRF.[87] Fitzgerald was very interested in prosecuting the cases criminally and, at his urging, the FBI opened a criminal investigation of BIF and GRF in October 2001. The intelligence cases continued as well, and the electronic surveillance continued. Because the wall between criminal and intelligence matters still existed, they decided to have separate case agents for the criminal and intelligence investigations. The lead intelligence case agents moved to the criminal case, and two new agents were assigned to the intelligence cases. The new intelligence agents were responsible for passing information over the wall to the criminal agents.

Fitzgerald immersed himself in the case and took a major role. He directed the FBI to interview al Qaeda cooperators from the New York cases, who provided considerable information on BIF and some on GRF as well. One cooperator, an admitted former al Qaeda member and Bin Ladin associate, said that BIF engaged in financial transactions for al Qaeda in the early 1990s. He also described how al Qaeda would take cash from charitable NGOs, which would then cover the transactions with false paperwork. After

---

[87] Fitzgerald took office pursuant to an interim appointment on September 1, 2001; he was formally appointed and confirmed by the Senate in October. Fitzgerald had extensive experience prosecuting terrorism cases as an Assistant U.S. Attorney in New York, where he prosecuted the Landmarks and Embassy Bombings cases and served nearly six years as co-chief of the Organized Crime and Terrorism Section.

opening the criminal case, the agents also were able to issue grand jury subpoenas for additional phone and bank records.

OFAC involvement and the shutdown of BIF and GRF

While the Chicago agents and prosecutors were starting to think about bringing criminal cases against BIF and GRF, policymakers in Washington were thinking about disrupting al Qaeda financing using whatever tools they had. BIF and GRF came to the attention of OFAC, which began to consider them for possible designation as a supporter of al Qaeda. To this end, OFAC dispatched two analysts to Chicago in early December 2001 to review the FBI files and begin putting together the evidentiary packages that would support designations.

These plans were dramatically accelerated when CIA analysts, drawing on intelligence gathered in an unrelated FBI investigation, expressed concerns that GRF could be involved in a plot to attack the United States with weapons of mass destruction (WMD). Neither the Chicago agents nor the FBI headquarters analysts, who had extensive knowledge of GRF, were consulted on this analysis, which a Chicago FBI supervisor characterized as baseless. The WMD fears led to a plan to enter and search the overseas offices of GRF and BIF to obtain swabbings and other evidence related to possible WMD deployment. BIF was included because the two charities were thought to be related. Although the WMD allegations were never corroborated, the events of 9/11 led to an understandably cautious approach in dealing with potential threats of mass casualties.

At the same time, OFAC received word from the General Counsel of Treasury, who was coordinating the interagency effort against terrorist financing, that it needed to designate BIF and GRF immediately. OFAC had not yet developed the evidence necessary for a designation under IEEPA. As a result, OFAC relied on a provision of IEEPA clarified by the Patriot Act, which provides that OFAC could freeze the assets belonging to a suspected terrorist supporter "during the pendency of an investigation." Only a single piece of paper, signed by the director of OFAC, was required.[88] OFAC announced this action on December 14, 2001, thereby effectively shutting down both charities in the United States while gaining additional time to develop the evidentiary packages necessary for permanent designations. This extraordinary power enabled the government to stop the charities' operations without any formal determination of wrongdoing.

The raids on a number of overseas offices also occurred on December 14, 2001, conducted, in various locations, by NATO troops and U.S. government personnel. NATO troops raided two GRF offices, and NATO publicly stated that GRF "is allegedly involved in planning attacks against targets in the U.S.A. and Europe."[89] At the same time, Albanian National Police, accompanied by an FBI agent, raided the GRF office in Tirana and the home of a GRF employee, seizing $20,000 and taking swabbings for residue of WMD.

---

[88] According to OFAC, in practice, an interagency group discusses and agrees to any designation.
[89] Shenon, "A Nation Challenged: The Money Trail", New York Times, Dec. 18, 2001.

The original plan did not call for searches or takedowns of the GRF and BIF offices in Illinois. Rather, the FBI was to use its FISA warrants to monitor the charities' reaction to the overseas searches. This plan went awry when word of the impending action apparently leaked to GRF. FBI personnel learned that some of the targets of the investigations may be destroying documents.[90] As a result, the FBI decided to do an unprecedented "overt" FISA search of both GRF and BIF offices, which was hastily assembled and conducted. Following a chaotic process, the government agents searched both BIF and GRF offices in Illinois on December 14, 2001, carting away substantial evidence. The agents also searched the residence of GRF executive director and Arnaout.

On December 14, 2001, the INS detained GRF fund-raiser Rabih Haddad, one of the subjects of the Detroit investigation, on the basis that he was out of his allowed immigration status, having overstayed a student visa issued in 1998. Following bond hearings that were closed to the press, public, and Haddad's family, an immigration judge denied bail and ordered Haddad detained.[91]

While officials and investigators around the world moved to eliminate the perceived WMD threat and shut down the operations of BIF and GRF, investigators working on the 9/11 attacks sought to understand a curious connection between hijackers Nawaf al Hazmi and Khalid al Mihdhar and a GRF fund-raiser. On 9/11, the FBI learned that two days before, hijackers Hazmi and Mihdhar had dropped off bags at an Islamic prayer center in Maryland. The bags, to which the hijackers had affixed a note stating "[a] gift for the brothers," contained fruit, clothing, flight logs, and various other materials. The FBI launched an investigation to determine if the imam of the prayer center played any roles in the attacks. The investigators quickly determined in addition to his other responsibilities, the imam worked part-time raising money for GRF, at the direction of its executive director in Illinois. The FBI investigated his involvement with 9/11 for one and a half years. It ultimately concluded that he had no role in supporting the 9/11 attacks, although the investigating agents considered him to be a supporter of and fund-raiser for the international jihadist movement.

BIF and GRF challenge the government's actions

The charities aggressively denied any connection to terrorism and condemned the raids and assets freeze. GRF's lawyer immediately called the government's action "a terrible, terrible, terrible tragic mistake," and stated, "If they're investigating terrorism, they're not going to find anything here." Another GRF spokesman said the government seized

---

[90] Press leaks plagued almost every OFAC blocking action that took place in the United States. The process had extremely poor operational security. In a number of instances, agents arrived at locations to execute blocking orders and seize businesses only to find television news camera crews waiting for them.

[91] *See Detroit Free Press v. Ashcroft et al*, 303 F.3d 681 (6th Cir. 2002) (setting out background). The hearing was closed pursuant to a September 21 directive from the chief immigration judge that immigration judges close immigration proceedings in certain "special interest" cases defined by the chief judge.

resources that GRF used to "prevent the slow starvation and gruesome death in parts of the Muslim world that rely on such badly needed aid."[92]

On January 28, 2002, GRF sued the Secretaries of Treasury and State, the Attorney General, and the Directors of OFAC and the FBI in federal court in Chicago. GRF requested that the government "unfreeze" its assets and return the items it seized during the December 14 searches. Two weeks later, GRF filed a motion for a preliminary injunction, contending that the government's blocking of its assets and records violated the law and Constitution.[93] BIF filed a similar suit on January 30, 2002, and a similar motion on March 26, 2002. BIF's complaint proclaimed its activities "entirely lawful," and contended that since its founding in 1992 it "has provided tens of millions of dollars worth of humanitarian aid in a dozen countries around the world, as well in the United States."[94]

Upon filing the complaint, BIF's lawyer said, "The government's actions threaten to destroy our essential constitutional liberties. If we no longer live in a society where we are secure from unreasonable searches and from the taking of liberty and property without any form of due process, then the terrorists will have succeeded in an even greater degree of destruction than the devastation of Sept. 11."[95] Despite the blocking of its assets, BIF and GRF could retain counsel because OFAC granted them "licenses" to do so. A license is written authorization from OFAC to spend money in ways otherwise prohibited by the blocking order, such as the release of blocked funds to pay for legal services.

BIF also sought a license to dispense the bulk of the funds blocked by the government, which totaled $700,000–800,000, to fund its overseas charitable causes, including a tuberculosis hospital for children in Tajikistan and the Charity Women's Hospital in Makhachkala, Daghestan. BIF supported its request with evidence of its charitable work, including affidavits from nurses in the hospital attesting to the importance of BIF's donations. According to BIF's counsel, the organization wanted to give away $500,000 of the blocked funds rather than let legal bills consume the money, and it even offered to have FBI agents accompany the funds overseas to their charitable destination. OFAC did not grant the license due to concerns that even funds sent to seemingly legitimate charities can be at least partially diverted to terrorist activities and OFAC's extremely limited ability to monitor the use of funds overseas. OFAC did license BIF and GRF to sustain some operations—retaining some employees and paying utilities, taxes and U.S. creditors—but most of the employees had to be let go, and the charities could neither raise new funds nor distribute existing funds overseas.[96]

---

[92] Deanna Bellandi, "Two Chicago-area Muslim Charity Groups Raided by Federal Agents; Assets Frozen," Associated Press, Dec. 15, 2001.

[93] *See, Global Relief Foundation, Inc. v. O'Neill et al.*, 207 F. Supp. 2d 779 at 787 (N.D. Ill. 2002), *affirmed* 315 F.3d 748 (7th Cir. 2002) (quoting complaint).

[94] *Benevolence International Foundation Inc. v. Ashcroft*, (N.D. Ill.), Complaint.

[95] Laurie Cohen, "2nd Muslim Charity Sues U.S. Officials on Terrorism," Chicago Tribune, Jan. 31, 2002, p. 1.

[96] Ultimately, the charities' legal bills consumed most of the frozen money, which angered donors who had intended their donations be used for humanitarian relief. See, e.g., Gregory Vistica, "Frozen Assets Going

Supporters of GRF fund-raiser Rabih Haddad, who was detained on immigration violations, rallied to his defense. Pointing out that Haddad had condemned the 9/11 attacks and contending he was a moderate and respected religious leader in the Detroit community, they considered his detention in solitary confinement on what appeared to be a minor visa violation as a prime example of discrimination against Muslims and an overzealous government response to 9/11, in violation of basic civil rights. For example, a sympathetic story in a London paper quoted U.S. Representative John Conyers: "The treatment of Rabih Haddad by the Immigration and Naturalization Service over the past several weeks has highlighted everything that is abusive and unconstitutional about our government's scapegoating of immigrants in the wake of the September 11 terrorist attack."[97]

Efforts to develop criminal cases against BIF and GRF

After the preliminary designations and searches of December 14, 2001, the FBI and U.S. Attorney's Office in Chicago focused their attention on developing a criminal case. To do so, they initially faced major logistical challenges. The Illinois searches yielded an enormous amount of information, including hundreds of tapes and videos that had to be translated and reviewed, and many computer hard drives. According to the legal requirements imposed by FISA, all of this information had to be reviewed for "minimization." Since the evidence was seized under intelligence authorities, the Justice Department could use only that evidence relevant to an intelligence investigation or a crime such as terrorism. The logistical difficulties were compounded by the charities' civil litigation, the blocking order and OFAC's continued need for access to the materials so that it could build a case for permanent designations. The latter issue caused considerable frustration and confusion, as there were no rules about exactly what information in the FBI files OFAC could lawfully see. In addition, the lead case agents, who had been intelligence agents, lacked any significant federal criminal investigative experience, let alone experience in preparing a complex, document-intensive financial investigation for prosecution.

The criminal investigation of BIF received a huge boost in March 2002. The Chicago agents, who had been working with Bosnian officials on the case, provided the Bosnians with enough evidence to gain legal authority to conduct a criminal search of BIF's offices there. An FBI agent accompanied the Bosnians on the search to ensure a proper chain of custody necessary for the admission of anything found into a U.S. criminal proceeding. This search yielded compelling evidence of links between BIF's leaders, including Arnaout, and Usama Bin Ladin and other al Qaeda leaders, going back to the 1980s. The material seized included many documents never before seen by U.S. officials, such as the actual minutes of al Qaeda meetings, the al Qaeda oath, al Qaeda organizational charts,

---

to Legal Bills," *Washington Post*, Nov. 1, 2003, p. A6. According to OFAC, when BIF exhausted the pool of blocked BIF funds, OFAC also issued licenses authorizing BIF to establish and maintain a legal defense fund in which to accept donations to offset its legal expenses.

[97] Andrew Gumbel, "The Disappeared," The Independent, Feb. 26, 2002.

and the "Golden Chain" list of wealthy donors to the Afghan mujahideen, as well as letters between Arnaout and Bin Ladin, dating to the late 1980s. It was an enormous break.

The Bosnian documents helped kick BIF investigation into high gear. Meanwhile, the GRF investigation temporarily took a back seat. On April 30, 2002, Arnaout and BIF were charged with two counts of perjury; the charge was based on a declaration that Arnaout had filed in the civil case against OFAC, in which he asserted that BIF never supported persons engaged in violence or military operations. Arnaout was taken into custody and denied bail. In September, the court dismissed the charges because established Supreme Court precedent held that the particular criminal statute under which he was charged did not apply to the out-of-court statements in Arnaout's declaration.[98] The government filed a criminal obstruction of justice case against Arnaout that same day, on the basis of the same false declaration. BIF was not charged again.

The government came back with a more substantive indictment of Arnaout in October 2002, directly alleging that BIF supported al Qaeda.[99] The indictment alleged that Arnaout operated BIF as a criminal enterprise that for decades used charitable contributions to support al Qaeda, the Chechen mujahideen, and armed violence in Bosnia. The government modified the allegations against Arnaout in a superseding and then a second superseding indictment, the latter of which was filed on January 22, 2003. It charged Arnaout with one count each of racketeering conspiracy under RICO (the Racketeer Influenced and Corrupt Organization Act), conspiracy to provide material support to terrorists, providing material support to terrorists, conspiracy to launder money, and wire fraud and two counts of mail fraud.

Attorney General John Ashcroft personally came to Chicago to announce the filing of the October indictment in a high-profile press conference. His public statements emphasized BIF's alleged support for al Qaeda and recounted much of the historic evidence linking Arnaout to Bin Ladin, including a recitation of the most significant al Qaeda documents seized at the BIF's office in Bosnia. Condemning BIF and Arnaout, the Attorney General declared, "There is no moral distinction between those who carry out terrorist attacks and those who knowingly finance those attacks."[100] BIF's lawyer believed that the Attorney General's inflammatory comments about al Qaeda and Bin Ladin compromised Arnaout's right to a fair trial before an impartial jury and characterized the press conference as "astounding" and "egregious." The trial judge also took notice, later referring to the extensive publicity the case received "in the wake of the Attorney General's remarkable press conference announcing this indictment."[101]

---

[98] *United States v. Benevolence International*, 02 CR 414, 2002 U.S. Dist. Lexis 17223 (Sept. 13, 2002) (court opinion and order).
[99] *United States v. Arnaout*, Second Superseding Indictment at ¶ 3 (same language in initial indictment).
[100] Attorney General Remarks, Chicago, October 9, 2004 (www.usdog.gov/ag/speeches/2002/100902agremarksbifindictment.html, accessed Apr; 1, 2004).
[101] *United States v. Arnaout,* 02 CR 892 (Jan. 28, 2003) (unpublished court order).

The indictment itself contained almost no specific allegations that BIF funded al Qaeda.[102] Instead, the charges focused primarily on BIF's diversion of charitable donations to fund Chechen and Bosnian fighters. At the same time, the indictment highlighted Arnaout's historical relationship with Bin Ladin and BIF's links to certain al Qaeda leaders, including BIF's origins with LBI, the Saudi entity Batterjee created in 1987 in large part to support mujahideen then fighting the Soviets in Afghanistan, and the handoff of nominal control of BIF from Batterjee to Arnaout. The indictment described Arnaout's history of supporting armed jihad, including Arnaout's having worked in the 1980s for the Mektab al Khidmat[103] and LBI to support various mujahideen—among them, those under the command of Usama Bin Ladin.[104]

The indictment charged Arnaout with racketeering conspiracy under RICO, alleging that Arnaout, Batterjee, and others operated BIF as a criminal enterprise and used the cover of a legitimate Islamic charity to support armed jihadist combatants. The government contended that BIF fraudulently solicited and obtained donations by falsely representing that the funds would be used solely for humanitarian purposes, while concealing that some of the donated funds were used to support armed fighters engaged in violence overseas. Through these illicit diversions, the indictment alleged, BIF provided a variety of military supplies, including boots, uniforms, and communications equipment, as well as an X-ray machine to fighters in Bosnia-Herzegovina and Chechnya. The indictment alleged that the conspirators engaged in various acts to conceal their support of armed militants and BIF's relationship to al Qaeda and other extremists.

The indictment also alleged that Arnaout and others provided material support to "persons, groups and organizations engaged in violent activities—including al Qaeda[.]"[105] The charge contains no specific claims about providing funds to al Qaeda, although it alleges that in 1998 Arnaout facilitated the travel of a key al Qaeda member into Bosnia-Herzegovina and that a leading al Qaeda member served as a BIF official in Chechnya.[106] An additional count in the indictment charged Arnaout with providing material support to persons engaged in violent activity by supplying 2,900 pairs of steel-reinforced anti-mine boots to Chechen fighters. The remaining counts charged Arnaout with money laundering and fraud in connection with BIF's activities.

The government indictment drew heavily on the documents seized from the BIF office in Bosnia that directly linked BIF and Arnaout to the formative period of al Qaeda. These links included (1) notes summarizing meetings during which al Qaeda was founded in Afghanistan in August 1988, and which specify the attendance of Usama Bin Ladin at the

---

[102] The government did not charge BIF with providing material support to a designated foreign terrorist organization (FTO) in violation of 18 USC 2339, which would seem like a logical charge had the government been able to prove that the BIF funded al Qaeda after it was designated an FTO in 1999.

[103] As discussed above, the Mekhtab al Khidemat was an organization primarily operated by Sheik Abdullah Azzam and Usama Bin Ladin to provide logistical support to the mujahideen in Afghanistan.

[104] Of course, Arnaout's defenders point out that supporting bin Ladin in the 1980s when he was fighting in a cause supported by the United States is hardly evidence of supporting terrorism.

[105] Second Superseding Indictment, count 2.

[106] See discussion later in this chapter regarding OFAC designation of the BIF for more detail on the key al Qaeda operative whose travel the BIF allegedly facilitated.

original oath of allegiance (*bayat*) that prospective members made to al Qaeda; (2) a list of wealthy mujahideen sponsors from Saudi Arabia, including references to Bin Ladin and Batterjee; (3) various documents showing Arnaout's substantial role in procuring weapons for the mujahideen in the 1980s or early 1990s; and (4) a 1988 newspaper article showing a picture of Arnaout and Bin Ladin.[107]

Arnaout initially pled not guilty to all charges and mounted a vigorous legal defense. OFAC refused to license BIF to use its blocked assets to pay for Arnaout's criminal defense on the grounds that BIF's funds could not be used by Arnaout in his individual capacity. Although Arnaout personally was not designated and could use whatever funds he had to defend himself, the OFAC refusal impaired Arnaout's ability to pay his counsel and caused considerable bitterness among his supporters.

OFAC Designations

Following its blocking of BIF's and GRF's assets pending investigation, OFAC continued to try to develop the evidentiary case it believed necessary to make permanent designations. Meanwhile, the charities' finances were effectively frozen, with the exception of the licenses discussed above. At least one senior Treasury official was concerned about the potential length of a temporary blocking order. On April 12, 2002, roughly four months after the blocking order was issued, the Treasury General Counsel wrote to other senior Treasury officials that "common fairness and principles of equity counsel that we impose a reasonable end date on the duration of such orders."[108] On October 18, 2002, OFAC designated GRF a specially designated global terrorist (SDGT) pursuant to Executive Order 13224, thereby freezing its assets and blocking transactions with it. As a result, four days later, the United Nations listed GRF as an organization belonging to or associated with al Qaeda. BIF met the same fate, as a result of OFAC action on November 19 and UN action on November 21.

The OFAC designations of BIF and GRF relied on the material gathered by the FBI during its pre-9/11 investigations and, in the case of the former, on the materials obtained in the March 2002 search of BIF's Bosnian offices. In its official Statement of the Case that provides support for the designation, OFAC traced BIF's founding by Batterjee and "the close relationship between Arnaout and Usama bin Ladin, dating from the mid-

---

[107]The government later put together this evidence and much more in an evidentiary proffer it submitted to the court in advance of trial.

[108] Treasury Memorandum, April 12, 2002. The memo proposed a six-month limit for discussion purposes, and offered a "clear recommendation" that temporary blocking orders be pursued with "due diligence and an anticipated end date." In May and June 2002, OFAC provided GRF and BIF, respectively, with notice of its intent to designate them and provided them with time to respond. The lengthy duration of the temporary designations resulted in part from extensions of time requested by BIF and GRF. These requests were necessary, at least in part, because OFAC continually added additional documents to the administrative record, and BIF and GRF wanted time to review and respond to them before any permanent designation was issued. In addition, BIF and GRF were only slowly getting access to their own records, which the government had seized, and they wanted additional time to use these records in their defense.

1980s and continuing at least until the early 1990s."[109] OFAC drew links between BIF and Bin Ladin by noting (1) in 1998, BIF provided direct logistical support for an al Qaeda member and Bin Ladin lieutenant, Mamdouh Mahmud Salim, to travel to Bosnia-Herzegovina;[110] (2) telephone records linked BIF to Mohammed Loay Bayazid, who had been implicated in al Qaeda's effort to obtain enriched uranium; (3) in the early 1990s, BIF produced videotapes that eulogized dead fighters, including two al Qaeda members; and (4) in the late 1990s, a member of al Qaeda's Shura Council served as an officer in BIF's Chechnya office. OFAC cited a number of ways in which BIF's activities differed from its ostensible purpose (e.g., it altered its books to make support for an injured Bosnian fighter appear as aid to an orphan), the purchase of equipment for Chechen fighters, and the newspaper article the FBI agents had found in the trash, in which someone had highlighted the weaknesses in the U.S. defenses against bioterrorism.

As for GRF, OFAC's internal documents supporting the designation spelled out its ties to al Qaeda leaders, including (1) evidence that GRF provided $20,000 to a suspected al Qaeda fund-raiser in November 2001; (2) the phone contacts between GRF's executive director and the mujahideen leader associated with al Qaeda leadership; (3) the phone contacts linking GRF to Wadi al Hage, UBL's personal secretary, who was convicted in the United States for his role in the 1998 embassy bombings; and (4) funds that GRF received from Mohammed Galeb Kalaje Zouaydi, a suspected al Qaeda financier in Europe who was arrested in Spain in 2002.

OFAC's unclassified Statement of the Case laid out the extensive evidence indicating GRF's role in supporting jihad. This evidence included the pictures of sophisticated communications equipment the FBI had found in the trash, photographs of jihadists both alive and dead, and documents establishing GRF's enthusiastic support for armed jihad. For example, a GRF pamphlet from 1995 stated, "God equated martyrdom through JIHAD with supplying funds for the JIHAD effort. All contributions should be mailed to: GRF." Another GRF publication stated that charitable funds "are disbursed for equipping the raiders, for the purchase of ammunition and food, and for [the mujahideen's] transportation so that they can raise God the Almighty's word[;] . . . it is likely the most important . . . disbursement of Zakat in our times is on the jihad for God's cause[.]"[111]

OFAC's assertions and the resulting UN actions publicly designated BIF and GRF as supporters of al Qaeda and effectively shut down these operations around the world.

---

[109] OFAC BIF Statement of the Case.

[110] Salim was later indicted for conspiracy to kill U.S. nationals, an overt act that included the 1998 embassy bombings. While in custody, he assaulted a corrections officer, inflicting grievous and permanent injury. Testimony in the 2001 embassy bombing trial also implicated Salim in al Qaeda's efforts to develop WMD.

[111] OFAC GRF Statement of the Case.

BIF and GRF Challenges to OFAC's Actions

GRF failed in its efforts to challenge OFAC's initial asset blocking in court. On June 11, 2002, the court denied GRF's claim for an injunction requiring the government to "unfreeze" its assets and return its property. The court held that GRF was not entitled to an injunction because it had failed to establish a reasonable likelihood of success on its claims that the U.S. government had violated its constitutional rights or the laws of the United States.[112] GRF's appeal was denied, and the U.S. Supreme Court refused to consider the case.[113] Although its legal challenge to the preliminary designation failed, GRF has continued to litigate the issue of whether sufficient evidence existed to justify its designation as an SDGT. As of this writing, that litigation is pending in federal district court in Chicago.

BIF's challenge to having its assets blocked pending investigation was stayed until the criminal case was resolved, and eventually it was dismissed. BIF elected not to challenge OFAC's designation of it as an SDGT. By that time, BIF was focused on the criminal issues, and, in any event, it was clear that BIF was dead as an organization.

Counsel for BIF and GRF expressed great frustration with the OFAC process, including the blocking of assets without any adversarial process adjudicating culpability, their view that the process lacked defined standards, their perception of OFAC's unresponsiveness to attorney inquiries and licensing requests, the use of classified evidence unavailable to the defense, and OFAC's reliance on evidence that would not be admissible in a judicial proceeding. For example, BIF's counsel was stunned to see that the administrative record supporting BIF's designation included newspaper articles and other rank hearsay. To BIF and GRF's counsel, experienced lawyers steeped in the federal courts' rules of evidence and due process, the OFAC designation process seemed manifestly unfair. In response, OFAC points out that the courts have upheld the process and standards it uses in designations, as well as the use of classified information, news articles and other hearsay in support of the designations. OFAC further maintains that its administrative record fully supports the designations of BIF and GRF.

Vigorous Defense in the Criminal Case

Before his plea, Arnaout vigorously litigated the criminal charges against him. As the case moved closer to trial, the government submitted a lengthy statement of facts setting forth the historical evidence tying Arnaout to Bin Ladin and al Qaeda. This proffer, which included multiple voluminous appendixes, drew heavily on the documents seized in Bosnia. The government did not provide specific evidence that BIF funded al Qaeda.

---

[112] *Global Relief Foundation v. O'Neill et al.*, 207 F. Supp. 2d 779, 809 (N.D. Ill. 2002).
[113] *Global Relief Foundation v. O'Neill et al*, 748 (7th Cir. 2002), *cert denied*, 124 S. Ct. 531 (2003).

Rather, it relied heavily on evidence that predated both BIF's creation and Bin Ladin's having become an avowed enemy of the United States.

Through his counsel, Arnaout asked the court to exclude all evidence related to al Qaeda, Bin Ladin, or other terrorist groups. To Arnaout, the government's case essentially boiled down to diverting charitable funds to support Chechen and Bosnian fighters, and had nothing to do with bin Ladin, terrorism, or al Qaeda. The proffer demonstrated, he contended, that "the United States intends to try Enaam Arnaout not for acts he committed in violation of United States laws, but rather for associations he had over a decade ago, before he relocated to this country, with people who were at the time America's allies but who are now its enemies."[114] The court reserved ruling on the evidence until trial, but in a ruling ominous to the government held that Arnaout "persuasively argues that a significant amount of the government's . . . proffer contains materials that are not relevant to him nor probative of the charges in the indictment(s), but rather are highly prejudicial matters suggesting guilt by association."[115]

Conviction and Sentence

On the morning that trial was to commence, Arnaout pled guilty to one count of racketeering conspiracy for fraudulent diversion of charitable donations to promote overseas combatants. He admitted that BIF solicited donations by representing the money would be used to provide humanitarian relief to needy civilians, while concealing "from donors, potential donors, and federal and state governments in the United States that a material portion of the donations received by BIF based on BIF's misleading representations was being used to support fighters overseas."[116] The supplies Arnaout admitted that he and others agreed to provide included boots for fighters in Chechnya, boots, tents, uniforms for soldiers in Bosnia-Herzegovina, and uniforms for a provisional but unrecognized government in Chechnya. The court later determined that the amount of funds diverted from humanitarian relief to support these fighters totaled $315,624.[117] Arnaout never admitted to supporting al Qaeda or any other terrorist group. To the contrary, as the presiding federal district court judge pointed out, "In its written plea agreement, the government agreed to dismiss sensational and highly publicized charges of providing material support to terrorists and terrorist organizations."[118]

The court sentenced Arnaout to more than 11 years in prison, but flatly rejected the government's request that it apply the sentencing enhancement for crimes of terrorism, which would have mandated a 20-year prison sentence. The court said plainly, "Arnaout does not stand convicted of a terrorism offense. Nor does the record reflect that he

---

[114] Defendant's Motion *in Limine* to Exclude Evidence of Historical Events (January 13, 2003).

[115] Order, Jan. 30, 2003. Separately, the court rejected the government's proffer as insufficient to satisfy the hearsay exception for co-conspirator statements. *U.S. v. Arnaout*, 2003 U.S. Dist. Lexis 1635 at *1 (Feb. 4, 2003). This order made it more difficult and riskier for the government to offer such statements at trial.

[116] Plea Agreement at 4.

[117] *U.S. v. Arnaout*, 282 F. Supp. 2d 838, 840 (N.D. Ill. 2003).

[118] *United States v. Arnaout*, 282 F. Supp. 2d at 843.

attempted, participated in, or conspired to commit any act of terrorism."[119] Moreover, the court held that the offense to which Arnaout pled guilty, racketeering conspiracy, was not a crime of terrorism as defined by law. The court further held that applying the enhancement would be improper because the "government has not established that the Bosnian and Chechen recipients of BIF aid were engaged in a federal crime of terrorism, nor that Arnaout intended the donated boots, uniforms, blankets, tents, x-ray machine, ambulances, nylon and walkie-talkies to be used to promote a federal crime of terrorism."[120] The court did increase Arnaout's prison time on the grounds that he diverted humanitarian aid from the destitute population BIF was aiding to armed fighters. Both the government and Arnaout appealed the sentence. Arnaout challenged the court's enhancement of his sentence for diverting funds from needy civilians, and the government challenged the refusal to apply the terrorism enhancement. A decision is pending.

Although Arnaout pled guilty to a serious felony and received a long prison sentence, many people in the Islamic and Arab communities concluded that Arnaout had been vindicated of any charge of supporting terrorism. They interpreted the judge's refusal to apply the terrorism sentencing enhancement as a major defeat for the government. As Al Jazeera told its online readers, "The U.S. government had hoped for a high profile 'terrorism' conviction, but the judge said the case had not been made."[121] The charge Arnaout pled to, although undeniably serious, fell far short of what the judge derisively called "sensational and highly publicized" charges of supporting terrorists, which the Attorney General himself had announced with great fanfare. A BIF lawyer believes that Arnaout's case, along with the shutdown of BIF, hurt and angered the Muslim community in the Chicago area. She fears that the bad feelings left by the case substantially reduce the likelihood of cooperation with law enforcement in the future.

Senior FBI agents in the Chicago office, who devote substantial effort to community outreach, agreed that the plea and the court's refusal to sentence Arnaout as a terrorism offender led many in Chicago's large Islamic community to see him as vindicated and to believe the government unjustly targeted him for prosecution—"picking on a poor guy" who is standing up for Muslims, as one agent described it.[122] These agents, as well as the case agents, agree that accepting a plea to a serious RICO (Racketeer Influenced and Corrupt Organization Act) charge was the right decision, but believe a trial would have allowed the government to lay out all its evidence against Arnaout in open court. They believe the community then would have seen what the agents saw—that Arnaout and BIF were supporting terrorism.

---

[119] *Id.*

[120] *Id.* at 845.

[121] Http://english.aljazeera.net (accessed Dec. 31, 2003).

[122] Commission Staff Interview.

Status of the GRF Criminal Case

The government's criminal investigation of GRF included the review of the voluminous documents and computer records seized from the GRF office and interviews with GRF personnel. Despite this effort, the government has to date filed no criminal charges against GRF or its leadership, and any such charges appear increasingly unlikely. GRF steadfastly denies any wrongdoing and its supporters view the government's failure to follow the OFAC blocking with a criminal indictment as a vindication of the organization. GRF's counsel contends that GRF never provided a single dollar to fund terrorism and that the government's evidence of suspicious links with terrorists all have innocuous explanations. He asserts GRF is an entirely innocent victim of the government's attempt to take some actions to respond to public panic caused by 9/11.

The government never proved a criminal case against GRF fund-raiser Haddad. Instead, Haddad was deported to his native Lebanon in July 2003 after an immigration judge found him ineligible for asylum because he was a security danger to the United States, a decision which was affirmed by the Board of Immigration Appeals. The decision to deport him rather than continue the criminal investigation was made in Washington, without consultation with the Detroit case agent who had investigated Haddad. Despite the findings of the immigration judge, Haddad's deportation generated considerable sympathy for him and condemnation of an alleged violation of his civil rights by the U.S. government. The government contends that ample evidence demonstrated that Haddad had significant terrorist ties and was a substantial threat to the United States.[123]

Lessons of BIF/GRF

The agents and officials in these cases faced one of the most important and difficult issues in the fight against al Qaeda and jihadist fund-raising: there is a difference between troubling "links" to terrorists and compelling evidence of supporting terrorists. This gives rise to a further issue: how much information does the government need before it can take action against a potential terrorist fund-raiser?

Law enforcement officials had concluded that both BIF and GRF had substantial and very troubling links to al Qaeda and the international jihadist movement. Government agents had little doubt that the leadership of these organizations endorsed the ideology of armed jihad and, in many cases, supported an extremist and jihadist ideology. Both of these organizations raised large amounts of money in the United States, which they sent overseas, often to or through people with jihadist connections. When the money went overseas, it became virtually untraceable, since it could be converted to cash and sent

---

[123]It is not our purpose to assess Haddad's culpability, but we recognize the decision not to criminally prosecute him does not amount to an exoneration. A decision about whether to prosecute an individual can turn on a number of factors other than his guilt, including whether unclassified evidence is available to use in court against him.

anywhere in the world. Moreover, BIF, at least, was plainly funding armed jihadist fighters.

But there is another side to the story. Despite these troubling links, the investigation of BIF and GRF revealed little compelling evidence that either of these charities actually provided financial support to al Qaeda—at least after al Qaeda was designated a foreign terrorist organization in 1999. Indeed, despite unprecedented access to the U.S. and foreign records of these organizations, one of the world's most experienced and best terrorist prosecutors has not been able to make any criminal case against GRF and resolved the investigation of BIF without a conviction for support of terrorism. Although the OFAC action shut down BIF and GRF, that victory came at considerable cost of negative public opinion in the Muslim and Arab communities, who contend that the government's destruction of these charities reflects bias and injustice with no measurable gain to national security.

The cases of BIF and GRF reveal how fundamentally 9/11 changed law enforcement and the approach of the U.S. government to those suspected of financing terrorists. In the past, suspicions of terrorist connections often resulted in further investigation but not action. The FBI watched jihadist sympathizers send millions of dollars overseas because they did not have a sense of urgency about disrupting the fund-raising and, in any event, had no practical way to do so. The 9/11 attacks changed everything. Suddenly, letting money potentially earmarked for al Qaeda leave the United States became another potential mass casualty attack. The government after 9/11 had both the will and the tools to stop the money flow. Thus, the government targeted and destroyed BIF and GRF in a way that was inconceivable on September 10.

But the question remains, was the destruction of BIF and GRF a success? Did it enhance the security of the United States or was it a feckless act that violated civil rights with no real gain in security? A senior government official who led the government's efforts against terrorist financing from 9/11 until late 2003 believed the efforts against the charities were less than a full success and, in fact, were a disappointment because neither charity was publicly proved to support terrorism. The former head of the FBI's Terrorist Financing Operations Section believes that strong intelligence indicated GRF and BIF were funding terrorism and, although the evidence for a strong criminal terrorism case may have been lacking, the government succeeded in disrupting terrorist fund-raising mechanisms. At the same time, he believes the cases have not been successful from a public relations perspective because there have been no terrorism-related convictions.

BIF and GRF still contend they never supported terrorism, and decry the government's conduct as counterproductive and abusive. A BIF lawyer said she understands the government's desire to take decisive action after 9/11 but thinks in moving against BIF the government overreached, lost sight of what the evidence showed, sought to graft irrelevant, dated al Qaeda allegations onto a simple fraud case, and ignored the rules of fairness and procedural safeguards that make our system the best in the world. In her view, the U.S. government "needs to be better than that," especially in times of crisis when our values are put to the test.

Our purpose is not to try to resolve the question of whether BIF or GRF actually provided funds to terrorists. We can, however, come to some understanding about whether the government action against them was justified. Reviewing the materials, classified and unclassified, available to the government makes it clear that their concerns about BIF and GRF were not baseless. There may not have been a smoking gun proving that these entities funded terrorism, but the evidence of their links to terrorists and jihadists is significant. Despite the charities' humanitarian work, responsible U.S. officials understandably were concerned about these organizations sending millions of dollars overseas, given their demonstrable jihadist and terrorist ties. Moreover, Arnaout has admitted to fraudulent conduct, which in and of itself constitutes a serious felony, even though it does not prove he funded al Qaeda.

At the same time, the government's treatment of BIF and GRF raises substantial civil liberty concerns. IEEPA's provision allowing blocking "during the pendency of an investigation" is a powerful weapon with potentially dangerous applications when applied to domestic institutions. This provision lets the government shut down an organization without any formal determination of wrongdoing. It requires a single piece of paper, signed by a midlevel government official. Although in practice a number of agencies typically review and agree to the action, there is no formal administrative process, let alone any adjudication of guilt. Although this provision is necessary in rare emergencies when the government must shut down a terrorist financier before OFAC can marshal evidence to support a formal designation, serious consideration should be given to placing a strict and short limit on the duration of such a temporary blocking. A "temporary" designation lasting 10 or 11 months, as in the BIF and GRF cases, becomes hard to justify.

Using IEEPA at all against U.S. citizens and their organizations raises potentially troubling civil liberties issues, although to date the courts have rejected the constitutional challenges to IEEPA in this context.[124] As the Illinois charities cases demonstrate, IEEPA allows the freezing of an organization's assets and its designation as an SDGT before any adjudication of culpability by a court. The administrative record needed to justify a designation can include newspaper articles and other hearsay normally deemed too unreliable for a court of law. A designated entity can challenge the designation in court, but its chances of success are limited. The legal standard for overturning the designation is favorable to the government, and the government can rely on classified evidence that it shows to the judge but not defense counsel, depriving the designated entity of the usual right to confront the evidence against it. Still, because of the difficulties of prosecuting complex terrorist-financing cases the government may at times face the very difficult choice of designating a U.S. person or doing nothing while dollars flow overseas to potential terrorists.[125]

---

[124] As noted above, the GRF challenge to IEEPA's constitutionality failed in court. *See also Holy Land Found. For Relief and Dev. v. Ashcroft*, 219 F. Supp. 2d 57 (D.D.C. 2002) (upholding use of IEEPA against purported charity accused of funding terrorism).

[125] The IEEPA process gives the designated person fewer rights than in the somewhat analogous circumstance of civil forfeiture, in which the government seeks to take (as opposed to freeze) property that

Finally, we need to keep BIF and GRF in mind as we evaluate the efforts (or lack of efforts) of our allies as they respond to intelligence concerning persons allegedly financing terrorism. Several former government officials have criticized the Saudi government for its failure to prosecute individuals for financing terrorism. As one put it, Saudi Arabia needs a "Martha Stewart"—a high-profile donor whose prosecution can serve as deterrent to others. Much of the frustration with the Saudis results from their apparent lack of will to prosecute criminally those persons who U.S. intelligence indicates are raising money for al Qaeda. Although willing to take other actions based on the intelligence—such as removing someone from a sensitive position or shutting down a charity—the Saudis have failed to impose criminal punishment on any high-profile donor. BIF and GRF should remind us that terrorist links and evidence of terrorist funding are far different things. Saudi Arabia and other countries certainly have at times been recalcitrant in seeking to hold known terrorist fund-raisers accountable for their actions. But in criticizing them, we should remember that in BIF and GRF, the total political will, prosecutorial and investigative talent, and resources of the U.S. government have so far failed to secure a single terrorist-related conviction.

---

it claims was derived from or used to commit specific crimes or unlawful acts. In seeking forfeiture where no crime is charged, the government must file a civil lawsuit and bear the burden of proof by a preponderance of the evidence (the standard used in most civil cases) that the property in question is forfeitable. The defendant gets the same type of discovery of the evidence available to any other litigant, such as taking sworn depositions and obtaining documents. Moreover, the defendant has the right to avoid forfeiture by demonstrating that he is an innocent owner, that is, he obtained or possessed the property in question without knowing its illegal character or nature.

Chapter 7

Al Haramain Case Study

The al Haramain Islamic Foundation (al Haramain or HIF) is one of the most important and prominent Saudi charities.[126] Al Haramain has been on the radar screen of the U.S. government as a potential terrorist-financing problem since the mid- to late 1990s, when the U.S. government started to develop evidence that certain employees and branch offices might be supporting al Qaeda and related terrorist groups.[127]

The U.S. government, however, never moved against al Haramain or pushed the Saudi government to do so until after 9/11. Terrorist financing simply was not a priority in its bilateral relationship with the Saudis before 9/11. Even when discussing terrorist financing with the Saudis, the U.S. government was more concerned about issues other than Saudi charities and al Haramain.[128] Meanwhile, the Saudis were content to leave the issue unexplored.

After the 9/11 attacks, a more focused U.S. government sought to work with the Saudis to stem the flow of funds from al Haramain to al Qaeda and related terrorist groups. Progress was initially slow; though some U.S.-Saudi cooperation on al Haramain occurred within the first six months after 9/11, it was not until the spring of 2003 that the U.S. government and the Saudi government began to make real strides in working together to thwart al Haramain.

Background

Al Haramain, a Saudi Arabia–based nonprofit organization established in the early 1990s, has been described by several former U.S. government officials as the "United Way" of Saudi Arabia. It exists to promote Wahhabi Islam by funding religious education, mosques, and humanitarian projects around the world.[129]

At its peak, al Haramain had a presence in at least 50 countries. Al Haramain's main headquarters are in Riyadh, Saudi Arabia, but it maintains branch offices in a number of

---

[126] See chapter 1 for the scope of this analysis.

[127] This chapter is derived from a review of internal government document and interviews with government policy makers. It was especially aided by the commission staff's ability to access and review NSC subgroup minutes of meetings, as well as internal memoranda from the NSC, State, Treasury and the intelligence community.

[128] Our investigation has focused on al Haramain in the context of al Qaeda financing. Although much of our analysis may apply to the financing of other terrorist groups, we have made no systematic effort to investigate any of those groups, and we recognize that the financing of other terrorist groups may present the U.S. and Saudi governments with problems or opportunities not existing in the context of al Qaeda.

[129] The Web site uses the term *salafi*, which is the preferred term of Saudi practitioners of Wahhabism. Some argue that Wahhabism is a virulent form of religious extremism, while others have a more benign view of it. See chapter 2 for more information.

countries to facilitate the distribution of charitable funds. Some of these offices are staffed by Saudi citizens; others are managed by the nationals of the countries involved. Estimates of its budget range from $30 to $80 million. It claims to have constructed more than 1,299 mosques, it funds imams and others to work in the mosques, and it sponsors more than 3,000 "callers to Islam" for tours of duty in different locations "to teach the people good and to warn them from wrongs." HIF provides meals and assistance to Muslims around the world, distributes books and pamphlets, pays for potable water projects, sets up and equips medical facilities, and operates more than 20 orphanages.

Although both the Saudi government and al Haramain say that it is a private organization, al Haramain has considerable ties to the Saudi government. Two government ministers have supervisory roles (nominal or otherwise) over al Haramain, and there is some evidence that low-level Saudi officials had substantial influence over various HIF offices outside of Saudi Arabia. The Saudi government has also historically provided financial support to al Haramain, although that may have diminished in recent years.

Charity and charitable organizations, like al Haramain, are extremely important to Saudi society. As discussed in more detail in chapter 2, religious and civic duty and government and religious functions in Saudi Arabia are intertwined. This dynamic creates complications for the Saudi government as it seeks to stem the flow of funds from Saudi Arabia to al Qaeda and related terrorist groups, and difficulties for the U.S. government as it seeks to engage the Saudis on terrorist financing.

Before 9/11

After the East Africa bombings in the summer of 1998, the U.S. government began to give more attention to terrorist financing. The National Security Council established a subgroup of the Counterterrorism Security Group to focus the U.S. government's efforts on terrorist financing.[130] As a result of this focus, and the consequent discovery that al Qaeda was not financed from Bin Ladin's personal wealth, the NSC became increasingly interested in Saudi charities and Bin Ladin's use of charities to fund terrorism.[131]

By no later than 1996, the U.S. intelligence community began to gather intelligence that certain branches of HIF were involved in financing terrorism. Later, the U.S. intelligence community began to draw links among HIF, the 1998 East Africa bombings, jihad actions in the Balkans, Chechnya, and Azerbaijan, and support for al Qaeda generally. The United States shared some of its information with the Saudis in an effort to spur action, including evidence that al Haramain officials and employees in East Africa may have been involved in the planning of the 1998 embassy bombings. The United States sought information and reports from the Saudis on employees of al Haramain around the globe and their connections to Bin Ladin, but received no substantive responses.

---

[130] Terrorist financing was also a component of the larger strategic plan Richard Clarke developed after the embassy bombings.

[131] The U.S. government's efforts to understand al Qaeda financing, and its engagement with Saudi Arabia, are described in chapter 3.

The Saudis took little initiative with respect to their charities. They did not make tough decisions or undertake difficult investigations of Saudi institutions to ensure that they were not being used by terrorists and their supporters. Although the Saudis did institute "Guidelines for Preventing Money Laundering" in 1995 and "Regulations on Charitable Organizations and Institutions" in 1990, these were very loose rules whose enforcement was doubtful. Moreover, the regulations covered only domestic charities, through the Ministry of Labor and Social Affairs, and exempted all charities set up by royal decree.

There may have been a number of reasons for Saudi inaction. Certainly, as we have discussed elsewhere (see chapter 2), the prominence of religion-based charities in Saudi culture may have made the Saudis reluctant to entertain the idea that charities might be involved in clandestine activities. Some in the United States suspected that the Saudis were complicit or at least turned a blind eye to the problem posed by charities during this period, although others vehemently disagreed.

Ultimately, however, the U.S. government simply did not ask much of the Saudis on terrorist financing, and the Saudis were content to do little. We did not provide sufficient information for the Saudis to act against charities like al Haramain, did not push the Saudis to undertake investigations of charities like al Haramain, and did not request real cooperation from the Saudis on intelligence or law enforcement matters relating to charities like al Haramain.

Other areas of U.S. policy involving the Saudis took precedence over terrorist-financing issues such as those concerning al Haramain. The U.S. government wanted the Saudis to support the Middle East peace process, ensure the steady flow of oil, cut off support to the Taliban, continue various mutually beneficial economic arrangements, and assist in the containment of Iraq. Given these other interests, stopping the money flow to terrorists was not a top priority in the U.S.-Saudi relationship.

Saudi policy was formulated at a very high level in the U.S. government. During the late 1990s, the U.S.-Saudi relationship was handled primarily by the U.S. government's most senior officials, including the secretaries of key departments (collectively referred to as the "Principals"), and often even by the President alone. This situation reflected the significance of the U.S. interests involved, considerable Saudi ties to senior U.S. officials, and U.S. willingness to accede to the strong Saudi preference for bypassing the U.S. bureaucracy. One former NSC official noted that before 9/11, lower-level officials in both governments generally handled terrorist financing, especially given the weakness of the intelligence on terrorist financing and the issue's low priority. The officials with knowledge about it were not the ones interacting with the Saudis, and those who were interacting with the Saudis did not push the issue of terrorist financing because their concerns were different.

Moreover, the U.S. government had too little unilateral intelligence on HIF and on al Qaeda's funding mechanisms generally to press the Saudis. The Principals did not want to confront the Saudis with suspicions; they wanted firm evidence. One NSC official indicated that there was some intelligence regarding charities, but it did not rise to the level of being actionable against any specific charity. As he said, "One individual could be dirty, but it would be difficult to justify closing down a charity on that basis." Occasionally the U.S. government provided select pieces of information out of context, but this method lessened the impact of the intelligence.

After 9/11

As we described in chapter 3, the 9/11 attacks generated a sudden and high-level interest in terrorist financing. Attention invariably turned to Saudi Arabia. The U.S. and Saudi governments initially agreed on a joint strategy, represented by the mutual U.S.-Saudi action against two branches of al Haramain in March 2002 designating them as financiers of terror.[132] But it was not until the spring of 2003 that the U.S. government developed a coherent strategy on engaging the Saudis on terrorist financing and specified a senior White House official to deal with the Saudi government on these issues. These elements enabled the U.S. government to capitalize on a new Saudi commitment to countering the financing of terrorism after the Riyadh bombings on May 12, 2003.

From 9/11 to March 2002: The U.S. government's initial efforts to organize the interagency process and engage the Saudis

Two things occurred immediately after 9/11: first, the U.S. government formed what turned out to be a generally effective interagency coordinating committee on terrorist financing; second, this group began discussing possible action to take against al Haramain.

Immediately after 9/11, the U.S. government, for the first time, developed a generally effective mechanism to coordinate agencies' approach to terrorist finance. Initially, an ad hoc gathering of agency representatives met under the auspices of the NSC to discuss and coordinate terrorist-financing issues. In March 2002, this ad hoc group was formalized by the NSC as the Policy Coordinating Committee (PCC), chaired by the Treasury Department with representatives from eight agencies with relevant subagencies. The PCC was designed to recommend to the President policy initiatives and actions aimed at destroying the financial infrastructure of terrorism.

After 9/11, there was constant discussion at the PCC about how to engage the Saudi government on terrorist financing. The U.S. government had new, aggressive legal authorities under Executive Order 13224 and UN Security Council Resolution 1373 (see chapter 5). The major issue was whether to use these coercive tools unilaterally or take a more diplomatic approach in engaging Saudi Arabia and their charities. On the one hand, using these tools against al Haramain, one of the most important Saudi charities, could be

---

[132] For an explanation of the IEEPA and UNSC process, see chapter 5, concerning al-Barakaat.

counterproductive without Saudi support.[133] On the other hand, using these strong tools could send an unequivocal message that the U.S. government and the international community were serious about fighting terrorist financing.

After considering the options for designating al Haramain, the PCC decided to try to engage the Saudis constructively on this charity. The United States wanted many things from the Saudis: information about the hijackers, action against al Qaeda cells training and operating in Saudi Arabia, intelligence sharing, and access to detained individuals. Terrorist financing was not the only element of the U.S.-Saudi counterterrorism relationship, nor the only objective of U.S. counterterrorism policy. The concern was that if the U.S. government pressed the Saudis on al Haramain, the Saudis' cooperation with the United States on counterterrorism issues or other issues would be jeopardized.

Moreover, as was the case before 9/11, the intelligence was simply not strong enough against the HIF headquarters to push the Saudi government to take aggressive action against the whole organization. As an early 2002 strategy paper emphasized, the United States needed to gather more solid, credible evidence on al Haramain, which could be released to the Saudi government as a way to ensure continued Saudi cooperation. Although the intelligence community expressed repeated concerns that al Haramain was deeply corrupted, others argued that there was little actionable intelligence on the charity. The intelligence presented to the policymakers was either dated, spoke to fund-raising for "extremism" or "fundamentalism" and not for terrorism, or lacked specificity. Indeed, because of the lack of specific intelligence, the U.S. government was in "asking mode" on al Haramain when interacting with the Saudis.

There was also the sense that the Saudi government would prefer to cooperate quietly with the U.S. government for internal political reasons. Perhaps they did not want to create the impression that charities were under attack. U.S. officials agreed to pursue quiet cooperation as long as the U.S. government saw concrete results. Although the United States saw no concrete results until 2003, it stuck with its plan to engage the Saudis quietly on terrorist-financing matters.

This cooperative approach was in evidence in the first interactions between U.S. and Saudi officials on al Haramain. In late November 2001, Assistant Secretary of State William Burns traveled to the Kingdom and shared U.S. concerns about terrorist financing with his Saudi interlocutors.[134] Al Haramain was not a subject of the questions but was listed in the talking points for the trip as an entity of concern.

Then, on January 17, 2002, Assistant Secretary Burns and Ambassador Robert Jordan provided the Saudi Crown Prince Abdullah and Foreign Minister Prince Saud al Faisal with a proposal for a joint U.S.-Saudi freeze of the accounts of eight Saudi entities and

---

[133] Within weeks after 9/11, the United States used its new powers of designation to freeze the assets of a prominent Saudi citizen, Yasin al Qadi. Apparently this unilateral action had created backlash in the Saudi government.
[134] An OFAC team received a one page response in Arabic from Saudi Arabia to these concerns in January 2002. This response was never supplemented by the Saudi government.

individuals, including the al Haramain offices in Bosnia and Somalia. In their discussions, the governments focused their attention on the U.S. proposal relating to the two al Haramain branch offices.

In Saudi Arabia at the end of January, Richard Newcomb, the director of Treasury's Office of Foreign Assets Control (OFAC), also raised the possibility with his Saudi interlocutors of joint designations. His talking points included two pages of classified intelligence on al Haramain (and other charities) to provide the Saudis. The Saudis agreed to "look into" the U.S. concerns on al Haramain. In addition to proposing joint designations, the U.S. delegation expressed "concern" over several other HIF branches, including those in Pakistan and Kenya (both designated in January 2004), and requested information from the Saudis.

On February 5, 2002, the Saudi government issued an official statement acknowledging "reports" of abuses by individuals affiliated with foreign offices of HIF and committed publicly to take actions to prevent such abuse. However, the Saudis were slow to respond to the U.S. proposal on the two al Haramain offices. The issue was taken up by senior levels in the U.S. government. For example, Treasury Secretary Paul O'Neill raised the proposal on his March 2002 trip to Saudi Arabia.

Eventually, the Saudi government agreed to the joint designation of the two al Haramain offices, although it did not agree to designate the other six entities or individuals originally proposed. On March 11, 2002, the U.S. and Saudi governments designated the Somali and Bosnian offices of al Haramain, freezing their assets and prohibiting transactions with them. Two days later the United Nations added the two branch offices to its list of sanctioned entities under UNSCR 1267 and subsequent related resolutions.

From March 2002 to January 2003: The U.S. loses traction

In early 2002, senior-level government officials started developing a new U.S. strategy toward Saudi Arabia on counterterrorism generally; terrorist financing would necessarily play a part. Because the strategy was so politically sensitive, the task of developing it was given to a small group within the NSC. As a result, PCC efforts to deal with the Saudis on terrorist financing were placed on hold for most of 2002, while the NSC drafted the strategy with a small team of agency representatives.

During that time, the U.S. government engaged the Saudis only sporadically on HIF. Although in the spring of 2002 the U.S. government requested specific information from Saudi Arabia on HIF associates, no action was to take place until the larger Saudi strategy on counterterrorism had been finalized.

During the summer and fall of 2002, the U.S. government received information that the Bosnian and Somali offices of al Haramain, whose assets were supposed to have been frozen and offices shut down, had reopened or were still active in some fashion. In September 2002, the U.S. government decided to approach the Saudi government about the reopenings of the Bosnian and Somali branches of HIF. The topic was raised at a senior level by U.S. government officials in Washington and through official visits to the region in the fall of 2002. The Saudis indicated they were unaware of the reopenings but said they would work with the U.S. government on the issue.

During 2002, the Saudis repeatedly said they would be prepared to act against al Haramain if the U.S. government provided them with more information, especially about specific branch offices and individuals. Some thought that this was perhaps simply lip service. For instance, in October 2002 Under Secretary of State Alan Larson raised with the Crown Prince strong concerns about the activities of several al Haramain offices. The Crown Prince responded that he was ready to act on any specific information the United States could provide. Some viewed Saudi requests for information from the United States as somewhat disingenuous given Saudi Arabia's ability to gather information on HIF and its supporters. Others were not so sure the Saudis had that ability. Perhaps even a tit-for-tat dynamic was at work: the U.S. government did not share intelligence that the Saudis thought we had, and which in many cases we did have, so the Saudi government feigned ignorance in order not to share its intelligence with the United States.

In December 2002, the Deputies Committee (DC), which consists of deputy secretaries of key departments and generally oversaw the activities of the PCC, approved the 12-step program for reinvigorating U.S. policy toward Saudi Arabia on counterterrorism overall. Much of the Saudi strategy dealt with terrorist financing. The steps included naming a senior interlocutor on terrorist finance, sharing more concrete and actionable intelligence with the Saudis, providing expertise in money laundering and investigative techniques, encouraging more public discussion of the business risks generated by opaque financial structures, pressuring Saudi nongovernmental organizations (NGOs) to adopt better oversight practices, and encouraging better use of the media to combat terrorist financing.

Concurrently with the approval of the Saudi strategy, the DC formally pushed forward a "nonpaper"[135] on al Haramain. Its goal was to compile U.S. government information on HIF, urge the Saudis to take specific actions, and set time frames for such actions. Agencies were tasked and the nonpaper was finalized by January 2003. Attention from the DC gave the nonpaper sufficient strategic importance for agencies to devote resources to developing it and motivated the approval of the release of information.

Two relatively new appointees, State Department Coordinator for Combating Terrorism Cofer Black and Special Assistant to the President and Senior Director on Combating Terrorism at the NSC Rand Beers, presented the nonpaper on al Haramain to Saudi officials during a previously planned trip on counterterrorism at the end of January 2003. At last, the U.S. government was providing the Saudis with the information that they had long requested and that the U.S. government had previously failed to supply. The mood was optimistic. A Department of State memo from January 2003 referring to al Haramain and other cases of concern suggested that "there is every indication that the Saudis are

---

[135] A "nonpaper" is generally understood to be an official but not definitive statement on an issue by a U.S. government agency.

ready to work with us on these specific cases now that we have specific information for them to act upon."

The nonpaper set out al Haramain's ties to terrorism, with details on various individuals, branch offices, and methods of transferring funds. The nonpaper suggested that many al Haramain field offices and representatives operating throughout the world, as well as its headquarters in Saudi Arabia, appeared to be providing important support to al Qaeda. The nonpaper recited prior U.S. requests for information from the Saudis and specific points of intelligence the United States had shared with the Saudis since 1998, and it noted that the United States had shared with the Saudis very little information between 9/11 and its delivery.[136] The nonpaper contained substantial information, including details on the role of the HIF headquarters in supporting terrorist organizations. Reflecting the new U.S. strategy, the U.S government was more direct and forceful in its message and gave the Saudi government concrete challenges to meet.

While the nonpaper represented a new and effective tactic, its delivery illustrated a shortcoming in the U.S. government's approach to Saudi Arabia on terrorist financing: Cofer Black and Rand Beers were new faces for the Saudis on this issue, and their portfolios were much broader than the fight against terrorist financing. The U.S. government had used a number of messengers, and there was no single person sending the Saudi government a clear message; each individual spoke about terrorist financing and HIF in the context of his or her predetermined and wide-ranging agenda; each individual spoke to different interlocutors with differing responsibilities and chains of command; and despite the sensitivity of the issue, not all the officials were senior. A U.S. official on the PCC said that Saudi representatives complained that junior U.S. officials were, in essence, bothering them. This failure to focus U.S. engagement of the Saudis was most apparent during our efforts to raise the reopenings of the Bosnian and Somali offices with Saudi officials. Within a six-week period in the fall of 2002, about five emissaries from the United States approached the Saudi government. Our efforts suffered from the diffusion of the message and, in the words of one senior U.S. official, the U.S. government allowed itself to be "gamed" by the Saudis because it failed to speak with one voice.

Moreover, it was acknowledged that the Saudis would be more likely to follow the leadership of the U.S. government on this subject if a senior White House official served as the interlocutor on terrorist financing to the Saudi government. In fact, the Saudis requested such an appointment in the fall of 2002. The U.S. government agreed the idea was a good one, but could not settle on an appropriate individual for the role until more than six months later. This failure to appoint a senior White House official in a timely fashion arguably caused a crucial delay in U.S. efforts to engage the Saudis on terrorist financing and al Haramain. One U.S. terrorist-financing official said the Saudis did not take terrorist financing seriously until this appointment was made. They looked at U.S. actions and concluded that terrorist financing was not as important to the United States as other issues.

---

[136] At that time, most of the intelligence on HIF released to the Saudis since 9/11 related to the Bosnian and Somali offices of HIF, in connection with the U.S.-Saudi joint designation of these offices in March 2002.

From 9/11 to May 2003: A lack of real cooperation from the Saudis

After 9/11, Saudi government officials appeared to be in denial that vast sums of money were flowing from Saudi Arabia to al Qaeda and related terrorist groups, or that the government had any responsibility in connection with these money flows. Some in the U.S. government thought that it simply never occurred to the Saudi government that a charity could be a conduit for terrorist financing. As well, some argued that charities' record keeping and the Saudi government's controls were insufficient for the Saudi government to know of al Haramain's links to terrorist organizations.

Even after the Saudi government froze the assets of the Bosnian office in March 2002, one senior Saudi government official denied in the press that the al Haramain office in Sarajevo was engaged in illicit activities. He claimed that the U.S. government had apologized to HIF for designating the wrong office. Another senior Saudi official characterized any terrorist financing out of the Kingdom as involving isolated cases and government controls as sufficient to prevent further problems; a third described HIF's clandestine activities as outside activities. We know these descriptions were inaccurate, as the U.S. and Saudi governments continued to take action against al Haramain and its employees.

Despite having frozen the accounts of entities and individuals listed by the United Nations under UNSCR 1373, the Saudis did little else initially. They insisted that their then 12-year-old charities law would suffice, as would their then 7-year-old anti-money-laundering statute. Foreign operations of charities were not regulated until 2002, when the Ministry of Islamic Affairs was put in charge of overseeing them. In the summer of 2002, the Saudis claimed that all out-of-country charitable activities had to be reported to the Foreign Ministry, but later in the year a representative of the Foreign Ministry said he knew of no such regulation. They claimed that they were reviewing all domestic charities in 2002 but took no actions and did not inform the U.S. government of any findings, even while clandestine activity continued. They repeated promises throughout 2002 to establish a High Commission that would oversee all charitable activities, and then claimed to have created such an entity in December 2002. By late fall of 2002 the Saudi government said it was moving to regulate charities further, but the U.S. government had not seen any documentation to that effect as of spring of 2003.

The Saudis responded to the increase in U.S. pressure, exemplified by the delivery of the al Haramain nonpaper in early 2003, by articulating additional counterterrorism policies. The measures were to include Ministry of Islamic Affairs preclearance of transfers of charitable funds overseas, host government approval of all incoming charitable funds from Saudi Arabia, and monitoring of charities' bank accounts through audits, expenditure reports, and site visits. Also in the spring of 2003, the Saudi Arabia Monetary Authority (SAMA) was said to have instituted a major technical training program for judges and investigators on terrorist financing and money laundering.

On al Haramain, the Saudi press reported in February 2003 that the Saudi government was planning to restructure the charity. The Saudi government had also reportedly initiated an investigation of al Haramain and was examining the personal accounts of senior officers. However, the Saudis resisted taking action against a top HIF executive despite U.S. requests. In April 2003, the Saudi government said that a new Board of Directors would be appointed for al Haramain, no new offices would be permitted, no third-country nationals would be hired, all overseas offices were to have their own local lawyers and accountants, and a licensing procedure would be implemented. Again, there was a sense that the Saudis wished to take such actions quietly. On May 8, 2003, the U.S. embassy in Riyadh reported that the Saudi government would close ten al Haramain branch offices pending review of their finances. This claim was reiterated several times by Saudi or HIF officials over the summer of 2003.

Although these measures were all steps in the right direction, the Saudi government generally failed to carry out a number of the actions pledged. For instance, they did not close the branch offices of HIF as promised. As well, the Saudi government remained cautious about speaking publicly about counterterrorism issues and ramping up its reforms. Some in the U.S. government thought that public statements by the Saudi government could have gone a long way toward deterring Saudi financial support for terrorists. Admittedly, the Saudis were, and still are, cautious about how any reforms and close cooperative efforts with the United States are perceived in the Kingdom.

Underlying the Saudi government's reluctance to act against charities funneling money to terrorists lay several issues.[137] First, at the time the Saudi government did not view al Qaeda as a domestic threat. The Saudis simply may not have believed that al Qaeda would attack it, despite the known hatred of al Qaeda and Bin Ladin for the Saudi regime. The signs were there, however, and even the U.S. government had warned the Saudis of possible upcoming attacks in the Kingdom.

Second, the Saudi government's efforts on terrorist financing were domestically unpalatable. It had been content for many years to delegate all religious activities, including those of charities, to the religious establishment and was reluctant to challenge that group. Since the Saudi government did not view al Qaeda as a domestic threat at that time, it could not justify the potential domestic rancor that would have resulted from a strong program against terrorism financing. The challenge was to find a way to increase oversight over charities, mosques, and religious donations without endangering the country's stability. Of course, by failing to reassert some measure of control over the religious establishment, the House of Saud was just as likely to endanger its stability.

---

[137] In addition to the points stated below, some with the U.S. government have speculated that the Saudi government resisted investigating al Haramain and other charities for fear that such investigations might unearth information implicating, or at least unflattering to, senior members of the Saudi government in the clandestine activities of the charity. The Commission staff has found no evidence that the Saudi government as an institution or as individual senior officials individually funded al Qaeda.

Third, the Saudi government did not have the technical capabilities to stem the flow of funds to terrorists from charities in Saudi Arabia. The Mubahith lacked the necessary investigative expertise to track financial crimes. In addition, as described in an internal OFAC document from April 2002, "The SAG [Saudi Arabian government] does not have the legal or operational structures in place at this time to effectively implement the U.N. resolutions relating to the prevention and suppression of the financing of terrorist acts."[138] Although the Saudis claimed to be developing procedures to track all donations to and from charities in October 2002, by January 2004 they were described as just starting to have such capabilities. Moreover, tighter control over money flows can be achieved only if the banks in Saudi Arabia are capable of monitoring and freezing funds. In 2002, the U.S. intelligence community was highly skeptical that Saudi banks had the necessary technical abilities.

The U.S. government was willing, and made several offers, to provide the Saudis with the necessary training. In 2002, the Saudis were described as "reluctant to host trainers from U.S. agencies on issues related to terrorist financing. This reluctance is partly cultural—an attitude that training implies a lack of equality between the parties." The U.S. government sent a Financial Services Assessment Team (FSAT) to Saudi Arabia in April 2002 to learn about Saudi financial systems and structures and ascertain opportunities for U.S. assistance and training, but the Saudis failed to schedule several key meetings during this trip.

May 2003: Turning a corner

On May 12, 2003, al Qaeda operatives detonated three explosions in an expatriate community in Riyadh, killing Westerners and Saudi Arabians. Since then, the Saudi government has taken a number of significant, concrete steps to stem the flow of funding from the Kingdom to terrorists. The Saudi government, in one of its more important actions after the bombings, removed collection boxes in mosques, as well as in shopping malls, and prohibited cash contributions at mosques. This action was important because terrorist groups and their supporters have been able to siphon funds from mosque donations. Its sensitivity cannot be overestimated. U.S. Ambassador to Saudi Arabia Jordan described the removal of the collection boxes as a "cataclysmic event." It was a real action that the Saudi public has both seen and been affected by; it has forced everyone to think about terrorist financing.

On May 24, 2003, the Saudi government followed up with comprehensive new restrictions on the financial activities of Saudi charities. These included a requirement that charitable accounts can be opened only in Saudi riyals; enhanced customer identification requirements for charitable accounts; a requirement that charities must consolidate all banking activity into one principal account, with subaccounts permitted for branches but for deposits only, with all withdrawals and transfers serviced through the main account; a prohibition on cash disbursements from charitable accounts, with

---

[138] Department of the Treasury, "Note to File," undated, but probably October 2002.

payments allowed by check payable to the first beneficiary and deposited into a Saudi bank; a prohibition on the use of ATM and credit cards by charities; and a prohibition on transfers from charitable accounts outside of Saudi Arabia.

Also, after the May 12 bombings the Saudis initiated action to capture or otherwise deal with known al Qaeda operatives, financial facilitators, and financiers in Saudi Arabia. Early in this campaign, the Saudis killed a key al Qaeda leader and financial facilitator known as "Swift Sword" in a firefight. The arrests and deaths of financial facilitators such as Swift Sword have been a blow to al Qaeda and have hampered its fund-raising efforts in the Kingdom.

The May 12 bombings caused the Saudis to become more receptive to disrupting al Qaeda financing than ever before; the Saudis appeared ready to take seriously the cooperative aspect of "quiet cooperation." At the same time, the U.S. government finally developed a coherent approach to working with the Saudis on combating terrorist financing. The United States had an agenda, the Saudi strategy, and was able to engage the Saudis more forcefully on the issues than it could have otherwise. Most importantly, the U.S. government raised the terrorist-financing dialogue to the highest levels. Fran Fragos Townsend, then deputy assistant to the President and deputy national security advisor for combating terrorism, was designated the senior White House liaison on terrorist financing, and President Bush has publicly stated his confidence in her.

The U.S. government was therefore in a position to test the Saudis' new focus on terrorist financing. Townsend traveled to Saudi Arabia in early August 2003 and again in September 2003. One product of the early high-level meetings was the establishment of the joint task force on terrorist financing, described below.

Despite the positive atmosphere of the August meetings, one area of continuing concern was that the ten al Haramain branches the Saudi government had committed to closing in May 2003, before the bombings, were apparently still operating. There was apparently some question as to whether the al Haramain head office really had control over its branch offices and therefore whether closing the branch offices was the responsibility of the Saudi government or the host governments. Some in the U.S. government believe this discussion to be specious, since resources regularly flow from the head office to the branches. They argue, plausibly, that even if the Saudi government itself cannot control the flows of funds, it can pressure the headquarters to cut off these resources to the branches or pressure the heads of governments of the countries where the branch offices are located to close those offices.

In the fall of 2003, the Saudi government passed new anti-money-laundering and terrorist-financing legislation. This law updated the 1995 anti-money-laundering law and improved reporting and record-keeping requirements, created new interagency coordination mechanisms, and established a financial intelligence unit to collect and analyze suspicious financial transactions. Also that fall, the Saudi government permitted a team of assessors from the Financial Action Task Force (FATF) and the Gulf Cooperation Council to visit the Kingdom to evaluate its anti-money-laundering and terrorist-financing laws and regulations. Finally, in September 2003 the Saudi government questioned the executive director of HIF, Abd al-Rahman Bin Aqil.

The joint task force on terrorist financing started operations in the fall of 2003 as well. The task force consists of staff from both the United States and Saudi Arabia. The task force seeks to identify and financially investigate persons and entities suspected of providing financial support to terrorist groups. The U.S. government offered the Saudis training in conducting financial investigations, and the Saudis "readily accepted." This training focused on the value of tracking financial transactions in an investigation and provided practical case studies. The Saudi trainees were dedicated and enthusiastic, although very much in need of training. One FBI official said, "I cannot overemphasize the importance of this initiative and the efforts on the part of both our countries to make it work."[139]

In November 2003, another bombing in Riyadh further jolted the Saudi government to take action on terrorist-financing issues and cooperate with the U.S. government. One U.S. government assessment described the impact of the 2003 Riyadh bombings on the Saudis, in conjunction with the May 12 bombings, as "galvanizing Riyadh into launching a sustained crackdown against al-Qaida's presence in the Kingdom and spurring an unprecedented level of cooperation with the United States." Similarly, it noted that "the attack of 9 November [2003], which resulted in the deaths of a number of Muslims and Arabs during the holy month of Ramadan, transformed Saudi public acceptance of the widespread nature of the threat in the Kingdom."[140] As a result, the Saudi government may have more latitude to act against terrorist financing than ever before.

Similarly, FBI officials have ranked Saudi cooperation on terrorist-financing issues as "good" since the May 12 and November 8, 2003, Riyadh bombings. The Saudis have aggressively interrogated people in their custody about financial matters, including questions posed by the U.S. government, and have provided actionable intelligence to the U.S. government. A senior CIA counterterrorism official agreed that there had been progress in our cooperation with the Saudis. He described it as "not perfect" but a big improvement from the difficult days before 9/11. In a sign of the level of U.S. confidence in the Saudi effort, the U.S. government is now releasing very sensitive intelligence to the Saudis.

By late fall of 2003, Saudis confirmed that since 9/11 they had taken several significant steps to modify their rules and regulations to stem the flow of funds to terrorists. In addition to the new charities regulations, the removal of zakat boxes, and the task force, as described above, the Saudi government said it had established the High Commission to oversee all charities, contributions, and donations; required all charities to undergo audits and institute control mechanisms to monitor how and where funds are dispersed; directed all Saudi charities to suspend activities outside Saudi Arabia; and investigated numerous

---

[139] Testimony of Thomas J. Harrington, Deputy Assistant Director, Counterterrorism Division, Federal Bureau of Investigation, before the House International Relations Subcommittee on the Middle East and Central Asia, March 24, 2004.
[140] Department of State, *Patterns of Global Terrorism 2003*, April 2004, p. 67.

banks accounts suspected of having links to terrorism and frozen more than 40 such accounts. The Saudi government has apparently also regulated hawalas through a mandatory licensing requirement and legal, economic, and supervisory measures and sought to decrease demand for unlicensed hawalas.

With respect to al Haramain, the Saudi and U.S. governments took further action at the end of 2003 and into 2004. On December 22, 2003, the U.S. and Saudi governments designated Vazir, an NGO in Bosnia, and its representative a terrorist supporter. It was determined that Vazir was simply another name for the previously designated al Haramain office in Bosnia. Then, in January 2004 the United States and Saudi Arabia jointly designated four additional branches of al Haramain, in Indonesia, Kenya, Tanzania, and Pakistan. The two governments held an unprecedented joint press conference in Washington to announce the designation. The names of these branches were subsequently submitted to the United Nations, which instituted an international freeze on their assets. Also, in January 2004 Executive Director Aqil was removed from his position. One public explanation was that the firing related to recent incidents involving HIF's operations in Bosnia.

On February 19, 2004, federal law enforcement took action against both the al Haramain branch in Ashland, Oregon, and the imam of the HIF mosque in Springfield, Missouri. The FBI and the IRS conducted searches of the Ashland offices of HIF as part of an investigation into alleged money laundering and income tax and currency reporting violations. Treasury took the additional step of freezing, during the pendency of an investigation, the accounts of the branch in Oregon and the mosque in Missouri.

The Saudis continue to make changes to their charities laws and regulations. Rules implementing the anti-money-laundering and terrorist-financing law were issued in February 2004. Also in February 2004, FATF issued its report indicating that Saudi Arabia was in compliance or near-compliance with international standards for almost every indicator of effective instruments to combat money laundering and terrorist financing.

On February 29, 2004, the Saudi government announced that it had approved the creation of the Saudi National Commission for Relief and Charity Work Abroad to take over all aspects of overseas aid operations and assume responsibility for the distribution of charitable donations from Saudi Arabia. Although the U.S. government had no details about this commission as of the end of March 2004, one former U.S. government counter-terrorist-financing official said that such an entity could, in theory, replace charities such as al Haramain by subsuming all of HIF's activities into its own. Al Haramain was said to be in the process of restructuring its administration and revising its financial regulations. Al Haramain was planning to refocus its charity work on Saudi Arabia, according to a statement by its new director, Sheikh Dabbas al Dabbas.

Continuing the pressure on al Haramain, the U.S. and Saudi governments jointly designated five additional branches of al Haramain (Afghanistan, Albania, Bangladesh, Ethiopia, and the Netherlands) on June 2, 2004. The United States also designated former

Executive Director Aqil. These names were subsequently submitted to the United Nations for an international freeze on their assets.

Lessons Learned

The U.S. government's efforts to address issues raised by al Haramain before and after 9/11 teach some critical lessons. First, to cause the Saudi government to move against terrorist financiers, the U.S. government has to acquire and release to the Saudis specific intelligence that will enable them to take the necessary action. Thus, the U.S. government was able to get the Saudis to take concrete actions against al Haramain, and charities generally, after it released the nonpaper containing specific intelligence about al Haramain and its employees to the Saudis in January 2003. Previously, the U.S. government appears, for the most part, to have tried to encourage the Saudis to act on the basis of little more than U.S. suspicions or assurances that the United States had intelligence it could not release.

Second, counter-terrorist-financing efforts are an essential part of the overall set of counterterrorist activities and must be fully integrated into the broader U.S. counterterrorism strategy toward Saudi Arabia. Without such integration, those working on terrorist financing might not be aware of other bilateral counterterrorism issues. The U.S. government might then have the appearance of sending mixed or inconsistent messages on counterterrorism to the Saudis. Once the broader Saudi strategy was approved, the U.S. government was able to develop a consistent message across counterterrorism issues. It could push the Saudis more forcefully on terrorist-financing issues, including al Haramain, by, for example, delivering the nonpaper in January 2003. In direct response to the nonpaper, the Saudi government announced its decision to close ten branch offices of al Haramain.

Third, U.S. counter-terrorist-financing strategy must be presented to the Saudi government by a high-level U.S. government representative. The perils of not speaking through a single high-level interlocutor were clear in the case of the reopenings of the Bosnian and Somali offices of al Haramain, as discussed above, when, as one key terrorist-financing official believed, the Saudis "gamed" us. It was not until the appointment of a senior White House official that the U.S engagement of the Saudi government on terrorist financing yielded its most concrete results. A PCC participant said the Saudis did not take terrorist financing seriously until Townsend was appointed. She has been able to apply consistent pressure, over a period of time, with the full backing of the White House.

Fourth, the U.S. government needs a distinct interagency coordinating committee focused on terrorist financing to ensure that terrorist-financing issues are not lost in the overall counterterrorism effort. The PCC proved to be generally effective in focusing the U.S. government on terrorist financing and retaining the momentum of the immediate post-9/11 period. It enabled different branches of the U.S. government to vet the information on al Haramain and assess the options. It ensured that al Haramain–related issues were not lost in the larger counterterrorism picture but were assessed periodically with the full attention of the interagency representatives.

At the same time, the coordinating committee must be fully integrated with the overall counterterrorism effort so that terrorist financing can be made part of the high-level diplomacy necessary to win the cooperation of key allies like Saudi Arabia. One way to achieve this goal is give the NSC the lead on the PCC, as is currently the case. The NSC is better able than any individual agency to integrate terrorist financing into counterterrorism through its leadership of the Counterterrorism Security Group; the NSC is better able to see how the different terrorist-financing tools fit together; the NSC is better able to task agencies and force agencies to reallocate resources; NSC leadership is more efficient because it has the authority to resolve more issues rather than forcing them up to the DC level; the NSC has the best access to information, especially regarding covert action; and the NSC is not operational and is therefore more neutral. Throughout the interagency process on al Haramain, NSC leadership of the PCC might have been useful to expedite the process and clarify the U.S. position.

The concept of a "terrorist-financing czar" has been proposed at times; while perhaps it could have been useful before 9/11, it would serve little purpose today and could detract from the U.S. government's current efforts and recent successes. Terrorist financing is already on the agenda of senior officials, so there is no need for a czar to draw attention to the issue. Each of the relevant agencies has established new sections on terrorist financing or augmented existing groups to work on terrorist-financing issues. Further elevating the issue might overemphasize it or, at the very least, detract from current progress in the larger counterterrorism fight. Action against terrorist financing is only one tool in the fight against terrorism and must be integrated into counterterrorism policy and operations. A czar would undermine this goal. Such a position would also dilute the power of a unified message and the benefits of a single messenger on all terrorism-related issues that the leadership of the NSC seeks to provide.

Challenges Ahead

Much remains to be done to address terrorist-financing issues in Saudi Arabia and the activities of Saudi charities, such as al Haramain, around the globe. Saudi Arabia has worked hard to institute an improved legal and regulatory regime. It remains to be seen if the new laws and regulations will be fully implemented and enforced, and if further necessary legal and regulatory changes will be made. The Saudis still have not established the National Commission as they promised in February 2004 and have not demonstrated that they are willing and able to serve as the conduit for all external Saudi donations in lieu of Saudi charities.[141] Moreover, it is imperative that the Saudi government develop its capabilities to monitor cash flows; otherwise, it will not be able to assess a given entity's or individual's compliance with the new laws and regulations. The Saudi government's acceptance of training from the United States and other

---

[141] The impact of the Saudi government's June 2004 announcement of the formation of such a commission remains to be seen.

countries would demonstrate its willingness to assure that gains in expertise and capabilities are ongoing.

It remains to be seen whether the Saudi government will be willing to make politically and religiously difficult decisions. The action it has taken in 2004 against several al Haramain branch offices is unquestionably significant. Although the government has frozen the assets of branches of al Haramain, it has not used its leverage with the head office to ensure that no funds flow to the designated branches.[142] Similarly, the Saudis have yet to hold prominent individuals—like the former head of al Haramain, for instance—accountable for terrorist financing. Such actions would send a signal both to potential targets and to the Saudi public that the Saudi government is serious about stemming the flow of funds to terrorists and their supporters.

We are optimistic that the U.S. and Saudi governments are on the right track in their mutual efforts on terrorist financing. Neither country can afford to lessen the intensity of its current approach. The Saudi government has come far in recognizing the extent of its terrorist-financing problem. We cannot underplay, however, the reluctance of the Saudi government to make the necessary changes between 9/11 and late spring of 2003. It remains to be seen whether it has truly internalized its responsibility for the problem. A critical part of the U.S. strategy to combat terrorist financing will be monitoring, encouraging, and nurturing Saudi cooperation while simultaneously recognizing that terrorist financing is only one of a number of crucial issues on which the U.S. and Saudi governments need each other.

---

[142] Again, the impact of the Saudi government's June 2004 announcement dissolving al Haramain remains to be seen.

Appendix A: The Financing of the 9/11 Plot

This appendix provides additional detail on the funding of the 9/11 plot itself and how the Commission staff investigated the plot financing.

Staff Investigation of the 9/11 Plot

The staff's investigation of the 9/11 plot built on the extensive investigations conducted by the U.S. government, particularly the FBI. The government thoroughly examined the plot's financial transactions, and the Commission staff had neither the need nor the resources to duplicate that work. Rather, the staff independently assessed the earlier investigation. We had access to the actual evidence of the plotters' financial transactions, including U.S. and foreign bank account statements, fund transfer records, and other financial records. We also had access to the FBI's extensive work product, including analyses, financial spreadsheets and timelines, and relevant summaries of interviews with witnesses, such as bank tellers, money exchange operators and others with knowledge of the conspirators' financial dealings. We were briefed by and formally interviewed the FBI agents who led the plot-financing investigation, sometimes more than once.

In addition to the FBI, we met with key people from other agencies, including the CIA and the Financial Crimes Enforcement Network (FinCEN), who had relevant knowledge about the plot financing. Commission staff also interviewed law enforcement officials from other countries who had investigated the 9/11 plot, reviewed investigative materials from other countries, and interviewed relevant private-sector witnesses. Finally, the staff regularly received relevant reports on the interrogations of the plot participants now in custody.

Financing of the Plot

To plan and conduct their attack, the 9/11 plotters spent somewhere between $400,000 and $500,000, the vast majority of which was provided by al Qaeda. Although the origin of the funds remains unknown, extensive investigation has revealed quite a bit about the financial transactions that supported the 9/11 plot. The hijackers and their financial facilitators used the anonymity provided by the huge international and domestic financial system to move and store their money through a series of unremarkable transactions. The existing mechanisms to prevent abuse of the financial system did not fail. They were never designed to detect or disrupt transactions of the type that financed 9/11.

Financing of the hijackers before they arrived in the United States

Al Qaeda absorbed costs related to the plot before the hijackers arrived in the United States, although our knowledge of the funding during this period remains somewhat murky. According to plot leader Khalid Sheikh Muhammad (KSM), the Hamburg cell members (Muhamad Atta, Marwan al Shehhi, Ziad Jarrah, and Ramzi Binalshibh) each received $5,000 to pay for their return from Afghanistan to Germany in late 1999 or early 2000, after they had been selected to join the plot, and the three Hamburg pilots also received additional funds for travel from Germany to the United States. Once the nonpilot muscle hijackers received their training, each received $2,000 to travel to Saudi Arabia to obtain new passports and visas, and ultimately $10,000 to facilitate travel to the United States, according to KSM.[143]

We have found no evidence that the Hamburg cell members received funds from al Qaeda earlier than late 1999. Before then, they appear to have supported themselves. For example, Shehhi was being paid by the UAE military, which was sponsoring his studies in Germany. He continued to receive a salary through December 23, 2000. The funds were deposited into his bank account in the United Arab Emirates and then wired by his brother, who held power of attorney over the account, to his account at Dresdner Bank in Germany (although there is no evidence that al-Shehhi's brother knew about or supported the plot).[144] Binalshibh was employed intermittently in Germany until November 1999. Jarrah apparently relied on his family for support. Indeed, Binalshibh said that Jarrah always seemed to have plenty of money in Germany because his parents gave it to him.

Notwithstanding persistent press reports to the contrary, there is no evidence that the Spanish al Qaeda cell, led by Barkat Yarkas and including al Qaeda European financier Mohammed Galeb Kalaje Zouaydi, provided any funding to support 9/11 or the Hamburg plotters. Zouaydi may have provided funds to Mamoun Darkazanli, who knew the Hamburg plotters as a result of being a member of the Hamburg Muslim community, but there is no evidence that he provided money to the plot participants or that any of his funds were used to support the plot.

Mounir Motassadeq, the Hamburg friend of the hijackers, held power of attorney over Shehhi's Dresdner Bank account, from November 24, 1999, until at least January 2001. Motassadeq told the German investigators that he held the power of attorney to handle routine payments—for rent, tuition, and the like—for Shehhi when he traveled to his homeland. On one occasion he transferred DM 5,000 from Shehhi's account to Binalshibh's account while they were both out of town. Motassadeq's role in managing Shehhi's account was part of the conduct that led to his conviction in Germany for complicity in 9/11, a conviction that was subsequently reversed.

Al Qaeda also paid for the training camps at which the 9/11 hijackers were selected and trained. We have not considered this expense as part of the plot costs, because the camps

---

[143] Another person, who operated a safehouse in Pakistan through which the hijackers transited, independently recalled that an al Qaeda courier provided at least one hijacker with $10,000 at KSM's direction.

[144] Al-Shehhi's last payment, received in December 2000, does not appear to have been moved to his account in Germany.

existed independently of the plot. The marginal cost of training the hijackers is a plot cost, but any estimate of it would be little more than a guess.

Financing of hijackers in the United States

The best available evidence indicates that approximately $300,000 was deposited into the hijackers' bank accounts in the United States by a variety of means. Just prior to the flights, the hijackers returned about $26,000 to one of their al Qaeda facilitators and attempted to return another $10,000, which was intercepted by the FBI after 9/11. Their primary expenses consisted of tuition for flight training, living expenses (room, board and meals, vehicles, insurance, etc.), and travel (for casing flights, meetings, and the September 11 flights themselves). The FBI believes that the funds in the bank accounts held by the hijackers were sufficient to cover their expenses.[145] The FBI, therefore, believes it has identified all sources of funding. Our investigation has revealed nothing to suggest the contrary, although it is possible that the $300,000 estimate omits some cash that the hijackers brought into the United States and spent without depositing into a bank account or otherwise creating a record.[146]

Al Qaeda funded the hijackers in the United States by three primary and unexceptional means: (1) wire or bank-to-bank transfers from overseas to the United States, (2) the physical transportation of cash or traveler's checks into the United States, and (3) the use of debit or credit cards to access funds held in foreign financial institutions. Once here, all the hijackers used the U.S. banking system to store their funds and facilitate their transactions.

The hijackers received assistance in financing their activities from two facilitators based in the United Arab Emirates: Ali Abdul Aziz Ali, a.k.a. Ammar al Baluchi (Ali), and Mustafa al Hawsawi. To a lesser extent, Binalshibh helped fund the plot from Germany.

---

[145] FBI Assistant Director, Counterterrorism Division, John S. Pistole, stated during a congressional hearing last fall that "the 9/11 hijackers utilized slightly over $300,000 through formal banking channels to facilitate their time in the U.S. We assess they used another $200-$300,000 in cash to pay for living expenses . . ." Senate Committee on Banking, Housing, and Urban Affairs, September 25, 2003, FDCH Political Transcripts at page 5. His statement concerning additional cash was apparently made in error. The FBI personnel most familiar with the 9-11 investigation have uniformly disagreed with it, and the FBI has never conducted any financial analysis that supports it. Although some FBI personnel involved in the early days of the investigation after 9/11 believed the hijackers had substantially more cash than that which was deposited in their accounts, the FBI view after more thorough investigation is to the contrary.

[146] We will never know the exact amount of funds the hijackers deposited into their accounts, as they made transactions which made it difficult to trace the money. For example, at times they made substantial cash withdrawals, followed by substantial cash deposits. It is impossible to tell if the deposit reflected new funds or merely the return of funds previously withdrawn but not spent. Nor is a complete analysis of their expenditures possible. They conducted many transactions in cash. Although the FBI has obtained evidence of many these transactions, there surely were many others of which no record exists. Additionally, gaps remain in our understanding of what exactly the hijackers did in U.S., so it is possible that they spent funds on activities of which we have no knowledge. Because the hijackers' activities and expenses are not fully known, we cannot say with certainty that every dollar has been accounted for. We believe, however, that the identified funding was sufficient to cover their known expenses and the other expenses they surely incurred in connection with their known activities.

Wire transfers

Upon their arrival in the United States, the hijackers received a total of approximately $130,000 from overseas facilitators via wire or bank-to-bank transfers. Most of the transfers originated from the Persian Gulf financial center of Dubai, UAE, and were sent by plot facilitator Ali. Ali is the nephew of KSM, the plot's leader, and his sister is married to convicted terrorist Ramzi Yousef. He lived in the UAE for several years before the September 11 attacks, working for a computer wholesaler in a free trade zone in Dubai. According to Ali, KSM gave him the assignment and provided him with some of the necessary funds at a meeting in Pakistan in early 2000. KSM provided the bulk of the money later in 2000 via a courier.[147] Although Ali had two bank accounts in the UAE, he kept most of the funds for the hijackers in a laundry bag at home.[148]

Ali transferred a total of $119,500 to the hijackers in the United States in six transactions between April 16, 2000, and September 17, 2000. Nawaf al Hazmi and Khalid al Mihdhar, the first hijackers to arrive, received the first wire transfer. On April 16, 2000, Ali, using the name "Mr. Ali," wired $5,000 from the Wall Street Exchange Centre in Dubai to an account at the Union Bank of California. The funds flowed through a correspondent account at the Royal Bank of Canada. Ali brought the $5,000 to the Exchange Center in cash. The Wall Street Exchange Center required identification, and it made a copy of Ali's work ID, along with his cell phone number and work address—all of which helped the FBI identify him and his subsequent aliases after 9/11. Ali wired the money to the account of a San Diego resident whom Hazmi met at a mosque and had solicited to receive the transaction on his behalf.[149]

Ali wire transferred a total of $114,500 to the plot leaders Shehhi and Atta after their arrival in the United States. Ali did not return to the Wall Street Exchange Centre. Instead, using a variety of aliases, he sent the money from the UAE Exchange Centre in Dubai, where no identification was required. On June 29, 2000, Ali, using an alias, sent a $5,000 wire transfer to a Western Union facility in New York where Shehhi picked it up. Over the next several months, Ali sent four bank-to-bank transfers directly to a checking account jointly held by Shehhi and Atta at SunTrust Bank in Florida: $10,000 on July 18, $9,500 on August 5, $20,000 on August 29, and $70,000 on September 17. On three of these occasions he used an alias; once he went by "Mr. Ali." In each case, Ali brought cash in UAE dirhams, which were then changed into dollars; the transaction receipts reflect the conversion. All of the bank-to-bank transactions flowed through the UAE Exchange's correspondent account at Citibank. Although Ali made the last five

---

[147] Ali also said KSM gave him money at various other face to face meetings and also wired him money. He used these funds both to support the hijackers and to buy things for KSM. He also occasionally fronted his own money in support of the hijackers, to be reimbursed by KSM. As a result, he could not be sure exactly where he got every dollar he spent.

[148] Ali's bank records show his accounts never contained sufficient funds to account for the money he sent to the United States, lending credence to his claim he kept the money in a laundry bag at home.

[149]. The person who received the funds came forward shortly after 9/11 to explain that he may have unwittingly aided two men who turned out to be hijackers. The FBI interviewed him extensively and satisfied itself that he did not knowingly aid the hijackers.

transactions using various aliases, he provided enough personal information to enable the FBI to unravel the aliases after 9/11.[150]

In any event, aliases were not the key to Ali's security. Instead, he relied on the anonymity provided by bustling financial center of Dubai and the vast international monetary system. His employment as computer wholesaler provided perfect cover. Ali said he sent the final $70,000 in one large transfer because Shehhi had called and asked him to "send him everything." According to Ali, KSM was displeased when he later learned of the transfer because he thought the size of the transaction would alert the security services. The amount did not worry Ali, however, because he knew that Dubai computer companies frequently transferred such amounts of money. Ali said he experienced no problem with this transfer, or any transfer in aid of the hijackers.[151]

Binalshibh also played a role in financing the plot by wiring, in four transfers, more than $10,000 from Germany to the United States. On June 13, 2000, Binalshibh sent $2,708.33 from Hamburg to Shehhi in New York via a Traveler's Express/Moneygram transfer. On June 21, 2000, he sent $1,803.19 from Hamburg to Shehhi in New York by the same means. Binalshibh also sent two Western Union transfers from Hamburg to Shehhi in Florida, wiring $1,760.15 and $4,118.14 on July 25 and September 25, 2000, respectively. Binalshibh apparently funded these transfers by withdrawing money from Shehhi's account at Dresdner Bank.

In addition, Binalshibh, using an alias, sent $14,000, in two installments, to Zacarias Moussaoui in early August 2001. Binalshibh received the money for these transfers from Hawsawi, wired in two installments on July 30 and July 31.[152]

As it turned out, none of the wire transfers associated with the plot—from Dubai or Germany—raised any significant suspicion or concern. They were essentially invisible in the billions of dollars in wire transfers that take place every day throughout the world.

Physical importation of cash and traveler's checks

The hijackers also brought into the United States a substantial amount of cash and traveler's checks, beginning with the first hijackers to come to the United States, Mihdhar and Hazmi. Following their January 15, 2000, arrival in Los Angeles, they opened an account at Bank of America in San Diego with a $9,900 deposit on February 4, 2000. They likely brought in more cash they deposited, as they surely had to pay for goods and services in the period between their arrival in Los Angeles and the opening of their Bank

---

[150] The FBI effort was made possible by unprecedented cooperation from the UAE, which provided copies of the paperwork Ali used and allowed the FBI to interview witnesses. Later Ali confirmed he sent the wire transfers.

[151] Central Banker Sultan bin Nasser al-Suweidi was quoted in the press earlier this year as contending that the UAE reported to U.S. officials Ali's large wire transfer to Al-Shehhi a year before 9/11. *See* Associated Press, *Dubai Banks Remain Focus of Terror Funding Investigation* (Jan. 17, 2004) (printed from WSJ.Com, 2/5/05). We have found no evidence the UAE provided any such notification. We have been told Al-Suweidi later backed off the statement in discussions with the FBI.

[152] Binalshibh and Al-Hawsawi both used aliases for these transactions.

of America account in San Diego, roughly three weeks later. The $16,000 that KSM said he gave Hazmi to support his and Mihdhar's travel and living expenses in the United States is the likely source of their funds.[153]

Shehhi apparently also brought some cash into the United States. He purchased $2,000 in traveler's checks from a New York bank on May 31, 2000, two days after his arrival in New Jersey. He had apparently withdrawn these funds from his Dresdner Bank account before he left Germany. Similarly, on June 28, two days after arriving in the United States, Jarrah opened an account at a bank in Venice, Florida, with a $2,000 cash deposit, apparently funds he had brought into the country.

The 13 muscle hijackers who arrived in the United States between April 23 and June 29, 2001, brought with them cash or traveler's checks for their own expenses and to replenish the funds of the hijackers who had previously arrived. These funds seem to have been provided directly to the muscle hijackers by plot leader KSM when he met with them in Pakistan before they transited the UAE en route to the United States, although their Dubai facilitators may have provided some additional funding.[154] Ali recalled that the hijackers arrived in Dubai with money to purchase plane tickets and traveler's checks, but said he may have provided some of them with additional funds. Hawsawi said he spent approximately $7,000–$9,000 in expenses for the hijackers in the UAE.

Investigation has confirmed that six of the muscle hijackers who arrived in this period purchased traveler's checks totaling $43,980 in the UAE and used them in the United States.[155] Beyond these confirmed funds, the muscle hijackers almost surely brought in more money in cash or traveler's checks that has not been identified. Some of the newly arrived muscle made substantial deposits shortly after entering the United States, and other hijackers made deposits soon after the muscle arrived. For example, Satam al Suqami and Waleed al Shehri arrived in the United States from the UAE on April 23, 2001, and opened a bank account at SunTrust in Fort Lauderdale on May 1 with a deposit of $9,000. It appears likely that Suqami or Shehri brought in cash or purchased traveler's checks in the UAE, although such a purchase has not been identified. Similarly, on June 1, 2001, $3,000 was deposited into Jarrah's SunTrust account and $8,000 was deposited into the Shehhi/Atta joint account. These funds may have been cash or traveler's checks that investigation has not yet identified, purchased and brought into the United States by

---

[153] There has been substantial speculation that al-Mihdhar and al-Hazmi received the money in Thailand in January 2000, where they traveled with senior Al-Qaeda operative Khallad bin Attash, and where we know Khallad received funds from another al Qaeda operative. It now seems unlikely that the hijackers received funds from Khallad in Thailand in light of KSM's account of providing them with funds and Khallad's own account in which he explained Al-Mihdhar and Al-Hazmi made a spur of the moment decision to go to Bangkok with him after their initial meeting in Malaysia, largely to obtain Thai stamps on their passport, which they hoped would help ease their entry in the United States by making them appear more like tourists. Other evidence corroborates Khallad's account, and it seems more likely the hijackers received operational funds from KSM in Pakistan, as he described, than on a trip they decided to make on the spur of the moment.

[154] As noted above, KSM said he gave each of the muscle hijackers $10,000 to facilitate their travel to the United States.)

[155] 5 The FBI has confirmed purchases by Majed Moqed, Wail Al-Shehri, Ahmed Al-Haznawi, Saeed Al-Ghamdi, Hamza Al-Ghamdi, Ahmed Al-Nami.

one or more of the three additional muscle hijackers—Hamza al Ghamdi, Ahmed al Nami, or Mohand al Shehri—who had entered the United States on May 28, 2001.[156]

Plot facilitators Ali and Hawsawi provided logistical assistance to the muscle hijackers as they transited the UAE en route to the United States, including assistance in purchasing plane tickets and traveler's checks. Phone records indicate that Ali aided the hijackers through May 2001 and that, thereafter, Hawsawi became the primary facilitator. A notebook Al-Hawsawi maintained shows payments he made to or on behalf hijackers transiting the UAE in June.

Ali has confirmed his role in assisting the muscle hijackers while they were in the UAE. KSM provided them with Ali's phone number, and they called him upon their arrival. He assisted them in purchasing airline tickets, traveler's checks, and Western-style clothes; arranged hotels and food; and also taught them Western skills, such as ordering at fast-food restaurants. It is not clear why Hawsawi got involved in the plot. Ali said he requested that KSM send someone to Dubai to assist him with the transiting operatives because he feared the time required to support the hijackers and train them to adapt to Western life would impinge on his day job with the computer company. According to Ali, KSM then directed Hawsawi to help him; but by the time Hawsawi arrived, Ali discovered the hijackers were not staying very long in Dubai and did not demand much of his time. It is hard to imagine that Ali was so concerned about his day job, but no other reason for Hawsawi's involvement is readily apparent.

Hawsawi has acknowledged aiding some of the muscle hijackers in the UAE. In addition, he assisted and provided funds to Mohamed al Kahtani, who was selected as a hijacker and flew to Orlando before being denied access to the United States. Kahtani had $2,800 cash in his possession when he arrived at the airport in Florida.

The hijackers who traveled internationally after arriving in the United States also carried funds back with them. For example, Mihdhar purchased $4,900 in traveler's checks in Saudi Arabia shortly before he returned to the United States on July 4, 2001, after an extended absence. According to Hawsawi's notebook, Hawsawi gave the funds to Mihdhar in the UAE in June 2001 to buy these checks. In some instances, we cannot determine whether the hijackers brought in more cash from overseas travel. For example, in the weeks after Shehhi returned to Florida from a trip to Egypt on May 2, 2001, several large deposits were made into his SunTrust account ($8,600 on May 11 and $3,400 on May 22). It is unclear whether the deposits came from funds Shehhi received overseas, funds brought by the muscle hijackers arriving in late May, or funds previously withdrawn and not spent.

Zacarias Moussaoui brought more money into the United States than any other person associated with the 9/11 attacks. Moussaoui declared $35,000 to Customs when he arrived in the United States from London on February 23, 2001, and he deposited $32,000 into a Norman, Oklahoma, bank three days later.

---

[156]. Some hijackers declared funds when they entered the U.S., but others, who we know had funds with them, did not.

Accessing overseas accounts

The hijackers also financed their activities in the United States by accessing funds deposited into overseas accounts. There are two primary examples of this method. Hani Hanjour maintained accounts at the Saudi British Bank in Saudi Arabia and at Citibank in the UAE. While in the United States, he accessed his foreign accounts through an ATM card to finance his activities. Approximately $9,600 was deposited into the Saudi British Bank account, and $8,000 into the Citibank account. Ali said he provided Hanjour with $3,000 to open the Citibank account and deposited another $5,000 into that account while Hanjour was in the United States.[157]

One of the muscle hijackers, Fayez Banihammad, also set up an overseas account to provide funding in the United States. On June 25, 2001, with the aid of Hawsawi, Banihammad opened two accounts at the Standard Chartered Bank in the UAE and deposited about $30,000 in UAE dirhams. According to Hawsawi, Banihammad brought the funds with him to open the accounts when he came to the UAE. Hawsawi was given power of attorney over the accounts on July 18, 2001. The accounts were accessible by an ATM card and a Visa card. Hawsawi received the Visa card from the bank after Banihammad departed for the United States and apparently sent it to Banihammad in the United States by express delivery. After his arrival in the United States on June 27, Banihammad made cash withdrawals with both cards to help fund the plot in the United States, and he used the Visa card to purchase the 9/11 plane tickets for himself and one of the muscle hijackers and to pay his Boston hotel bill on the morning of 9/11. Hawsawi apparently bolstered Banihammad's financing with a deposit of $4,900 on August 20, 2001, into Banihammad's SCB account.

No aid from U.S. persons

No credible evidence exists that the hijackers received any substantial funding from any person in the United States. With one possible minor exception discussed below, the FBI's investigation has not revealed any evidence that any person in the United States knowingly provided any funding to the hijackers. Extensive investigation by Commission staff has revealed nothing to the contrary.

Despite persistent public speculation, there is no evidence that the hijackers who initially settled in San Diego, Mihdhar and Hazmi, received funding from Saudi citizens Omar al Bayoumi and Osama Bassnan, or that Saudi Princess Haifa al Faisal provided any funds to the hijackers either directly or indirectly. A number of internal FBI documents state without reservation that Bayoumi paid rent on behalf of Mihdhar and Hazmi, a claim reflecting the initial view of some FBI agents. More thorough investigation, however, has determined that Bayoumi did not pay rent or provide any funding to the hijackers. On one

---

[157] Hanjour also received $900 from his brother, who is not believed to be a witting supporter of the plot. The origin of the rest of the funds is unclear, although Hanjour may have received funds when he transited Pakistan in June 2000.

occasion he did obtain a cashier's check to assist Mihdhar and Hazmi pay a security deposit and first month's rent, but the hijackers immediately reimbursed him from their funds.

The one person who evidence indicates may have provided money to a hijacker in the United States was Yazeed al Salmi, a Saudi citizen who came to the United States on a student visa in August 2000; he settled in San Diego, where he came into contact with future hijacker Nawaf al Hazmi. On September 5, 2000, $1,900 was deposited into Hazmi's San Diego Bank of America account from a set of $4,000 in traveler's checks that Salmi had purchased in Riyadh, Saudi Arabia, on July 16, 2000. Little more is known about this transaction. After September 11, Salmi was detained as a material witness because of his contact with Hazmi, and was debriefed extensively by the FBI. He even testified to the grand jury before being deported to Saudi Arabia. Unfortunately, the FBI did not learn that Salmi's traveler's checks wound up in Hazmi's account until after he was deported, and Salmi never informed his interrogators of the matter. In June 2004, Salmi was interviewed regarding the transaction, and claimed not to recall it. There are no other known witnesses to this transaction.

Did Salmi fund Hazmi, knowingly or otherwise? It appears likely that Hazmi did nothing more than facilitate a transaction for Salmi. Indeed, Hazmi's bank records reveal that he withdrew $1,900 in cash the same day he deposited the $1,900 in traveler's checks. This large withdrawal is unusual for Hazmi, as he tended to make much smaller cash withdrawals or use his debit card. Moreover, Salmi did not yet have a bank account in the United States at the time of the transaction, so it is entirely possible that he simply asked Hazmi to do him the favor of cashing the traveler's checks for him.[158]

There is no evidence that Salmi ever provided Hazmi with any other funds. Neither Salmi's account at Bank of America nor Hazmi's account there reflects any other transfers or indicia of transfers. There is no evidence that any other person in San Diego provided Hazmi or any other hijacker with any funds.[159]

No hawalas, self-funding, or state support

The extensive investigation into the financing of the 9/11 plot has revealed no evidence to suggest that the hijackers used hawala or any other informal value transfer mechanism to send money to the United States. Moreover, KSM and the other surviving plot participants have either not mentioned hawalas or explicitly denied they were used. Wire transfers, physical importation of funds, and access of foreign bank accounts were sufficient to support the hijackers; there seems to be no reason al Qaeda would have used

---

[158] Al-Salmi opened an account at Bank of America on September 11, 2000, according to the account opening document.

[159] In September 2000, Al-Hazmi assisted another San Diego associate with a transaction by writing a check on his behalf. Thus, the associate provided Al-Hazmi with $3000, and Al-Hazmi immediately wrote a check for that amount on behalf of the associate. The transaction was a wash, which resulted in no funding of Al-Hazmi.

hawalas as well. Although al Qaeda frequently used hawalas to transfer funds from the Gulf area to Pakistan and Afghanistan, we have not seen any evidence that al Qaeda employed them in moving money to or from the United States.[160]

The hijackers were apparently not expected to provide their own financing once they arrived in the United States. There is no evidence that any of them held jobs in the United States, with the exception of Nawaf al Hazmi, who worked part-time in a gas station for about a month, earning $6 an hour. As discussed above, Shehhi received a salary from the UAE military though December 23, 2000, but did not do any work for this money. There is no evidence to suggest that any of the hijackers engaged in any type of criminal activity to support themselves. Finally, there no evidence that any government funded the 9/11 plot in whole or part.

Hijackers use of U.S. banks

While in the United States, the hijackers made extensive use of U.S. banks. They chose branches of major international banks, such as Bank of America and SunTrust, and smaller regional banks, such as the Hudson United Bank and Dime Savings Bank in New Jersey. Plot leaders Atta and Shehhi may have chosen SunTrust because their Florida flight school banked there and directed its students to use it as well. The muscle hijackers who later linked up with Atta and Shehhi also opened accounts at SunTrust. There is no information available as to how or why the hijackers chose other banks. The hijackers typically opened checking accounts and Visa debit card accounts at the same time.

All of the hijackers opened accounts in their own name, using passports and other identification documents. Contrary to numerous published reports, there is no evidence the hijackers ever used false Social Security numbers to open any bank accounts. In some cases, a bank employee completed the Social Security number field on the new account application with a hijacker's date of birth or visa control number, but did so on his or her own to complete the form. No hijacker presented or stated a false number.

The hijackers were not experts on the use of the U.S. financial system. For example, the teller who opened the initial Atta-Shehhi joint account at SunTrust in July 2000 said she spent about an hour with them, explaining the process of wiring money. On one occasion in June 2001, the hijackers aroused suspicion at a SunTrust branch in Florida while attempting to cash a check for $2,180. Shehhi presented identification documents with different addresses, and the bank personnel thought the signature on the check did not match his signature on file. The bank manager refused to sign the check and issued an internal alert to other SunTrust branches to watch the account for possible fraud. The internal alert was a routine notice sent in accordance with SunTrust's loss avoidance procedures. SunTrust never considered reporting Shehhi to the government because it had no evidence he had done anything illegal. No one at SunTrust or any other financial institution thought, or had any reason to think, that the hijackers were criminals, let alone

---

[160] *See* chapter 2 re al Qaeda's use of hawala, generally.

terrorists bent on mass murder, and no financial institution had any reason to report their behavior to the government.

The hijackers' transactions themselves were not extraordinary or remarkable. The hijackers generally followed a pattern of occasional large deposits, which they accessed frequently through relatively small ATM and debit card transactions. They also made cash withdrawals and some occasionally wrote checks. In short, they used their accounts just as did many other bank customers. No one monitoring their transactions alone would have had any basis for concern.

Contrary to persistent media reports, no financial institution filed a Suspicious Activity Report (SAR) in connection with any transaction of any of the 19 hijackers before 9/11, although such SARs were filed after 9/11 when their names became public. The failure to file SARs was not unreasonable. Even in hindsight, there is nothing—including the SunTrust situation described above—to indicate that any SAR should have been filed or the hijackers otherwise reported to law enforcement.

Return of funds to al Qaeda

From September 5 through September 10, 2001, the hijackers consolidated their unused funds and sent them to Hawsawi in the UAE. On September 5, Banihammad wired $8,000 from his account at SunTrust Bank to his Standard Chartered Bank account in the UAE. On September 8 through 10, the hijackers sent four Western Union wire transfers totaling $18,260 to Hawsawi at two different exchange houses in the UAE. In addition, Hazmi and Mihdhar deposited their excess cash into an account held by Mihdhar at First Union Bank in New Jersey, bringing the balance to $9,838.31 on September 10. That same day, Hazmi and Hanjour sent an express mail package containing the debit card linked to Mihdhar's First Union account to a P.O. box in the UAE rented by Hawsawi. After the 9/11 attacks, a receipt for the sending of this package was found in Hazmi's car at Dulles International Airport, and the FBI intercepted the package.

Binalshibh said that when he spoke by phone with Atta in early September 2001, Atta said he wanted to return some leftover funds. At the time, Binalshibh was in Madrid trying to get a flight to Dubai, and had visa and passport problems. He explained his visa and passport issues to Atta and advised him to send the money to someone else. Atta then called Hawsawi to give him the information needed to pick up the wire transfers, as did the other hijackers who wired money to Hawsawi. Binalshibh and Atta also discussed the return of funds.

On September 11, Hawsawi used a blank check that Banihammad had provided him earlier and an ATM card to withdraw from Banihammad's Standard Chartered Bank account the approximately $7,880 in dirhams that Banihammad had wired there. He then deposited about $16,348 in dirhams to his own checking account at Standard Chartered Bank, reflecting the proceeds of the wire transfers he had received. Next, he transferred $41,000 from his checking account to his Standard Chartered Bank Visa card and left

Dubai for Karachi, Pakistan, leaving some funds in the account. On September 13, 2001, KSM used a supplemental Visa card issued for Hawsawi's Standard Chartered Bank account to make six cash withdrawals at ATMs in Karachi totaling about $900.[161] The remaining funds, roughly $40,000, were not withdrawn or transferred before the UAE froze the account after September 11. KSM has since acknowledged withdrawing funds returned by Atta to Hawsawi; he claimed he gave the money to a senior al Qaeda leader, Abu Hafs, in Kandahar. It is not clear if KSM was referring to the approximately $900 he withdrew from the account, or if Hawsawi had provided KSM with additional funds in cash after 9/11.

The hijackers' efforts during their final days to consolidate and return funds to al Qaeda reflect their recognition of the importance of money to the organization. Although some of the hijackers did squander relatively small amounts on superfluous purchases, including pornography, they generally consumed little, and plot leader Atta was especially frugal. Indeed, Binalshibh has explained that frugality was important to Atta because he did not want to waste funds he considered to be blessed and honored.

Funding of Other Plot Participants

In addition to the 19 hijackers, other plot participants received al Qaeda funding for their role in the plot. KSM said that he, Binalshibh, and Hawsawi each received $10,000 (in addition to the funds they provided the hijackers). The details of this funding are not entirely clear, but KSM said he personally used $6,000 of his money to rent a safehouse in Karachi. Ali required no support from al Qaeda, as he already lived and worked in the UAE. By contrast, al Qaeda had to pay for Hawsawi, the other UAE-based plot facilitator, because he traveled and was living there solely to support 9/11 and other al Qaeda operations. Hawsawi incurred substantial expenses on behalf of the plot, covering travel, apartment rental, car rental, and living expenses.

The available evidence does not make clear how Hawsawi received funds for his plot-related activities. He claimed he received $30,000 in cash from Hamza al Qatari—then an al Qaeda financial manager—that Hawsawi brought into the UAE with him. Hawsawi claimed he received no other funds except for approximately $3,000–$4,500 that Banihammad brought to him, which he assumes came from KSM or Qatari. Although Hawsawi claimed that these funds were sufficient for all his activities in the UAE, their total was clearly less than Hawsawi's known expenses in the UAE. These included aiding the 9/11 hijackers, financing his own living expenses, buying supplies for al Qaeda, wiring Binalshibh a total of $16,500, wiring funds to another likely al Qaeda operative in Saudi Arabia, and providing $13,000 to yet another al Qaeda operative who transited the UAE before departing for another operation on September 10, 2001. Moreover, KSM gave a different account of how Hawsawi was funded. In KSM's version, Hawsawi had a budget of $100,000 and KSM provided all the funds, either by courier or by the muscle hijackers as they traversed the UAE after picking up the money from KSM in Pakistan.

[161] The supplemental Visa card had been applied for on August 25, 2001 in the name of an alias used by KSM.

While in the UAE, Hawsawi received two wire transfers totaling about $6,500 from a Sudanese national then living in Saudi Arabia. Both the transfers were sent in August 2001 from the National Commercial Bank in Saudi Arabia to Hawsawi's Standard Chartered Bank account in the UAE. According to information provided by a foreign security agency, the sender claims he was asked to wire the funds by Uthman al Shehri, the brother of hijackers Waleed and Wail al Shehri. The purpose of the transaction remains unknown, and the relevant witnesses are currently beyond the reach of the U.S. government.

Binalshibh said that he met KSM in Karachi in June 2001; there KSM gave him a plane ticket to Malaysia, where he planned to meet with Atta.[162] Binalshibh said he also received $5,000 from Abu Hafs to support his travel in June. He may have received additional funds during this trip. According to Binalshibh, he was living on al Qaeda money when he returned to Germany in June 2001. On September 3, 2001, Hawsawi, using an alias, wired $1,500 from the UAE to Binalshibh, also using an alias, in Hamburg, presumably to pay for his subsequent travel from Germany, which took place on September 5.

Binalshibh also funded his activities in part by controlling Marwan al Shehhi's bank account, which he apparently accessed with an ATM card, and with the assistance of Motassadeq, who held power of attorney over the account. Binalshibh himself said that Shehhi left him "a credit card" when Shehhi departed Hamburg for the United States in mid-2000. For example, Binalshibh withdrew money from Shehhi's account to send $2,200 to the Florida Flight Training Center in August 2000 in apparent anticipation of his own arrival in the United States. Activity in Shehhi's German bank account indicates that Binalshibh was accessing his funds while he was in the United States.

In January 2001 Atta, sent a $1,500 wire transfer via Western Union from Florida to Binalshibh in Hamburg. There is no known explanation for this transaction, which seems especially odd because Binalshibh had access to Shehhi's German account at the time.

Total Cost

We estimate that the total cost of the 9/11 attacks was somewhere between $400,000 and $500,000. The hijackers spent more than $270,000 in the United States, and the costs associated with Moussaoui were at least $50,000. The additional expenses included travel to obtain passports and visas, travel to the United States, expenses incurred by the plot leader and facilitators, and the expenses incurred by would-be hijackers who ultimately did not participate. For many of these expenses, we have only a mixture of fragmentary evidence and unconfirmed reports, and can make only a rough estimate of costs. Adding up all the known and assumed costs leads to a rough range of $400,000 to $500,000. This estimate does not include the cost of running training camps in Afghanistan where the

---

[162] The meeting in Malaysia ultimately did not take place because Atta was busy awaiting the arrival of the additional hijackers in the U.S.; the meeting took place later in Spain.

hijackers were recruited and trained or the marginal cost of the training itself. For what its worth, the architect of the plot, KSM, put the total cost at approximately $400,000, including the money provided to the hijackers and other facilitators, although apparently excluding Moussaoui. Although we cannot know if this estimate is accurate, it seems to be reasonable, given the information available.

Ultimately, knowing the exact total cost of the plot makes little difference. However calculated, the expense—although substantial—constituted a small fraction of al Qaeda's budget at the time. As we discuss in chapter 2, al Qaeda's annual budget for the relevant period has been estimated to be about $30 million. Even today, with its estimated revenues significantly reduced, al Qaeda could still likely come up with the funds to finance a similar attack.

Origin of the Funds

To date, the U.S. government has not been able to determine the origin of the money used for the 9/11 attacks. As we have discussed above, the compelling evidence appears to trace the bulk of the funds directly back to KSM and, possibly, Qatari, but no further.[163] Available information on this subject has thus far has not been illuminating.[164] According to KSM, Bin Ladin provided 85–95 percent of the funds for the plot from his personal wealth, with the remainder coming from general al Qaeda funds. To the extent KSM intended to refer to wealth Bin Ladin inherited from his family or derived from any business activity, this claim is almost certainly wrong, because Bin Ladin was not personally financing al Qaeda during this time frame.[165] Ultimately the question of the origin of the funds is of little practical significance. Al Qaeda had many avenues of funding. If a particular source of funds dried up, it could have easily tapped a different source or diverted money from a different project to fund an attack that cost $400,000–$500,000 over nearly two years.

We know that a small percentage of the plot funds originated in the bank account of Shehhi, which apparently came from his military salary. Binalshibh drew on these funds to wire approximately $10,000 to Shehhi in the United States, as well as to support his own role in the plot to some degree. Al Qaeda does not necessarily have to completely fund terrorist operatives. Some, like Shehhi, have means and can fund themselves, at least in part, a factor that makes the fight on "terrorist financing" all the more difficult.

---

[163] FBI Assistant Director Pistole testified that the FBI had traced the funds back to certain bank accounts in Pakistan, *see* Senate Govt. Affairs Committee, July 31, 2003, but the FBI has clarified that Pistole meant the funds were traced back to KSM in Pakistan. No actual bank accounts there have been identified.

[164] Senior al Qaeda detainee Abu Zubaydeh has commented on the source of the funding; he said that KSM received funds for the 9/11 operation directly from UBL, bypassing al Qaeda Finance Chief, Shayk Said, and suggested that some of the funds came from money that Zubaydeh had provided UBL for use in an operation against Israel. Zubaydeh, however, apparently did not participate in the 9/11 planning, and his statements lack any foundation.

[165] Instead, al Qaeda relied on donations provided by witting donors and diverted from legitimate charitable donations by al Qaeda supporters. *See* chapter 2 (discussing al Qaeda financing). It is also possible KSM meant that Bin Ladin funded the plot with funds he kept under his personal control.

Appendix B: Securities Trading

This appendix describes the staff and U.S. government investigations into the issue of whether anyone with foreknowledge of the 9/11 attacks profited through securities trading, and explains the conclusion in the Commission's final report that extensive government investigation has revealed no evidence of such illicit trading.

Almost since 9/11 itself, there have been consistent reports that massive "insider trading" preceded the attacks, enabling persons apparently affiliated with al Qaeda to reap huge profits. The Commission has found no evidence to support these reports. To the contrary, exhaustive investigation by federal law enforcement, in conjunction with the securities industry, has found no evidence that anyone with advance knowledge of the terrorist attacks profited through securities transactions.

Commission Staff Investigation

Commission staff had unrestricted access to the U.S. government officials who led and conducted the investigation into securities trading in advance of 9/11. In addition to interviewing the key personnel, Commission staff reviewed the nonpublic government reports summarizing the investigative results as well as backup data, including spreadsheets, memoranda and other analyses, and reports of interviews with traders, securities industry participants, and other witnesses. We obtained and reviewed the reports of investigations done by certain major nongovernmental securities industries bodies who share responsibility with the government for monitoring securities trading in U.S. markets, including the New York Stock Exchange and the National Association of Securities Dealers Regulation, and interviewed witnesses from a key private-sector entity. Commission staff also reviewed information provided by foreign securities regulators, interviewed German law enforcement officials, and interviewed U.S. law enforcement personnel regarding their contacts with their foreign counterparts on securities trading.

In addition, Commission staff drew on its review of extensive classified intelligence concerning al Qaeda and how it manages its operations and its finances, as well as debriefings of al Qaeda detainees, including 9/11 plot leader Khalid Sheikh Mohammed and other plot participants. This information proved useful in evaluating how closely held al Qaeda kept the 9/11 operation and the likelihood it would seek to profit from the attacks through securities trading.

The U.S. Government Investigation of Trading in the United States

The Securities and Exchange Commission (SEC) and the FBI, with the involvement of the Department of Justice, conducted the investigation of the allegation that there was illicit trading in advance of 9/11; numerous other agencies played a supporting role.[166] The SEC's chief of the Office of Market Surveillance initiated an investigation into pre-9/11 trading on September 12, 2001. At a multi-agency meeting on September 17, at FBI headquarters, the SEC agreed to lead the insider trading investigation, keeping the FBI involved as necessary. The Department of Justice assigned a white-collar crime prosecutor from the U.S. Attorney's Office in Brooklyn to work full-time on the investigation; he relocated to Washington, D.C., on September 18.

The SEC undertook a massive investigation, which at various times involved more than 40 staff members from the SEC's Division of Enforcement and Office of International Affairs. The SEC also took the lead on coordinating intensive investigations by the self-regulatory organizations (SROs) that share responsibility for monitoring the U.S. securities markets, including, among others, the New York Stock Exchange, the American Stock Exchange, the National Association of Securities Dealers Regulation, and the Chicago Board Options Exchange. The investigation focused on securities of companies or industries that could have been expected to suffer economically from the terrorist attacks. Thus, the investigators analyzed trading in the following sectors: airlines, insurance, financial services, defense and aerospace, security services, and travel and leisure services, as well as companies with substantial operations in the area of the World Trade Center. The investigation also included broad-based funds that could have been affected by a major shock to the U.S. economy. Ultimately, the investigators analyzed trading in 103 individual companies and 32 index or exchange-traded funds and examined more than 9.5 million securities transactions.

The investigators reviewed any trading activity that resulted in substantial profit from the terrorist attacks. Investments that profited from dropping stock prices drew great scrutiny, including short selling[167] and the purchase of put options.[168] The SEC has long experience in investigating insider trading violations, which can involve the use of these techniques by those who know of an impending event that will make stock prices fall. The investigators also sought to determine who profited from well-timed investments in industries that benefited from the terrorist attacks, such as the stock of defense and security companies, and who timely liquidated substantial holdings in companies likely to suffer from the attacks.

---

[166] The SEC is an independent federal agency entrusted with enforcing the federal securities laws. Its Division of Enforcement has extensive experience in investigating insider trading. Because the SEC lacks authority to bring criminal cases, it regularly works jointly with the FBI and DOJ, as it did in this case, on potentially criminal securities law violations.

[167] Short selling is a strategy that profits from a decline in stock price. A short seller borrows stock from a broker dealer and sells it on the open market. At some point in the future, he closes the transaction by buying back the stock and returning it to the lending broker dealer.

[168] A put option is an investment that profits when the underlying stock price falls. A put option contract gives its owner the right to sell the underlying stock at a specified strike price for a certain period of time. If the actual price drops below the strike price, the owner of the put profits because he can buy stock cheaper than the price for which he can sell it. By contrast, a call option contract is an investment that profits when the underlying stock price rises. A call option contract gives its owner the right to buy the underlying stock at a specified strike price for a certain time period. People illicitly trading on inside information often have used options because they allow the trader to leverage an initial investment, so that a relatively small investment can generate huge profits.

The SEC investigators reviewed voluminous trading records to identify accounts that made trades that led to profits as a result of the attacks. The SEC followed up on any such trades by obtaining documents and, where appropriate, interviewing the traders to understand the rationale for the trades. The SEC also referred to the FBI any trade that resulted in substantial profit from the attacks—a much lower threshold for a criminal referral than it would normally employ. Consequently, the FBI conducted its own independent interviews of many of the potentially suspicious traders. The SROs, which have extensive market surveillance departments, played a key role in the SEC investigation by providing information and, in some cases, detailed reports to the commission. In addition, the SEC directly contacted 20 of the largest broker-dealers and asked them to survey their trading desks for any evidence of illicit trading activity. It also asked the Securities Industry Association—the broker-dealer trade group—to canvass its members for the same purpose.

The SEC investigation had built-in redundancies to ensure that any suspicious trading would be caught. For example, the SEC reviewed massive transaction records to detect any suspicious option trading and also obtained reports, known as the Large Option Position Reports and Open Interest Distribution Reports, that identified the holders of substantial amounts of options without regard to when those options were purchased. Similarly, to ensure full coverage, the SEC obtained information from a number of entities that play a role in facilitating short sales. Between these efforts, the work of the SROs, and the outreach to industry, the chief SEC investigator expressed great confidence that the SEC investigation had detected any potentially suspicious trade.

No Evidence of Illicit Trading in the United States

The U.S. government investigation unequivocally concluded that there was no evidence of illicit trading in the U.S. markets with knowledge of the terrorist attacks. The Commission staff, after an independent review of the government investigation, has discovered no reason to doubt this conclusion.

To understand our finding, it is critical to understand the transparency of the U.S. markets. No one can make a securities trade in the U.S. markets without leaving a paper trail that the SEC can easily access through its regulatory powers. Moreover, broker-dealers must maintain certain basic information on their customers. It is, of course, entirely possible to trade through an offshore company, or a series of nominee accounts and shell companies, a strategy that can make the beneficial owner hard to determine. Still, the investigators could always detect the initial trade, even if they could not determine the beneficial owner. Any suspicious profitable trading through such accounts would be starkly visible. The investigators of the 9/11 trades never found any blind alleys caused by shell companies, offshore accounts, or anything else; they were able to investigate the suspicious trades they identified. Every suspicious trade was determined to be part of a legitimate trading strategy totally unrelated to the terrorist attacks.

Many of the public reports concerning insider trading before 9/11 focused on the two airline companies most directly involved: UAL Corp., the parent company of United Airlines, and AMR Corp., the parent company of American Airlines. Specifically, many people have correctly pointed out that unusually high volumes of put options traded in UAL on September 6–7 and in AMR on September 10.[169]

When the markets opened on September 17, AMR fell 40 percent and UAL fell 43 percent. The suspicious options trading before the attacks fueled speculation that al Qaeda had taken advantage of the U.S. markets to make massive profits from its murderous attacks. The allegations had appeal on their face—just as al Qaeda used our sophisticated transportation system to attack us, it appeared to have used our sophisticated markets to finance itself and provide money for more attacks. But we conclude that this scenario simply did not happen.

Although this report will not discuss each of the trades that profited from the 9/11 attacks, some of the larger trades, particularly those cited in the media as troubling, are illustrative and typical both of the nature of the government investigation into the trades and of the innocent nature of the trading. The put trading in AMR and UAL is a case in point: it appeared that somebody made big money by betting UAL and AMR stock prices were going to collapse, yet closer inspection revealed that the transactions were part of an innocuous trading strategy.

The UAL trading on September 6 is a good example. On that day alone, the UAL put option volume was much higher than any surrounding day and exceeded the call option volume by more than 20 times—highly suspicious numbers on their face.[170] The SEC quickly discovered, however, that a single U.S. investment adviser had purchased 95 percent of the UAL put option volume for the day. The investment adviser certainly did not fit the profile of an al Qaeda operative: it was based in the United States, registered with the SEC, and managed several hedge funds with $5.3 billion under management. In interviews by the SEC, both the CEO of the adviser and the trader who executed the trade explained that they—and not any client—made the decision to buy the put as part of a trading strategy based on a bearish view of the airline industry. They held bearish views for a number of reasons, including recently released on-time departure figures, which suggested the airlines were carrying fewer passengers, and recently disclosed news by AMR reflecting poor business fundamentals. In pursuit of this strategy, the adviser sold short a number of airline shares between September 6 and September 10; its transactions included the fortunate purchase of UAL puts. The adviser, however, also bought 115,000 shares of AMR on September 10, believing that their price already reflected the recently released financial information and would not fall any further. Those shares dropped significantly when the markets reopened after the attacks. Looking at the totality of the adviser's circumstances, as opposed to just the purchase of the puts, convinced the SEC that it had absolutely nothing to do with the attacks or al Qaeda. Still, the SEC referred

---

[169] *See, e.g.,* September 18, 2001 Associated Press Report.
[170] A high ratio of puts to calls means that on that day far more money was being bet that the stock price would fall than that the stock price would rise. Such a ratio is a potential indicator of insider trading—although it can also prove to have entirely innocuous explanations, as in this case.

the trade to the FBI, which also conducted its own investigation and reached the same conclusion.

The AMR put trading on September 10 further reveals how trading that looks highly suspicious at first blush can prove innocuous. The put volume of AMR on September 10 was unusually high and actually exceeded the call volume by a ratio of 6:1—again, highly suspicious on its face. The SEC traced much of the surge in volume to a California investment advice newsletter, distributed by email and fax on Sunday, September 9, which advised its subscribers to purchase a particular type of AMR put options. The SEC interviewed 28 individuals who purchased these types of AMR puts on September 10, and found that 26 of them cited the newsletter as the reason for their transaction. Another 27 purchasers were listed as subscribers of the newsletter. The SEC interviewed the author of the newsletter, a U.S. citizen, who explained his investment strategy analysis, which had nothing to do with foreknowledge of 9/11. Other put option volume on September 10 was traced to similarly innocuous trades.

Another good example concerns a suspicious UAL put trade on September 7, 2001. A single trader bought more than one-third of the total puts purchased that day, establishing a position that proved very profitable after 9/11. Moreover, it turns out that the same trader had a short position in UAL calls—another strategy that would pay off if the price of UAL dropped. Investigation, however, identified the purchaser as a well-established New York hedge fund with $2 billion under management. Setting aside the unlikelihood of al Qaeda having a relationship with a major New York hedge fund, these trades looked facially suspicious. But further examination showed the fund also owned 29,000 shares of UAL stock at the time—all part of a complex, computer-driven trading strategy. As a result of these transactions, the fund actually *lost* $85,000 in value when the market reopened. Had the hedge fund wanted to profit from the attacks, it would not have retained the UAL shares.

These examples were typical. The SEC and the FBI investigated all of the put option purchases in UAL and AMR, drawing on multiple and redundant sources of information to ensure complete coverage. All profitable option trading was investigated and resolved. There was no evidence of illicit trading and no unexplained or mysterious trading. Moreover, there was no evidence that profits from any profitable options trading went uncollected.[171]

The options trading in UAL and AMR was typical of the entire investigation. In all sectors and companies whose trades looked suspicious because of their timing and

---

[171] The press has reported this claim, and the allegation even found its way into the congressional testimony concerning terrorist financing of a former government official. The government investigation would have detected such traders because the investigators focused on people who purchased profitable positions—regardless of when or whether or when they closed out the position. Moreover, officials at the SEC and the Options Clearing Corporation, a private entity that processes options trading, pointed out that any profitable options positions are automatically exercised upon the expiration date unless the customer explicitly directed otherwise. Any direction not to exercise profitable options is a highly unusual event, which the OCC double-checks by contacting the broker who gave them such instruction. The OCC personnel had no recollection of any such contacts after 9/11.

profitability, including short selling of UAL, AMR, and other airline stocks, close scrutiny revealed absolutely no evidence of foreknowledge. The pattern is repeated over and over. For example, the FBI investigated a trader who bought a substantial position in put options in AIG Insurance Co. shortly before 9/11. Viewed in isolation, the trade looked highly suspicious, especially when AIG stock plummeted after 9/11. The FBI found that the trade had been made by a fund manager to hedge a long position of 4.2 million shares in the AIG common stock. The fund manager owned a significant amount of AIG stock, but the fund had a very low tax basis in the stock (that is, it had been bought long ago and had appreciated significantly over time). Selling even some of it would have created a massive tax liability. Thus, the fund manager chose to hedge his position through a put option purchase. After 9/11, the fund profited substantially from its investment in puts. At the same time, however, it suffered a substantial loss on the common stock, and overall lost money as a result of the attacks.

In sum, the investigation found absolutely no evidence that any trading occurred with foreknowledge of 9/11. The transparency of the U.S. securities markets almost ensures that any such trading would be detectable by investigators. Even if the use of some combination of offshore accounts, shell companies, and false identification obscured the identity of the traders themselves, the unexplained trade would stand out like a giant red flag. The absence of any such flags corroborates the conclusion that there is no evidence any such trading occurred. Indeed, the leaders of both the SEC and FBI investigations into pre-9/11 trading expressed great confidence in this conclusion.

International Investigation

There is also no evidence that any illicit trading occurred overseas. Through its Office of International Affairs, the SEC sought the assistance of numerous foreign countries with active securities markets. The FBI also engaged with foreign law enforcement officials about overseas trading. There are two issues to consider with respect to the international investigation: overseas trading in U.S. securities and trading of foreign securities in overseas markets.

Trading of U.S. securities overseas

The SEC sought the assistance of countries where there was significant trading of U.S. securities. Each of these countries had previously entered into information sharing agreements with the SEC to cooperate in securities investigations, and each willingly cooperated in the 9/11 investigation. According to the SEC, there is generally little trading of U.S. securities overseas, since U.S. securities trade primarily in U.S. markets. Thus, unusual trading in U.S. securities would not have been very hard for foreign regulators to detect. Each country the SEC contacted conducted an investigation and reported back to the SEC that there was no trading in U.S. securities in their jurisdiction that appeared to have been influenced by foreknowledge of the 9/11 attacks.

The foreign investigators also helped investigate suspicious trading in the U.S. from offshore accounts. For example, the SEC investigation revealed that shortly before 9/11 an offshore account had taken a short position in a fund that tracked one of the major U.S. market indices—an investment that profited when the U.S. market declined. After 9/11, the offshore investor closed out the position, reaping $5 million in profit. The SEC's Office of International Affairs solicited help from a European country to investigate further. Although this trade was highly suspicious on its face, the European country's investigation revealed that this investor was an extremely wealthy European national who often speculated by taking short positions in the U.S. market. In fact, the same investor had employed this strategy to lose $8 million in the six months preceding 9/11.

Trading of foreign securities

There is also no evidence that insider trading took place in the stock of any foreign company. The SEC asked its foreign counterparts to investigate trading in securities that trade primarily on foreign markets subject to foreign regulation. Indeed, a number of companies that suffered serious economic losses from the 9/11 attacks were foreign companies, which traded mainly on foreign markets. In particular, the insurance companies with the largest potential losses included Munich Reinsurance Co., Swiss Reinsurance Co., and Allianz AG, all foreign-based companies that primarily traded overseas.[172] In addition to the SEC, the FBI team investigating the financial aspects of the 9/11 plot frequently dealt with foreign law enforcement officials after 9/11 and raised the trading issue.[173] Neither the SEC nor the FBI was informed of any evidence of any illicit trading in advance of 9/11 in any foreign securities.

Shortly after 9/11, Ernst Welteke, president of the German Central Bank, made a number of public statements that insider trading occurred in airline and insurance company stock, and also in gold and oil futures. These preliminary claims were never confirmed. In fact, German officials publicly backtracked fairly soon after Mr. Welteke's statement was issued. On September 27, a spokesman for the German securities regulator, BAWe (Bundesaufsichtsamt für den Wertpapierhandel), declared that while the investigation was continuing, "there is no evidence that anyone who had knowledge of the attacks before they were committed used it to make financial transactions."[174] On December 3, 2001, a spokesman for the BAWe said its investigation had revealed no evidence of illicit

---

[172] According to the SEC's Chief, Market Surveillance, the countries with the most significant relevant trading of foreign corporations stock were the UK and Germany. The UK quickly and publicly reported it had found no illicit trading. *See e.g.,* J. Moore, The Times, *Bin Ladin did not Deal* (October 17, 2001) (Chairman of Financial Services Authority reported that investigation failed to reveal evidence of irregular share dealings in London in advance of 9/11). Other countries publicly reported similar findings. *See e.g.,* Associated Press Worldstream, *Suspicion dispelled of insider trading in KLM shares before September 11 attacks* (reporting conclusion of Dutch government investigation that sharp drop in share prices of the national airline days before 9/11 were not caused by people who knew of terrorist attacks).

[173] The chief of the FBI team also raised the issue with CIA and asked it to be alert for any intelligence on illicit trading; he received no such reports from the CIA.

[174] Agence France Presse (Sept. 27, 2001).

trading in advance of 9/11 and that the case remained open pending new information. The spokesman said separate investigations by state authorities had also yielded no information and had been closed. [175]

Commission staff interviewed German law enforcement officials who said that exhaustive investigation in Germany revealed no evidence of illicit trading. Moreover, both SEC and FBI officials involved in the trading investigation told the Commission staff that German investigators had privately communicated to them that there was no evidence of illicit trading in Germany before 9/11. The FBI legal attaché in Berlin forwarded a lead to the German BKA (Bundeskriminalamt), which reported back that the trading allegations lacked merit. It appears, then, that Welteke's initial comments were simply ill-considered and unsupported by the evidence.[176]

Other investigation corroborates the conclusion of no illicit trading

Since 9/11, the U.S. government has developed extensive evidence about al Qaeda and the 9/11 attacks. The collected information includes voluminous documents and computers seized in raids in Afghanistan and throughout the world. Moreover, the United States and its allies have captured and interrogated hundreds of al Qaeda operatives and supporters, including the mastermind of the 9/11 plot and the three key plot facilitators. No information has been uncovered indicating that al Qaeda profited by trading securities in advance of 9/11. To the contrary, the evidence—including extensive materials reviewed by Commission staff—all leads to the conclusion that knowledge of the plot was closely held by the top al Qaeda leadership and the key planners. It strains credulity to believe that al Qaeda would have jeopardized its most important and secretive operation or any of its key personnel by trying to profit from securities speculation.

---

[175] *See* Australian Financial Review (Dec 3, 2001).

[176] The SEC investigated trading of American Depository Receipts (ADRs) in foreign companies. ADRs are receipts issued by a U.S. bank for the shares of a foreign corporation held by the bank. ADRs publicly trade on U.S. markets. This investigation revealed no illicit trading.